STEVE PRICE

STEVE PRICE

BE YOUR BEST

With Ben Blaschke — Foreword by Wayne Bennett

HACHETTE AUSTRALIA

HACHETTE AUSTRALIA

Published in Australia in 2008 by Hachette Australia
(An imprint of Hachette Livre Australia Pty Limited)
Level 17, 207 Kent Street, Sydney NSW 2000
Website: www.hachette.com.au

Originally published in 2008 by Hodder Moa
(An imprint of Hachette Livre NZ Ltd)

Text © SP Ten Limited
The moral rights of the author have been asserted.
Design and format © Hachette Livre NZ Ltd 2008

This book is copyright. Apart from any fair dealing
for the purposes of private study, research, criticism
or review permitted under the *Copyright Act 1968*,
no part may be stored or reproduced by any process
without prior written permission. Enquiries should
be made to the publisher.

CIP data is available from the National Library of Australia

Text design by Hachette Livre NZ Ltd
Cover design by Luke Causby, Blue Cork
Front cover photo courtesy of Action Photographics
Back cover photos courtesy of Action Photographics and Melba Studios
Printed in China by Everbest Printing Co. Ltd

Hachette Livre Australia's policy is to use papers
that are natural, renewable and recyclable products
and made from wood grown in sustainable forests.
The logging and manufacturing processes are expected
to conform to the environmental regulations
of the country of origin.

This book is for all the kids who dare to dream the dream. With support, belief in yourself, hard work and perseverance you, too, can one day live the dream.

Contents

Acknowledgements 9
Foreword — *By Wayne Bennett* 11

1   A New Beginning   17
2   Growing Up   27
3   The Price is Rising   38
4   Jo   45
5   A Change of Scenery   50
6   Learning the Hard Way   55
7   A Grand, Grand Final   62
8   War-torn   70
9   Back From the Dead   79
10   A Dream is Realised   84
11   A Picture Speaks a Thousand Words   91
12   Rock Bottom   97
13   My Mate Matthew   101

14	Top Dog	108
15	Crushed	115
16	Leading Light	128
17	Coffs Harbour	133
18	Guiding Stars	143
19	Falling Short	153
20	A Terrible Loss — *By Marie Moore*	163
21	Once Were Warriors	166
22	Rolling the Dice	174
23	Never Tough Enough	180
24	Charge Downs	184
25	All That Glitters is Gold	188
26	The Highest Honour	196
27	My Son Steve — *By Margaret Sullivan*.	208
28	State of the Game	213
29	The Future	221

Vodafone New Zealand Limited
20 Viaduct Harbour Avenue
Private Bag 92 161
Auckland 1030, New Zealand

Reception   +64-9-355 2000
Facsimile   +64-9-355 2688

12 August 2008

Dear Steve,

Congratulations on your book from all of us here at Vodafone.

We truly value and appreciate the relationship we have been able to build over the years. You are a great captain and a fantastic role model for the Vodafone Warriors and for New Zealand.

At Vodafone we are passionate about our brand and what it means to our customers. In your very first talk to our team, you outlined the Steve Price brand and what it meant for you, your family and your fans. We are excited that you will now be sharing the life lessons that created your brand with so many more of us through this book.

Your experiences from the world of sport and your belief in teamwork, ambition and achieving goals always provide great motivation and inspiration to the Vodafone team as well as to me personally.

Thanks for all you have done for Vodafone and for the Vodafone Warriors. We have had a great time working together. Long may it continue.

Go Steve Price! Go the Vodafone Warriors!

Yours sincerely

Russell Stanners
Chief Executive Officer
Vodafone New Zealand Limited

Acknowledgements

WELL, THIS is my chance to thank all of those people who have been a part of and had an influence on the life of Steve Price. So sit back with your cup of tea and enjoy.

Firstly, my wife Jo who has been there from the early days — and survived the good and bad times. Through everything, she has given me her unconditional love and support. Without her I may not have survived some of the tougher times. She has been my rock.

We have brought three beautiful kids into the world — Jamie-Lee, Kasey and Riley — and our world, like our mums', revolves around giving them every chance to be the best they can be.

Mum and Dad split up when I was young and Dad went in a separate direction, got remarried to Cindy and had a daughter Georgia who is my half sister. It has been difficult for Dad but he has always stayed in contact and will always be an important part of my life.

Mum never made an issue of the split. Instead, she tried to make life as normal as possible. She has been the one constant in my life — my role model and the backbone upon which I have often leant. She is always telling me how proud she is of me and my own family and of what I have achieved. The only thing I can say in reply is that nothing I have achieved would have been possible without her.

A huge support to Mum was, and still is, my stepfather Garry. Whilst he is not my dad, he is the next closest thing, having given me love, support, advice, strength and guidance that have been much needed and never taken for granted. Throughout my whole life Mum and Gaz have sacrificed so much so I could fulfil my dreams. That is something I will never be able to fully repay them for. To my little sister Wendo and brother Dan, your loyalty and true love is something very special.

To all my family members, including my special nephews and nieces, and the Prices, Sullivans, Christies, Pollards, Hendersons and Hinds, as well as my married-into family of Tate, Walton, Jackson and Dean, thank you for all your love and support. Also, to all of my loved ones who are no longer with us, who have passed away over the years, I will never forget you and thank you all for being there for me everyday.

A special thanks to Miss Colleen Prentice, my Sydney mum, and Sydney grandmother to the kids. Your love and loyalty are truly appreciated.

I have been very lucky to have fallen in love with the game of rugby league. Through my journey I have had many great mentors including people such as Greg Platz, Arthur Wrigley, Bill Pollard, Chris Anderson, Steve Folkes, Wayne Bennett, Billy Johnson, Garry Cszlowski, Graham Tucker, John Ackland, Ivan Cleary, Mal Meninga and, of course, Peter 'Bullfrog' Moore.

Other people whose friendship and advice I appreciate are: Don Gailer, Neil Mansell, Bill Baskett, John Bain, Bruce Sharrock, George Mimis, John Ballesty and Richard Shaw. If it wasn't for these people I wouldn't be as comfortable as I am, nor would I have had the opportunities I have been blessed with.

To all the other people who have been a part of my life, be it my school, teammates, coaches and staff, workmates, teachers, selectors, mentors and supporters: every time I go out and play or strive to achieve something I feel I am representing you all. I hope you all feel as proud as I do of where I come from and what I represent. I am sorry if I haven't named you, but so many people have had an influence on who I am that it would take a book to thank them all. Hopefully you will enjoy reading my story.

Finally, I want to thank Ben Blaschke for writing my book. You have made telling my story an absolute pleasure and I can't thank you and the publishers Hachette Livre enough for making this experience so truly great. Thank you and be good.

Steve Price
Auckland, August, 2008

Foreword
— By Wayne Bennett

IT WAS 1998 — the year he made his State of Origin debut for Queensland — that I finally met Steven Price, but I had actually come across him long before then. Seven years earlier I had received a phone call from a good friend of mine, Graham Tucker, asking me to come and look at this young kid playing for his Newtown side in the Under-18s grand final in Toowoomba. I had played with Graham for Queensland in the 1970s and had heard a bit about Steve because there was some publicity about him, so I rolled up to watch this promising young forward go round.

Well, I saw Steve but I also saw a kid playing for the opposition named Shane Webcke. Steve was obviously a well-credentialed player and he looked like he was going to do something in the game, but I decided to chase Shane instead because I knew that Steve was close to doing a deal with Canterbury. I thought to myself: 'This can only get into a bloody bun-fight here — just stay out of it Wayne. This guy Shane Webcke looks alright so let's grab him instead'.

I didn't speak to Steve that day and we had no direct interaction again until I chose him for game one of the 1998 State of Origin series. He wasn't necessarily a popular choice. I don't think everyone was a fan of him — there was nobody jumping over hurdles saying, 'You've got to have Steve Price in your Queensland team' — but it was the right time, right place and I liked what he brought to the game.

I thought he had something that Queensland needed. The game had just been reunited after the Super League war and even though he was young, he had been playing some pretty good football. I just had confidence in him. Steve always seemed to be in there competing every week. He did his job as a front-rower, which is not always glamorous, and I thought he was a long-term investment for Queensland which is all part of the process.

Of course, Steve didn't know that at the time and I didn't want him to know. I wanted to keep him on his toes even though that's not always the best way to go with 'Pricey'. His personality is such that he is a bit fragile that way — he wants people to like him. Well, I liked him but I didn't need to show it — I showed it when I picked him in the team!

But it was hardly an auspicious start. Steve came from a club that defended differently to most other clubs. Canterbury used an up-and-in style of defence in which they brought players out of the line while most sides tried to keep a straight line. You usually try and pick players without those different traits because you know how you want to play and what you've got to do to win, but we worked very hard that week to get it out of his game. We knew it was going to hurt us if Steve came out of the line — and as it turned out that's exactly what happened. Steve raced up to pressure their kicker on the last tackle and NSW raced through the gap to score.

But he knew he had done the wrong thing and if there is one thing about Steve Price it is that he doesn't like to fail you. If you show some confidence and belief in him he is a very loyal guy. I love that quality about him and it's something I noticed very early on. The key for Steve was not to carry the divot with him, as they say in golf, after he had made that mistake. I wasn't paying much attention to his apologies at halftime but my last comment before he ran back out for the second half was: 'Don't do it again'. Sure enough he went out, scored a try and we ended up winning the game 24–23.

Since then I've always been there for Steve if he has ever needed to discuss anything or ask my advice. I don't necessarily put myself in that position but I want my players to understand that, if they need to talk to me, I'm available to them. I can't live their lives for them and I can't be with them 24 hours a day but Steve is a smart learner and a smart guy — he welcomes those who can help him and he seeks advice and direction. While he has always made his own decisions, those occasions when he has called me have been when he has felt a specific need and has thought I might have something to add.

One of those occasions was in 2001 when he was playing poorly and had endured a really tough 18 months. He had been dropped from the Queensland side during

Foreword

the 2000 Origin series and hadn't played representative football since. I remember saying to him candidly, 'You've got to start running bloody hard again Steve. You're running across-field at the moment and you're looking for the soft landings'.

Steve was beside himself at the time. He was just so disappointed and he was copping a fair bit of criticism. He doesn't like that. I guess none of us do, but criticism doesn't work for Steve Price. He performs better with a pat on the back than a kick in the guts. There has to be an honesty to what you tell him and Steve handles that okay but he doesn't handle it when you're negative or trying to find fault with him. He understands that he has faults but he responds far better to positive reinforcement.

In 2001 I was trying to send him positive messages because there was no bigger fan of Steve Price than me. He missed out on the Queensland side again in 2001 and we won the series that year which really upset him but, to his credit, he turned it around and I brought him back the following year. He hasn't looked back since.

The other occasion that stands out when Steve asked for my advice was in 2004 when he was contemplating leaving the Bulldogs to join the Warriors. It was a huge issue for him at the time. I never really thought Steve would leave the Bulldogs but I understood his reasoning — he had been scarred too many times.

Steve was the face of Canterbury. When things started going pear-shaped he was the one guy who stood above it all. Captaincy has its responsibilities but the demands and expectations that were placed upon him during the salary cap crisis and then Coffs Harbour were way above what should be expected of the captain of a football club.

It was too great of a burden to carry. He did so with great dignity and class and the club was very fortunate to have him at that time, but it wore him down. He knew what he was — he was a football player and that's what he wanted to do — but at that period of his life his football was being affected because he was a diplomat and he was the club's spokesman.

I remember reading the newspapers in 2002 when they published the players' salaries and when I saw what some of his team-mates were earning I thought: 'My God, they've taken him for granted'. They took his loyalty for granted. Steve bled blue and white. He was Peter Moore's baby — he loved Peter Moore and he loved the Bulldogs. When he called to tell me he was considering an offer from the Warriors, he obviously had his reasons for considering such a huge move.

But the Warriors came at the right time for Steve. A lot of players in his position find it difficult to play for other Sydney clubs, and he could never have done that, but the Warriors were off-shore and they were made for him. They offered him the relief that he sought. I thought it was excellent timing.

Steve rang me a couple of times to discuss it but the last time he called I was driving down a highway somewhere in northern NSW. I was only there to offer an opinion but I've been in footy for a long time and I see how these players can get caught up in situations that they don't want to be in. I told him that the Warriors might provide the change he needed although the final decision had to be his.

I must admit that I was still a little surprised when he left the Bulldogs — one of the reasons I never tried to lure Steve to Brisbane was that I never really thought he would leave anyway — but it has turned out to be exactly what he needed. He did a great job at Canterbury in the way he handled himself but he has been simply outstanding in Auckland without all of the pressure he had to endure at the Bulldogs.

I'm told that they actually consider him more of a Kiwi than half of the Kiwi players these days!

But that's Steve Price. He can walk that divide between people because he is such a lovely person. He isn't brash or over-confident in himself. He has strong self-belief but he also possesses good morals and he cares about people.

In that sense he really hasn't changed too much from that first time I saw him play in his Under-18s grand final in Toowoomba. He has fulfilled what we saw in him as a kid and he has taken it to the umpteenth level, which is what it is all about. What you see on the field is what you see off the field. There aren't two Steve Prices and that is another of his endearing qualities. He has always carried himself well. He is a credit to the game because he has presented and conducted himself in the manner that you would expect from a mature person.

Of course, these days he seems to think he can coach too. I was fortunate enough to coach the All Golds team on their tour of the United Kingdom in late 2007 and I had Steve chirping in my ear the whole time: 'Why did you do this, why didn't you do that?' I said to him, after about 15 minutes, 'Is it your turn to coach now? Here, you can have a turn'. Steve likes to hold court and he likes to philosophise a little bit but that's what makes up the guy.

Foreword

At the end of the day he is an extremely loyal person. If you're loyal to him he will never let you down. He is a very solid individual and that's one of the things that people like about him — he is someone you can rely upon. That's important. I have always felt that I could rely on Steve. In the team environment, if it's a night out, he doesn't drink a great deal either. I've never seen him drunk. He is very committed and that's why his longevity has been there as well — he has committed himself to the game totally and he has done a hell of a job.

More importantly, he has continued to get better with age and has developed into a wonderful leader. I think of players such as Shane Webcke, Andrew Gee and Darren Lockyer as very special guys. Going forward, they are the guys I would like to see involved in the game as administrators and 'Pricey' is right up there with all of them.

I'm sure he will be involved in the game somewhere when he retires and I certainly hope he is. He would make an excellent CEO. It's not an easy position and it's not something you can just jump straight into but Steve is a wonderful leader of people and I just hope he chooses rugby league once his playing days are finished because he is a credit to our sport. The game would be better off if it had more Steve Prices.

1 A New Beginning

I ALWAYS thought I would be a Bulldog for life.

For as long as I could remember, there was no other place I was going to go and that was just the way it was. Whenever the time came for me to sit down with the club and discuss a new contract, talk would centre on the long term and my involvement with the Bulldogs after my playing career had come to an end. I was Steve Price — the Bulldog — and it was a part of my make-up.

I was 18 when I arrived in Sydney and 20 when Jo joined me two years later, and the Bulldogs have played a huge role in the people that we are today. We made friendships that will last forever because when you join the Bulldogs you're not alone — your family joins too. That's why they were known as 'The Family Club'. Your playing days might only represent a short period of your life but the club plays such an integral role that it never really comes to an end.

People often ask me why I left the Bulldogs and it's a very difficult question to answer. That's one of the reasons I decided to write this book.

A lot has happened to me during my career — both on and off the field. I've played in three grand finals and watched one from the sideline, won a premiership and was injured when we won another. I have lived out a childhood dream by representing Queensland and Australia, received my life membership with the club and was even named in the Bulldogs' greatest ever team at the 70th anniversary dinner in 2004. But I've also experienced some tough times as well — the salary cap scandal, the Coffs Harbour saga of 2004 and rumours that I was gay and had a gambling addiction.

This book provides me with an opportunity to set the record straight for the first time, but above all else I want it to give an insight into Steve Price the person — and central to that is my loyalty to those closest to me. It is for this reason that I feel compelled, first and foremost, to spell out my reasons for leaving the club that had played such an integral role in my family's life.

Like most Bulldogs fans, I believed it was a formality that I would play out my career with the Bulldogs. But a lot of things happened between 2002 and 2004 that changed my perspective.

One was the sacking of Garry Hughes. To this day I'm convinced that those involved in getting rid of Garry had no idea just how important he was to the Bulldogs. He was the glue that held the place together.

There were never any glitches when Garry was football manager — it was smooth sailing all the way. He had everything under control, knew exactly what to do in any given situation and, on those rare occasions where he didn't, he knew who to go to in order to get the right people involved. I'm quite certain that my contract situation in 2004 wouldn't have become a problem if Garry had still been involved.

One of the reasons that I had never come close to leaving the Bulldogs previously was because I had never actually been off-contract. Garry was the reason for that. But that was just the tip of the iceberg.

The roots of my decision to leave the Bulldogs date back to 2002, when the club was found guilty of massive salary cap breaches and consigned to the foot of the Telstra Premiership ladder. For me personally, I guess it all began on Monday 19 August 2002 — two days after *The Sydney Morning Herald* broke the biggest story of the year.

None of the players had any idea just how serious the salary cap situation was until we were called into a meeting that day and asked by Leagues Club chairman Gary McIntyre and his son David to take eight-percent pay cuts in order to help the Bulldogs get themselves back under the salary cap. We had decided as a group to turn down his wish initially but after the NRL announced the punishment our club would receive for the breach we all signed new contracts agreeing to the eight-percent cut. To alleviate our concerns, that extra eight percent was added as an incentive if we reached the finals in 2003.

I was off-contract that year and, although I had agreed to terms on a new two-year deal (2003–04) with our chief executive Bob Hagan a few months earlier, I was

A New Beginning

yet to put pen to paper. We had agreed in principle with a hand shake but I hadn't signed the NRL registered contract. That's where the problems began.

Bob resigned the week after the salary cap scandal broke — one of a number of officials who were to become casualties — and was replaced by Steve 'Turvey' Mortimer, who did a tremendous job under very difficult circumstances. When it came time to sit down with 'Turvey' towards the end of the season to discuss a new contract, my manager George Mimis and I said to him, 'We haven't signed a deal yet but we've agreed to one', to which he replied, 'Okay, well we'll put an offer to you and we'll get it signed off'. But when he put his offer to us it was nothing like what we had agreed to with Bob. When we handed 'Turvey' the document that stated what had been agreed upon he nearly had a heart attack! He said, 'That's impossible; we can't give you this type of contract'.

It wasn't exactly what we wanted to hear, but George came up with an idea. He suggested that I sign for two years as was originally planned, with an option in my favour for the third. That would give the club time to sort through some of their existing contracts. In other words, we were under the impression that I would be rewarded financially in 2005–06 for the considerable pay cut I had agreed to at the time in order to help out the club.

As it was, myself and a handful of other players who were coming off-contract in 2002 actually suffered far more financially than those players who weren't. Not only did we agree to smaller deals to help alleviate the Bulldogs' salary cap woes when we re-signed for 2003 and beyond, we then took an eight-percent pay cut *on top* of the new deal. The rest of the team only had to forego eight percent on what they were already being paid and, given that the eight percent had been added on as an incentive if we made the finals in 2003, they weren't really affected at all. The rest of us lost out pretty big.

IT WASN'T until 2004, the year I had my contract option coming up, that I started to realise the things I had been promised might not eventuate. For starters, the people who had made those promises — Steve Mortimer and Garry Hughes — had both been removed (Mortimer agreed to 'step down') following the Coffs Harbour scandal that had taken place in February of that year.

Of course, I still had every intention of re-signing with the Bulldogs. I wanted to sign a deal, I wanted to get it out of the road and I wanted a contract that justified my reasons for taking a pay cut back in 2002. I wouldn't say that I wanted to be rewarded for it but I did want something from the club that would basically say, 'Thank you for doing what you did because it got us out of a tight spot'. Instead, I didn't hear a word from them for months — despite the fact that they kept announcing the re-signing of other players.

It was April when I first began asking George to find out what was happening but all he knew was that the retention committee was meeting soon and my situation would be discussed.

It wasn't until mid-June that a concrete offer finally came through, which was all I had been asking for, but I was disappointed to discover that nothing had really changed from the deal I was already on. It was a difficult situation because Bulldogs chief executive Malcolm Noad didn't know the full story but I felt that I deserved better after all that I had done.

By then there was a rumour going around that the Warriors were pretty keen on making me an offer. George had heard the same thing and said to me, 'We've got the offer from the Bulldogs now but it's not really much better than what we're already getting. It's a little bit more but I suggest we just wait and see what the Warriors do'. I said, 'Okay, no worries'.

As I've already mentioned, the whole situation would never have gone this far if Garry was still at the club. It would have been dealt with in April. So it would be an understatement to say that I was a little bit upset with the whole thing by this stage.

I was in State of Origin camp with Queensland on 1 July when George rang me and said, 'Mate, you won't believe it but we've got the offer from the Warriors and it's pretty good — I think it is something we've got to seriously consider'. I told him that I wasn't going to make any sort of decision until Origin was over but that whatever happened, Jo and the kids had to be happy. I didn't want Jo to have to come over with me if she didn't want to be there. That was the most important thing for me and to the Warriors' credit they organised for Jo to travel to New Zealand and look around.

Jo didn't even want to do *that* originally — she had never been to New Zealand before and wasn't looking forward to going over by herself — but the Warriors were fantastic. George told her to keep an open mind, to be honest and truthful and that, if there was anything that she was questioning, to make sure she asked before it was too late. I was still in camp when I called her and said, 'What do you reckon?' She told me: 'It was actually pretty good, the people were really nice and I've got no problems. I think I could live there no problem'.

With that out of the way, leaving the Bulldogs was suddenly a very real possibility for the first time in my career — but it wasn't a done deal. The Bulldogs were obviously worried I might leave because they had decided to chase Parramatta prop Paul Stringer. They were hedging their bets under the pretence that Paul was good friends with Mark O'Meley and would be keen to sign if the opportunity arose. As it turned out, Parramatta knew exactly what the Bulldogs were up to, and that I wasn't going to be making a decision until Origin was over, so they gave Paul a deadline of midday on State of Origin day to re-sign — he either signed a new contract with Parramatta or took a gamble and risked being left without a club if I decided to stay with the Bulldogs. In the end he took a good offer from the Eels, I returned from Origin camp, and the Bulldogs began their last ditch attempts to keep me.

I had to have a laugh, however, when I received a phone call out of the blue one day from Kevin Campion. Apparently Bulldogs coach Steve Folkes had heard a rumour that 'Campo' and his wife had hated New Zealand when he had played for the Warriors a few years earlier, so he rang up Billy Johnstone — the Cowboys trainer at the time — and asked if he could get 'Campo' to give me a call and pretty much tell me what he thought.

So Kevin called me and said, 'Hi mate, I've just got a message from Billy to give you a call and just let you know how I found New Zealand — me and the missus. I'm not sure why because I would have thought they'd want to try and keep you at the Bulldogs, but I can't say a bad thing about the place! I don't know what they've been told but this is probably the worst thing they could do. I'm only going to tell you great things. The people are fantastic, the experience we had was brilliant and being an Aussie over there, we had absolutely no issue. Everyone looked after us as if we were their own, the missus loved it and we only came to the Cowboys because the Warriors didn't give us the opportunity that we were hoping for in the end. If it wasn't for that, we would have stayed for sure'.

Needless to say, I had a quiet chuckle about that.

THE DAY after State of Origin III — on the Thursday — I spent the whole day at the

Leagues Club with Steve Folkes, chairman George Peponis, Malcolm Noad — who had taken over from 'Turvey' as CEO, Leagues Club boss John Ballesty and our new football manager Brad Clyde. I arrived there at about 10 a.m. and didn't leave until nine o'clock that night. We spoke about a whole range of issues but the main thing for me was longevity — could the Bulldogs guarantee that I would be a part of the club going forward given everything that had happened over the previous two years?

They eventually came up with an offer that they said was the absolute best that they could do and we said we would consider it. I went straight home, sat down with Jo and we had a massive talk about all of the pros and cons of leaving the Bulldogs to join the Warriors.

George was still reluctant for me to leave because Steven Price leaving the Bulldogs was something that simply shouldn't happen. He actually said to me, 'Mate, I think you should stay. The Warriors are a little bit of an unknown, the jury is still out on Mick Watson and I'm a bit unsure about him'. He was certainly proved right about that one.

George and I were due to meet with the Warriors the next morning so he said to me: 'Depending on what happens we'll either tell the Warriors it's all over or we'll say it's all on and we'll tell the Bulldogs it's all over'. And that was the night that I made my decision. I said to Jo, 'I really think it's the right thing to go to the Warriors. There will be a few things that I want to sort out with my contract but that's the way I feel'.

I had already spoken to Wayne Bennett about my thoughts and he was very supportive as well. I asked him straight out, 'What do you think about the Warriors? Do you think it would be a good move if I was contemplating going there?' Straight away Wayne said to me, 'I think it would be good', because he knew everything that I had been through during the salary cap scandal. I had told him the scenario, he saw what my salary was in the newspapers and he said, 'Mate, if that's what you're getting it's not good. They should be looking after you a lot better than that and it seems like they are taking you for granted'.

I STILL love the Bulldogs — that will never change — but in 2004 I had started to see things differently. I've mentioned Garry Hughes' sacking. The biggest gripe I had about Garry's departure was the club's reason for doing it.

About a week after the Coffs Harbour scandal broke — when a woman claimed she had been sexually assaulted by a number of Bulldogs players after our trial match against Canberra — we copped a whole heap of criticism for players turning up to police interviews wearing shorts and t-shirts. Apparently those concerned were being disrespectful towards what was obviously a very serious issue.

The truth is that none of the players knew that they were required by police when they turned up to training that day — and shorts and t-shirts are what players wear before and after training. Not everyone wears a suit and tie to work. What happened was that the boys turned up for training, the club was then informed that they had to go into the city for interviews immediately and when they arrived they were suddenly confronted by a media throng. Later that night they were shown on every television channel turning up to their interviews wearing the wrong clothing and it looked as though the Bulldogs had absolutely no respect for the situation.

That wasn't the case at all but there was a lot of pressure from outside for the club to be seen to be taking action — and Garry turned out to be the fall-guy despite the fact that what happened wasn't his fault. That certainly got me thinking. It would never have happened under the previous administration because the club was all about the people and had always dealt with things internally.

For Garry to be fired over that really opened my eyes. He was a Bulldogs man through and through. He had played all of his footy there, his family was very, very involved in the club and he had been part of the administration ever since his playing days had come to an end. I had a wonderful relationship with him and if he had still been there I would never have left.

THE OTHER big change that contributed to my decision to leave the Bulldogs was the significant shift in culture. By this stage, the younger guys were starting to have a bit of an influence on that by going out and partying whenever they could. I was used to the family orientated club the Bulldogs had always been and I wasn't really jumping on board with where the club was going and what was being allowed to happen.

For the club to then say 'We can't really afford to pay you that much', when they were paying other players plenty, made me feel as though they considered them to be a more important part of where the club was going than I was.

But hey, if I couldn't change it, why fight it? I realised that it might be best to accept what was happening and go to a club where I could start to make a difference.

Maybe everything I had been through over the previous two years had started to wear me down. It was certainly a permanent cloud hanging over my head. I was starting to feel a little bit stale that pre-season and I was ready for a new challenge. I knew, too, that in two years' time the same salary cap excuse would be trotted out again. I wanted to sign a three-year deal but 'Folkesy' only wanted to sign me for two. He also wanted me to retire from representative football to focus solely on the Bulldogs. The greatest challenge for me as a player has always been to compete at the highest level — Tests and State of Origin — and I couldn't imagine having those goals taken away from me. I don't think I was asking too much.

I don't blame anyone for what happened. Once 'Turvey' and Garry left, Malcolm Noad and Brad Clyde came in and they just weren't aware of what had been promised two years earlier or of the loyalty that I had shown at the time. It's not always about money but I had put up with certain things for two years and it obviously wasn't going to get any better. Unfortunately, when I stuck up for myself I didn't get the response I was hoping for.

I still left the club on good terms and I've got absolutely no regrets. I would have finished at the Bulldogs a very happy person just like I'll finish at the Warriors a very happy person. I could have done either and I was very lucky to have been in that position with a number of tremendous opportunities open to me.

I WOULD soon learn that all wasn't quite as it seemed at the Warriors but in July 2004 I was extremely impressed with what the club had to offer.

The irony was that, on the morning I was due to meet with Warriors management at the Novotel in Brighton Le Sands, I hadn't actually had any personal contact with the club at all. I had barely even spoken to them on the phone. George was the one who had been dealing with them and Jo had been over to New Zealand to meet everyone but I'd really only seen them on TV.

One thing that the Warriors did do was send me a video with four of their players — Stacey Jones, Monty Betham, PJ Marsh and Richard Villasanti — saying how great it would be to have Steven Price come to the Warriors. That was a nice touch and something I hadn't expected. They also had no issue with me playing rep footy and actually encouraged it. To top it off, they were more than willing to offer me a three-year deal.

So I was fairly impressed with the club but I still wanted to speak to Wayne

Bennett again. George actually said to me: 'Don't talk to Wayne again because *you've* got to make the decision', but on the Friday morning that I was scheduled to meet with the Warriors for the first time I gave Wayne a call. I needed his support because he knew my situation and he was external enough not to be affected by emotion.

As far as George was concerned I was meeting with the Warriors to tell them I was staying with the Bulldogs. In reality I had spoken to Jo and had pretty much decided that if I was able to get some minor details sorted out with my contract then I was going to go to the Warriors.

That's exactly what I told Wayne. His response was: 'Mate, I don't think there is any problem with that. I think if anything it's a good decision for you at this stage of your footy career and your family life. It will be great for them as an experience and if you can achieve what you're setting out to achieve personally I think that will be a real credit to you as a person'. I told Wayne that I was proud of my career but that if I was able to make a difference at the Warriors and help build a successful culture it would be the icing on the cake. That had already been done at the Bulldogs but at that stage of my career I felt the things I had learnt over the years could really help a young club with potential. He agreed and that was all I needed to hear.

When I met with George that morning I said, 'George, I think I want to go to the Warriors'. He just stared at me and said, 'Are you serious?' He couldn't believe it.

But the Warriors were great. George went in first to discuss the minor contract alterations I wanted with their CEO Mick Watson, general manager Spiro Tsiros and football manager Don Mann. A few minutes later I was introduced to them and they said, 'No worries, that's sweet with us'. They were obviously pretty excited. Mick said to me, 'It's great news for our club to sign a guy like you and we just can't wait, we wish you all the best for the rest of the season' — and that was basically it. We went straight into George's office, signed a letter of intent and the deal was done.

THERE WAS one more thing that disappointed me about the whole contract situation. Straight after my meeting with the Warriors, I called Malcolm Noad to let him know that I was going to leave, that George would be in touch and that I wanted to wait until Monday — after our game against Melbourne — before making the announcement at a press conference. Malcolm's response was: 'There's nothing that we can do?' I replied, 'No, you've pretty much told me that this is everything you can do'.

Of course, the Bulldogs tried to come up with a better deal but by then it was too late. It has happened a couple of times in my life now that someone has said to me 'This is the absolute best that we can do' only to come up with a better offer at the very last minute. The Bulldogs had already told me two weeks earlier that they couldn't do any better but when they found out I was leaning towards the Warriors they suddenly found a bit of extra money in the coffers. That disappointed me. I thought that I'd been at the club long enough for people to be up front and honest with me.

Right through my whole career at the Bulldogs, every time it came time to sign a new contract the CEO would tell me: 'We've got no money left in the kitty, this is the best we can give you' — and I would cop it. 'No worries,' I'd say, 'I like it here and I can handle that'. Jo always said to me: 'I think they say that to you because they know you want to stay'.

But as I said, the past is the past and I hold no grudges. I'm proud about the way I left the Bulldogs. It was a business decision and at the end of the day I think the Bulldogs respected that.

I've never forgotten a conversation I had with former Bulldogs boss Peter Moore — who first brought me down to Sydney — about Chris Mortimer. Chris was at the Bulldogs for 11 years, had his testimonial, and then received an excellent offer to join Penrith in 1988. Apparently Peter said to him, 'Mate, I'll be very disappointed if you don't take that offer because you're towards the end of your career, I think you'll really help Penrith and you're looking after your family'. The other thing Peter said to Chris at the time was: 'You'll always be a Bulldog, no matter what happens. However many years you play at Penrith, you'll always be known as a Bulldog'.

I saw a real similarity between Chris Mortimer and myself because I *do* see him as a Bulldog. No matter how many years I was to play for the Warriors, I still felt that people would associate the majority of my career with the Bulldogs. And the link is still there. Whenever I'm back in Sydney I go into the Leagues Club or go down to the football club and say G'day to everyone. The Bulldogs played a very special role in my life. They made me the person and the player I am today and I'm never going to forget that.

2 Growing Up

I WAS born on 12 March 1974 — the first child of Margaret Christie and John Price. Mum and Dad were just starting out in a trailer-building business called Price's Trailer Sales back then and everything was going really well for them. My sister Wendy was born two years after me and we lived on a farm in Dalby — about 250 km north-west of Brisbane. That's where I have my first memories.

I had a three-wheeler motorbike that I used to ride around all over the place because we had plenty of space to have fun. Either that or I'd be on the ride-on mower with Dad.

I was also somewhat of a firebug. One morning I woke up early and found some newspapers on the bottom of one of those Bonaire air-conditioning coolers. Dad used to smoke so I grabbed his matches and decided it would be a good idea to light the whole thing up. The next minute there were flames everywhere and I'm panicking and yelling out to Dad. He jumped out of bed, came racing into the room and pushed the whole Bonaire unit straight out of the house. It literally flew out the door and down the stairs!

Another time there was a tarp for a trailer in the farm shed and I decided to see what would happen if I set that on fire too. I grabbed Dad's matches and the next minute he was having visions of his whole shed — trucks and all — going up in flames. It goes without saying that I was in a fair bit of trouble for that one.

I almost burnt my aunty's farmhouse down when my cousin and I decided it would be pretty cool to set fire to the bushes. But my firebug stage came and went pretty quickly — mainly because of the floggings I copped for nearly killing us!

We were pretty well known around Dalby. The farm we lived on was owned by my Pop Trevor while my Uncle Russell and my great grandmother also owned farms in the area. Pop had a business called Price's Machinery and he was renowned for being a wheeler and dealer. His nickname was 'Sarge' and he was always attending auctions to buy anything from machinery to cars and even furniture — whatever he could do up to sell at a better price. I loved the holidays because it meant I could go with Pop to his auctions and see how he went about his business.

My cousin Jason and I used to spend hours playing in the massive sandpit we had on the farm. I owned a heap of Tonka trucks so when he came over we would build a road through the middle of the sandpit, split the toys between us and each have our own side. Then we would start doing deals and that sort of thing — but inevitably there would be a blue. We'd start throwing sand at each other, start throwing punches and each walk away with black eyes!

I remember having a fight with a guy at school too during my first year there. We went to school in Dalby for only six months before we moved to Brisbane but I still found time for this fight, which was a kicking fight. The kid's name was Kevin Turner and we both had new boots that we each thought were better than the other's. We ended up having an argument so we decided we'd have a kicking fight to see who had the best boots. It wasn't a good idea — we were in terrible pain and neither of us really won. In the end, both pairs of boots worked pretty well!

I also had my first crush at school in Dalby. There was a girl who I thought was quite attractive and it was around the time that *Star Wars* was pretty big so I thought of myself as Luke Skywalker and she was my Princess Leia!

WE MOVED from the farm when Dad bought a townhouse on Kookaburra Street — where we lived for a couple of years when I was young — but it was around about that time that things started to turn sour between Mum and Dad. Dad received a pretty hefty tax bill one day that he couldn't afford to pay so the business went into receivership and we had to sell up. It must have put a lot of strain on their relationship and when I was six years old they split up.

Dad moved down the coast by himself while Mum, Wendy and I moved to Brisbane. I didn't realise at the time how tough Mum was doing it, but because we'd gone bankrupt we basically had nothing and she was working a couple of jobs just to keep us going.

We certainly didn't make it easy on her. I used to look after my sister when school finished each afternoon and we had made quite a few friends around the neighbourhood. Mum had a change jar on the fridge that she would throw all of her small change in to save a bit of money for us, but I used to raid it to buy lollies and share them around all of our friends! There was no way we could afford it — if anything, the other kids should have been buying lollies for us — but I didn't realise how hard it was for Mum at the time. It wasn't until quite a while later that she realised what was going on and she went off her head at me!

We had moved into an area in Brisbane called Acacia Ridge which was renowned as one of the tougher suburbs around but we couldn't really afford to live anywhere else. I remember a night early on when we went to visit Dad. Mum drove down to pick us up afterwards and when we arrived back home the whole unit had been ruined. Someone had broken in and stolen all of Mum's valuables — there was basically nothing left. That was terrible for her and I remember how upset she was.

But Mum was really conscious of trying to give us the best lifestyle that she could even though she didn't have any money. We didn't see a lot of Dad by this stage because of the divorce so we spent a lot of time with our grandfather, Mum's dad, who tried to help her out as much as he could.

Eventually we were able to move from the unit to a nearby house on Flaxton Street. I remember that place well because Flaxton Street had a huge hill that we used to race down. We would build go-karts with all of the other kids on the street and go flying down the big dipper with bark flying off everywhere. It was crazy when I look back on it.

I also played soccer for about 12 months but I quickly began to discover my love for rugby league. It would have been 1982 by this stage and Acacia Ridge was Souths Magpies territory. It was one of the strongest teams of the era with guys like Mal Meninga and Gary Belcher playing for it — all of these huge stars. One day Mum bought me a sweatshirt, more like a pullover really, but in the design of an actual jersey so it was white with the black V and all of the sponsors' names on it. That was my jersey so I thought I was a rugby league player, even though I wasn't playing rugby league at the time. It was my first real taste of rugby league and the excitement of the Magpies.

Mum also started seeing the man who would become my stepfather, Garry Sullivan, around this time. Garry worked for a company called John Bain Transport — who bought a lot of trailers from Dad when we were living in Dalby — so they had actually met quite a few years earlier. They started seeing each other after we had moved to Brisbane and eventually it started to become quite serious. We ended up moving to Toowoomba because Garry was located there and he thought it would be better for us to get out of Acacia Ridge.

But I made life pretty tough for Gaz. I wasn't happy about leaving Acacia Ridge because I quite liked it there and I also considered myself the man of the family — the tough guy. He was only trying to help but my opinion at the time was that he shouldn't be around. I guess I always hoped that Mum and Dad would get back together one day. I regret the way I acted now because I was just this snotty-nosed kid sticking up for my Mum and sister.

Anyway, we rented a place in Toowoomba on Drayton Road and I started going to Harristown Primary School. Not long after that we moved into the house that is still Mum's home now on Alderley Street — which Poppy Christie helped Mum and Gaz buy — and in 1983 they were married. I remember walking Mum down the aisle to give her away and I realised then that Mum and Dad wouldn't be getting back together. But I didn't ease up on Gaz and we had blues all the time.

There was one time I said something I shouldn't have or carried on like an idiot, probably both, and he sent me outside. Toowoomba is a pretty cold place, especially in winter, so I was outside for a few minutes and I must have known what was going to happen. After five minutes Mum and Gaz had come out to get me because they were worried about me freezing to death but they couldn't find me — I had snuck around the side of the house and actually jumped back in my bedroom window while they were outside panicking! That sort of thing happened quite regularly — I'm just surprised Gaz was so good to me with the way I treated him.

Mum and Garry ended up having my half-brother Daniel together in 1984 whom I had grand plans for. I decided that, whenever we played footy or cricket in the back yard, even though there was a 10-year age difference, I was going to make it really hard for him so that he would learn to be competitive. Well it worked — he is now the most competitive person I have ever met!

Unfortunately it came back to bite me. We were playing backyard cricket once,

I took off for a run, tripped over my own feet and broke my big toe. I was lying there in absolute agony but all Daniel did was pick the ball up, stroll over to the stumps and run me out!

IT WAS during that same year, in 1983, that one of my school mates, Wade Baartz, said to me, 'Why don't you come and play rugby league? I reckon you would be good at it'. I wasn't so sure. I was a fast runner as a nine-year-old but I certainly wasn't a big kid so I went home and spoke to Mum and Gaz about it.

It was Gaz that actually convinced Mum to let me play. She was doing the typical Mum thing, saying, 'Oh my little boy, he'll get hurt', but Gaz was a rugby league man and happened to be a financial member of the Newtown Rugby League Club. They had offered financial memberships to raise a bit of money and had asked people to become life members by paying $500. Gaz had paid the money so he was a member of Newtown and that's the club Wade asked me to play for.

As it turned out, even though Wade was in the same year as me at school, he was actually 12 months older than me so I couldn't play in his team. It nearly turned me off playing because he was the only reason I turned up in the first place, but Mum said, 'Why don't you go with the boys you're supposed to be with and see how it goes? Give it a go and if it's no good you can quit'. It ended up being the greatest thing I did because the boys who were in the older group found themselves in a bit of trouble — a few of them have ended up in jail — while the boys I was with enjoyed huge success going through the juniors.

But I remember turning up to my first training session and being terrified because I didn't know anyone. It was one of those situations where I didn't even catch a footy until late in the session because I was too busy looking at all of these other kids and wondering what I was doing there.

I remember my first game against Southport Tigers. It was a trial game and the other team was just huge. All the coach said to me was: 'When you get the ball just run as fast as you can and try to put it over the tryline'. I scored a try the first time I touched the ball but I must admit it was probably because I was so scared — I didn't want to get tackled so I ran around the outside and scored!

We had a great team back then and a few of us went on to play in the NRL. They included my best mate Ian Dunemann, his little brother Andrew, Russell Bussian and Toddy Miller. Ian was actually our goal-kicker that first year. We played barefoot on a full-sized footy field and wherever you scored you had to kick for goal from there. Being winter in Toowoomba it was freezing, we played at eight or nine o'clock in the morning so there was still ice on the ground . . . and Ian was a toe-poker! Even the thought of going out to play footy in the NRL with sleet on the grass absolutely terrifies me now but we did it without any second thought at the time. We just loved the game so much.

I had a daily routine each Saturday where I would come home after a game and watch Jerry Lewis and Dean Martin on TV. I would absolutely wet myself, laughing uncontrollably. That was always followed by the Saturday afternoon footy which at the time, more often than not, would feature Parramatta. If they won I would be so excited that I would run out into the backyard with my footy and start chipping and chasing over the clothesline pretending I was Peter Sterling or Brett Kenny. Mum wasn't too thrilled. There was a corner between the back shed and the house where Mum had a garden and I used to wet the whole area with a hose so that I could slide along and score tries like my heroes did when it was raining. We had red clay rather than dirt so I was always filthy by the time I came back inside.

I also gradually destroyed Mum's garden. She had these high plants with a really broad stem that I hated because if I slid into them I would always get jabbed or cut. As time went by I would slowly but surely get rid of bits of the garden until one day I accidentally took the whole lot out! I thought I was doing Mum a favour but she yelled at me for hours!

I'll never forget the day I burnt my leg in Mrs Dunemann's car — because I've still got the scar to prove it. I had stayed at their place the night before and Mrs Duney was driving us to the game. She always used to have everything ready to take to the footy — snacks and sandwiches — as well as a hot water flask in the back of her old Kingswood station wagon. Ian's younger brother Andrew and I were sitting in the back of the car when Mrs Duney ripped around a corner and, as she did so, the flask tipped over. Unfortunately the lid wasn't on properly and the water flew out everywhere. I had footy socks and tracksuit pants on where the water hit and all of a sudden I felt this burning sensation which got worse and worse because it was boiling water. Mrs. Dunemann pulled over to look at the burn and as she pulled my sock down it started pulling layers of skin off!

Me with my great grandmother, Old Nana Price, and right with Mum. I was only one year old at the time.

My father John and me in Dalby, back in 1976.

A family gathering at Surfers Paradise in 1975. From left is Auntie Sandra, me (aged about one), Mum, Dad, Nana Glad and my grandfather Trevor who I called Poppy Price.

My sister Wendy, stepfather Garry, me and Mum. I was 10 years old at the time.

My first day of school in 1980.

My Under-10s side at Newtown in 1984. We finished the season undefeated and won the Hamilton Cup and President's Cup. I'm standing third from the right in the back row.

My Darling Downs Primary School's rugby league 12-years team in 1986. We were crowned State Champions and won the Gary Balkin Trophy. I'm third from right in the back row again, wearing my favourite No.10 jersey. Second from left in the same row is a young kid by the name of Shane Webcke.

My first day of high school at Harristown State High in 1987. I'm pictured with my little brother Dan and Nana Christie.

Left: My future wife Jo before our Year 12 formal in 1991 and, right, my good friends Heath Farlow and Tony Crossley on the same day.

Top: My Year 7 class in 1986 at Harristown Primary School with me standing fifth from left in the back row and Jo one to the right of centre in the third row. We're pictured standing together right in the centre in our Year 11 photo at Harristown High School below.

Jo and I at Seagulls Stadium in 1991 after my Harristown State High School side played Palm Beach-Currumbin.

Me and my cousin Jason Price in 1992 at the farm where I lived as a kid. Behind us is my first car . . . 'Kermit the Ute'.

Right: As a bustling young forward playing for Harristown State High School against John Paul II, Marayong in the 1992 Commonwealth Bank Cup national semi-final. I threw an intercept for John Paul II to score but we scraped home 12–10.

Below: Peter 'Bullfrog' Moore drops me off at Sydney airport after our Commonwealth Bank Cup final in 1992.

Action Photographics

One of my very first games in first grade for the Bulldogs in 1994.

Growing Up

I actually played that day which is probably one of the stupidest things I've ever done. It was halfway through my first year, I loved playing and I didn't want to miss a game but all that kept happening each week was that the burn would blister up, the blister would burst and it would never really heal. Three months later it still hadn't healed because I kept playing and it started to get infected. Mum eventually said to me, 'If you don't look after it they'll end up cutting your leg off!' I went to the specialist and he told me the same thing so finally I took a break from playing and let my burn heal.

NEWTOWN WAS always a strong club, having produced Newcastle's Robbie O'Davis, Cronulla and St George fullback Kurt Wrigley, and my current Warriors team-mate Michael Witt, his brother Steve, Ben and Jaiman Lowe and Tony Jensen over the years.

We also had some excellent coaches when I was growing up. Wayne Simmons was my first coach but he was supported by his father-in-law who happened to be Gary Czislowski, who is Scott Czislowski's father and Ben Czislowski's grandfather. Gary said to us that year: 'Boys, I want you to go home and watch State of Origin tonight and whatever number you wear, find the player who wears the same number and do the same as him'.

I used to wear number eight for Newtown, which was lock at that time, and the player I watched represent Queensland that night was Bob Lindner. I watched everything he did and I liked how he played. He wasn't a dirty player, he wasn't a player who got the big wraps or the one who won games for his team but he always gave everything he had — particularly in Origin. I idolised him. Over the years he did some phenomenal things on the footy field and was a part of a fantastic era in State of Origin.

I also became a Parramatta supporter because during that time it was Parramatta and Canterbury who were the rivals and I didn't like Canterbury. They seemed like a dirty team and they had all of the so-called 'thugs' in their side. They were the intimidators whereas Parramatta had all of the class and grace. They had an exciting back line and obviously Ray Price played for them. I used to tell everyone at school that he was my uncle!

Back in the 1980s, Peter Sterling had his own sports store called Peter Sterling Sports. I used to buy *Big League* and *Rugby League Week* every week and they had an advertisement saying you could buy an authentic jersey, so I saved my money and sent away for a No 13 jersey just like my Uncle Ray's. When it arrived I used to wear it around and tell people that Ray had given it to me, so everyone thought I was pretty cool until they found out that I had made the whole thing up!

I actually got to meet Ray after the 1986 grand final. We had driven down to Brisbane airport to drop Gaz off and Ray happened to be there on his way to one of the islands for a holiday with his wife. When I saw him I raced over to Mum and said, 'That's Ray Price!' She said, 'Go and ask him for his autograph — the worst thing that can happen is he says no'. So I walked up to him and he was sensational. He signed my autograph, I told him my name was Price and he had a giggle about that. I also told him that I wanted to play first grade for Parramatta one day and how sad I was that he was retiring. He wished me luck, patted me on the head and sent me on my way. I'll never forget it.

I SHOWED plenty of promise as I moved through the junior grades and made the Toowoomba side and every other rep team from Under-9s right through to the Under-12s Queensland Schoolboys. I was fast and probably a little bit bigger than the other kids when I first started playing. But it was also around that time, as I was turning 12 and 13, that a lot of kids started to really develop physically. It was a tough time for a country kid like myself because the city teams were massive. They always seemed to develop a lot quicker so I really started to struggle from Under-13s right through to Under-15s.

The way the rep teams worked back in the Under-13s and -14s was that you would be picked from your club side to play for Toowoomba. You would then participate in the South East Queensland Carnival which was in Brisbane my first year and Chinchilla my second.

Schoolboys footy was similar. You had your Under-12s, Under-15s and Open Schoolboys teams so again there was the Toowoomba Schoolboys team, then Darling Downs which was very much like Toowoomba and South West, then Queensland Country or City — depending on where you were from — and then Queensland. That was in all three age groups.

I remember my first overseas tour, with Toowoomba, when I was 11. We went to New Zealand to play against some of their local rep sides and, as it turned out,

Growing Up

I came across a young halfback named Stacey Jones for the first time. I was talking to Stacey when I joined the Warriors and he's certain he played against us. He is a couple of years younger than me but he used to play up in his brother's age group and he remembers playing against a Toowoomba touring team.

I don't remember playing against Stacey too well but I do remember playing against this giant Maori girl. She scared the life out of us! This was down in Christchurch somewhere and she was only 11 but she was so big and mean. We still won the game but gee we were scared of this girl — I think I'd still be scared if I came across her now! The tour went for two weeks and covered both the North and South Islands. Each kid had to have an adult with them so Nanna Christie — Mum's mum — came over with me which was great for both of us.

Anyway, right up through to the Under-12s I had always made the Toowoomba team and that year I also made the Queensland Schoolboys. Then, all of a sudden, I couldn't make anything. I went from Queensland Schoolboys when I was 12 to not even making South East Queensland a year later.

I still thought I was going pretty well. I was making the Toowoomba teams but I wasn't taking the next step into the Queensland teams . . . and then I started getting put on the bench for Toowoomba! That was a huge wake-up call for me. Until then my aspirations were right on target, then all of a sudden I was playing poorly, I wasn't enjoying it as much and I lost a lot of confidence because I was so much smaller than the rest of the boys.

One day Mum pulled me aside and said to me, 'Okay, this is the scenario — you don't look like you're enjoying your footy and I'm not going to let you keep playing if you're not enjoying it. I don't want you to feel that you've got to play it for anybody else. You've got to want to play it yourself. I'm going to have someone come along today to watch you play and if, in their opinion, you're not playing like you enjoy it then you're not going to play anymore.'

I was crapping myself! I had no idea who this person was supposed to be so I tried as hard as I could, but it was obviously a test from Mum to get me going again. All of a sudden I went back to the basics and things started to improve.

But I consider myself lucky to have had so many good coaches as a kid. Every single one was outstanding and taught me the fundamentals of the game which has really helped my progress throughout my career. You see so many kids coming into first grade now, even coming into an NRL squad, that can't pass from right to left with any confidence, accuracy or consistency. There are all of these basic fundamentals of the game that they can't do and the reason is that when they first started playing their coaches didn't spend enough time getting the fundamentals right.

It's a bit of a nightmare for someone like Ivan Cleary at the Warriors who always has to go back to those basics because the Polynesian kids grow so fast that they've never needed a good passing game. They just run over the top of the little white kids and it's not until they reach first grade when all the other guys are the same size and the same strength that they start to struggle. So having that coaching when I was young was amazing. I was fortunate too that my stepfather Gaz had some wonderful friends such as John Bain, Bill Baskett and Neil Mansell who all owned transport companies and would sponsor me whenever I made a rep team, because Mum and Gaz couldn't afford to send me on the trips.

I went to three Queensland rugby league camps when I was young and it was one of the best things I ever did. We had guys like Danny Stains, Arthur Beetson and Ian Roberts coming to those camps and giving us hands-on training. Some of the great coaches would be there too — John Monie and Wayne Bennett — so as a 13- or 15-year-old you couldn't have anybody better to learn from.

I remember John Monie was at my first camp when I was 13 and he had every skill of the game in this course — chipping and chasing, regathering and tackling, stepping — all of that in the one continuous course and at the end of it he would give you a mark. Well he gave me a D for mine and I was shattered because I loved Parramatta and he was the Parramatta coach. I thought: 'There goes my chance to play for the Parramatta Eels'. The funny thing is that I met John a few years ago through Wayne Bennett and told him the story. I said, 'Hopefully it made you look bad with your marking system', but he turned it around on me and said, 'Maybe because I marked you harshly that day you went back and worked really hard at those skills and that's why you're where you are now'. It's probably true.

We were also pretty lucky in Toowoomba because every year we would have teams come up to play in the Tooheys Challenge (the ARL's pre-season knockout competition). It gave us that personal interaction with players and it was one of the greatest things the game could do from my perspective because it really gave me the passion and desire to excel and emulate those players one day.

Growing Up

To see the speed of the game, to meet the guys and see how big they were was actually quite intimidating because you wondered how you could ever reach their level. But it made me so determined and focused on succeeding that even Jo half expected me to dump her and marry a football when I grew up!

I would buy every single *Rugby League Week* and I had posters all over my room of all the players. I knew everything about rugby league: all the players, how many games they had played, how many tries they had scored. If I was asked any question about rugby league I could answer it on the spot just like that. It used to frustrate Mum because I would struggle with my school work. She used to say to me: 'You know how excited you get about *Rugby League Week*? Try and get just as excited about Maths or English'. Obviously that was never going to work. I would spend hours and hours in my room and Mum would think 'He's doing his homework' but I was reading *Rugby League Week*. That was my homework. But I was fit too because I played three games a week — school footy, rep footy and club footy — as well as mowing lawns to make a bit of pocket money.

I remember buying my first pair of footy boots. I was 11 at the time and one of our sponsors at Toowoomba said they would sponsor three of us with a tracksuit and a pair of footy boots before our trip to New Zealand. I walked into the sports store and said to Peter Duncan, who owned the shop, 'I don't care what brand I buy, I just want a pair of screw-in boots'. He said, 'What do you want screw-in boots for?' I told him, 'Because they're the best — they're comfortable and they're the best'. He just looked at me and said, 'What a load of rubbish. It's the worst thing for your feet. You shouldn't be wearing screw-in boots at your age — that's a joke'.

I was stunned. I loved the sound of screw-ins walking on the concrete and I used to see all of the Winfield Cup players wearing them so I thought that was what you had to do. But this guy ripped into us, convinced me to buy a pair of moulded boots and I didn't wear anything else until 2007. With the way the grounds are now, it's hard to find moulded boots that can survive on those surfaces so I reluctantly wear screw-ins now if I have to. Still, it goes to show you how much of an impact people can make when you're young. The funny thing about it is that those first boots of mine were Pumas and they had this certain smell that I'll never forget. I'm actually sponsored by Puma now and when I received my first pair from them two years ago I smelt that great smell again. It brought back a flood of memories from my early years.

3 The Price is Rising

BY THE time I was 15 I was enjoying my football again, was playing well and had renewed my ambition to one day play first grade in the ARL.

It was while I was at a Queensland rugby league camp in 1989 that I was first spotted by a guy called Mick Ryan, who had played for Canterbury, Newtown and the Roosters. Mick was doing his Level 2 coaching certificate and took our group for a few drills. He must have liked something about me because he mentioned to a contact at the Gold Coast Giants that there was this kid named Steven Price who they should look at. All of a sudden I would start running into people who were apparently keeping an eye on me, or my coach would tell me that people were watching.

As it turned out, my stepfather Garry was good friends with the father-in-law of Gold Coast trainer Billy Johnstone, who was going to be in town for Christmas. Gaz said to me, 'We'll try to get you to meet Billy and see what he says about getting to first grade.'

Billy proved to be a hard man to track down because he was catching up with family but I ended up calling him and going around to see him on Christmas Day, which was probably quite rude of me when I look back on it. I said to Billy, 'What do I have to do to get a scholarship or a contract with the Gold Coast?' He said to me, 'You've basically got to play for Queensland or the Australian Schoolboys. You do that and you'll get something. Have you done that?' I told him, 'I've played Under-12s' and he said, 'That's good but you have to make the older age groups'.

So that is exactly what happened. The following year we had a great season at

The Price is Rising

Harristown State High School — where we played in the state semi-final of the Commonwealth Bank Cup against a very good Palm Beach Currumbin team — after which myself, Ian and Andrew Dunemann and Russell Bussian were all signed to scholarships with the Gold Coast. That's when I first started to get to know Billy Johnstone — whom I've since had a lot to do with at the Bulldogs and while playing for Queensland and Australia — but I must admit he didn't talk to me for a couple of years when I left the Gold Coast to sign for Canterbury!

It was actually around this time too that I started coaching the Under-6s at Newtown. The first team I coached was my little brother Daniel's team which featured none other than my current Warriors team-mate Michael Witt. I did a lot of refereeing as well and Brent Tate — another Warriors team-mate these days as well as being my brother-in-law — played in one of the first games I officiated. Not surprisingly he carved them up.

IN 1992, Gaz was transferred to Adelaide to start and operate a new yard for the company he worked for, John Bain Transport. The family — Mum, my brother Daniel and my sister Wendy — joined him but I had signed a two-year scholarship with the Gold Coast and didn't want to throw that away. I had finished high school in 1991, when we made the Queensland semi-finals of the Commonwealth Bank Cup, and was supposed to join the Gold Coast the following season to play Under-21s but they decided I was a bit young and told me to stay in Toowoomba for another 12 months.

That threw a spanner in the works. With Mum moving to Adelaide I didn't know what I was going to do. I also wanted to be a policeman but I didn't have the marks to get in straight away. I ended up staying behind and living in our house by myself which made life difficult for Mum and Gaz because they had to send money back to me which they didn't really have to spare. But there were others to help me out too. I turned 18 in March and got my driver's licence so Uncle Russell let me borrow his green ute, which we used to call Kermit.

Jo's brother-in-law Brad was a butcher and would give me a really good deal on meat. I would also make the trip down the range and buy 20-kg bags of carrots and potatoes for next to nothing. All year I basically I lived on steak and vegetables!

Our house became a second home for most of my team-mates. If we all went out on a Friday night it ended up being the halfway house where all the boys would go because they'd had a few drinks and couldn't go home to their parents. You would wake up in the morning and there would be bodies lying on the floor everywhere! They used to eat all of my food too so come Monday there was nothing left, but I survived and it was a huge learning curve in how to look after myself.

For a little while at the start of the year, once I knew I was going to be staying in Toowoomba, I took a job as a furniture removalist delivering new furniture to customers. That only lasted for three-and-a-half weeks before I realised it wasn't going to be my future, so I was back to square one — stuck in Toowoomba with no job and no idea what I was going to do for the next 12 months.

Then my school coach from the year before, Brian Gardner, came around to visit. He said to me, 'We're going to have a really good team this year. I reckon you should come back to school'. I thought about it and realised that aside from having another year in the school football side, it also served my purpose of wanting to get into the police force if I went back and did well.

Mum wasn't happy about it though. She told me it would be a wasted year and a waste of time because I'd already done Year 12 and should be spending my time doing some sort of course.

Well, I ended up going against Mum's wishes, went back to school and everything started out really well. I was getting As in everything and because I had done Year 12 before I knew what to expect. I was on top of it all. Then the footy season kicked off and my studies started going downhill.

The footy team was strong though. We had an excellent squad of players and as time went by we started progressing through the regional games, then the preliminary state games and the Queensland final against St Pat's Mackay — a side that featured three future team-mates in Wendell Sailor, Chris Cheung and Dennis Scott. That took us to the national semi-finals against John Paul II, Marayong. I threw an intercept in the first half that helped them to a 10–0 lead but somehow we fought back in the second and ended up winning 12–10.

It was around the same time that I had my first contact of sorts with Bulldogs boss Peter 'Bullfrog' Moore. The Queensland Schoolboys Championships was on at the Gold Coast and there were a lot of talent scouts there keeping an eye on everyone. Obviously I was already signed to the Gold Coast but I'd heard that Peter and Bulldogs president Barry Nelson were going to be there and I wanted to impress them.

The Price is Rising

I was playing in the second row and we were winning one of our games pretty easily so I decided out of the blue that I would take a shot at goal. It was on the touchline and 'Bullfrog' and Barry were sitting right where the kick was to be taken from.

I still have no idea what I was thinking. I must have figured that if I was going to impress them, this was the way to do it — just imagine a wide running, ball-playing second-rower that can kick goals as well! So I set the ball up and took my time because I wanted to make sure it was perfect, but as I went to kick it my boot clipped the ground, took a chunk of grass out and sent this worm-burner shooting straight along the turf! I couldn't believe it. I ran back over halfway with my head down thinking: 'Well, if I ever had any chance of playing for the Bulldogs it's gone now'. That was the last I thought of it.

Then about two weeks later Mum received a phone call in Adelaide. She rang me straight away and said, 'That's weird, this guy named Peter Moore just rang'. Mum had no idea who he was although Gaz was running around like crazy going 'Oh my God, Peter Moore!'

The Australian Championships were coming up in Perth and I'd made the Queensland side on the bench, so Peter had called Mum to ask if it was okay for him to talk to me while we were over there. What we later found out was that Peter had actually been calling all of the people who had been involved with me — our neighbours, my headmaster at school, Newtown — to find out about me. He was doing his homework to see if I was the type of person that would fit into the Bulldogs culture.

Because I was with the Gold Coast I didn't think I would be going to the Bulldogs but I was still excited that someone like Peter Moore was interested in me. The problem was that I didn't get a lot of game time in Perth. I saw Peter there a few times but he hadn't said a thing to me and I started to wonder what was going on. I thought: 'That's strange, he called Mum to say he wanted to talk to me and now he is just brushing me'. Even worse, I could see him going up to all of my team-mates and chatting to them instead.

Having said that, it was a pretty good team — we had Brad Thorn, Matt Sing, Ian Dunemann and Anthony Fowler who played for the Gold Coast — and we played against guys like Steve Menzies, Matt Seers and Robert Mears. But I was getting pretty disappointed. I thought Peter was a liar until Anthony Fowler came back after his meeting with 'Bullfrog' and said to me, 'That was a waste of time — all he did was ask me questions about you!'

It was one of our last days in Perth when Peter finally walked up and introduced himself. He said to me, 'I gave your mum a call and asked if it was alright if I met with you. I haven't spoken to you or anything but I don't want you to be alarmed by that, it's just the way I do things. We are considering you, but don't be disappointed that you're on the bench and haven't had much time on the field. Don't think that that's something that is going to affect you. Whenever you get your opportunity, just do your best because it hasn't happened for you this tournament'. That was great advice and we left it at that for the time being.

CANTERBURY — BANKSTOWN RUGBY LEAGUE CLUB LIMITED
A.C.N. 001 869 405

Affiliated to the N.S.W. RUGBY FOOTBALL LEAGUE -- Headquarters: BELMORE SPORTS GROUND -- Postal Address: BOX 123, P.O., BELMORE 2192

Patrons:	President:	Chief Executive:	Telephones:
Right Hon. P. J. KEATING, P.M.	B. NELSON, J.P.	P. MOORE, O.A.M.	789 2922, 789 2199
Hon. L. McLEAY, M.P.			Fax: 789 4815
Hon. K. J. STEWART, A.O.			
W. J. DAVOREN, M.P.			

8th July, 1992

Mr S Price
Harristown Senior High School
HARRISTOWN   QLD   4350

Dear Steven,

Bad luck about Perth. You suffered from not being in the Queensland first 13. Actually, I thought that you would still go very close but it wasn't to be.

I know just how disappointed you must be but, in sport, you can benefit from these disappointments if you have mental toughness.

I will talk to Margaret in Adelaide and come back to you shortly.

Very Truly Yours,

Peter Moore.

P S MOORE, OAM
CHIEF EXECUTIVE

Peter 'Bullfrog' Moore penned this letter to me after the Perth experience. It was appreciated.

The Price is Rising

This was around the time that our Harristown side was progressing through the Commonwealth Bank Cup. Our state final was against St Pat's Mackay at Seagulls Stadium on the Gold Coast, which was a stadium that I loved playing at, and unbeknownst to me Mum flew up from Adelaide as a surprise. When she turned up at the game I nearly had a heart attack! I never expected her to be there and it was fantastic.

We beat St Pat's Mackay which meant that we were now in the Commonwealth Bank Cup final against Patrician Brothers, Fairfield. Peter organised for both Mum and my brother to fly to Sydney where they were picked up in his Mercedes — which had been washed and polished — and driven to their hotel. Ironically they stayed at the Novotel at Brighton le Sands where I would first meet with the Warriors years later. I wanted Jo to be there as well so I asked Neil Mansell — a family friend and successful transport owner in Toowoomba — if I could borrow enough money to pay for her flight. When Mum found out she told him that he wasn't to let me get away with not paying him back!

It was 1992 and the Commonwealth Bank Cup was a big deal back then so our game was right before Brisbane played Illawarra in Friday Night Football. They actually played reserve grade *before* our game!

Peter pulled out all the stops. He phoned Bob Millward, who was CEO of the Steelers at the time, and arranged for him, Mum, Daniel and Jo to gain entry to a private box. He introduced Mum as Margaret Sullivan and for good reason too. All of the other officials were flicking through their programmes to see who this Sullivan kid was but of course there was none listed. Peter said to them, 'Oh he's one of the young kids, he's on the bench, I don't even know if he's named so he might not even get a game tonight.' That was 'Bullfrog' at his best. I was actually the captain that night and he used to relay the story with a cheeky smile — another clever ploy that he got away with!

We had a late hiccup in our preparation for the game. Because we were coming from Queensland, the Commonwealth Bank gave us a budget of $9000 to get there and back. We decided that instead of flying down on the day of the game we would bus down early and stay in Wollongong for the week. We arrived on the Tuesday, with the game being on Friday night, and enjoyed a perfect preparation until Ian Dunemann sprained his ankle the day before the game while he was practising his kick-offs. He was one of our best players and we spent that entire night trying to reduce the swelling. We ended up needling him up for the game and he played but I'm sure it hindered him.

In the end we lost the final by one point, 17–16, thanks to a Garen Casey field goal. As captain it was particularly hard to deal with, coming so close to being the best schoolboy team in the country.

Having said that, playing in a Commonwealth Bank Cup final opened up a lot of opportunities. The Roosters was one club that contacted me and said, 'We have a camp coming up, it's a weekend camp, so come along because at the end of it there is a trial and you might be offered a contract'. The Steelers were keen too, while Peter had already spoken to Mum and basically offered me a contract.

I actually told Peter at the time that I wanted to go to the Roosters camp (mainly because I wanted the free tracksuit). He said to me, 'Okay mate, that's alright, you can see what it's like there', but he must have jumped straight on the phone to Mum because he told her: 'If Steve goes to the Roosters camp and gets hurt, our offer is null and void'. What Peter had done was send Mum flowers every week, he had taken her to Wollongong and was basically planting a seed about how great the Bulldogs would be for her son.

A few days later Peter faxed a letter to me which stated that if I signed I would be out of my Gold Coast contract and officially a Bulldog. I spoke to Mum and others whose opinions I respected about what would be best for me. Garry was obviously one of them, as well as Jo and her mother Carly. I also spoke with a lot of people who had been involved in my junior football career — Don Gailer, Greg Platz, Arthur Wrigley and Bill Pollard — and they all felt the Bulldogs offered the best environment for a young footballer. I knew about the successful history of the Bulldogs and the solid foundation they had laid over the years. The Gold Coast had only just started out and hadn't had much success, so I eventually decided to sign with the Bulldogs.

It was a tough decision but in the end I think Mum was quite pleased too — it was a chance for me to get out of my comfort zone and have to tough it out for myself. It could easily have ended differently but thanks to Peter's efforts I ended up a Bulldog and it turned out to be the greatest decision of my life.

4 Jo

ONE CONSTANT throughout my entire career — and most of my life in general — has been the support of my wife Jo. I'm not sure how I would have made it through the darker days of my life without Jo and my three wonderful kids Jamie, Kasey and Riley. That stability has played a crucial role in where I find myself today, both on the rugby league field and in life in general.

When I first moved to Sydney in late 1992 I didn't have that and I really struggled. I was homesick and my football reflected my mindset. When Jo moved down everything started to change for the better — even when we were going through some tough times financially or were missing our friends and family back home. We would get by because we had each other.

I believe one of the reasons for that is because we knew each other so well. We were best mates for a number of years before we started going out. Not only is she my wife, she's my best friend. She knows when I'm struggling or not feeling great. She knows what to do and what to say.

Because she knows me as Steven Price from Toowoomba she keeps me on level ground. If I think I'm going better than I actually am she'll let me know. She loves me to death and wants to keep me happy but she will also say whatever needs to be said.

The fact that we had our kids at quite a young age has helped us too because we had to grow up very quickly. It's a huge challenge to move to Sydney and have kids when you're 21 and living away from your family. Because we've really only had ourselves for a long time, we've had to live and learn our own way. We've never been afraid to make decisions on what's best for us. That's why we were confident that we could handle the move to New Zealand in 2005 — we had already done it 12 years earlier — and it has proved to be a great move for us.

Jo has been incredibly strong through all of the upheaval and the dramas that have followed my career — and there have been some massive issues we've had to deal with. From the salary cap in 2002 to sexual assault accusations against the Bulldogs, rumours that I was gay and also that I had a gambling problem — all of those have an impact upon the people that care about you most. They don't like to see it.

Particularly during the salary cap saga, Jo knew how much effort I had put in and how much it meant to me. To see it all taken away from us was extremely hard to take. That's one of the reasons why it's so important for her to know me. When we were going through that she was completely honest with me. And it probably affected Jo more than me because I was always busy doing media, training or playing while she was at home stewing and stressing about what people were saying. It's a lot harder on the families than the players because we go to training and we deal with it alongside the rest of the guys. The girls are very closely associated but they haven't got the same support to get them by. They can feel quite isolated and helpless. They're worried about you and they want you to be alright but they're the ones that are copping it even more.

When you look at all of the things we've had to go through, it just goes to show her character. We've both gone through our parents splitting up, and that's a terrible thing, but at least it's not out in the open for everyone to see. What I've had to deal with has been on the front and back pages of the newspaper.

You can imagine what it was like hearing rumours that your husband was going to move in with his gay lover. It was ridiculous but that rumour spread around the entire country. We even received a phone call from a guy in Perth that had heard it!

Coffs Harbour was another one. Ask any woman how they would handle that and they won't be able to give you an answer. To know that your husband was at the same hotel at the same time as sexual assault allegations were made against 'unidentified members' of his team must have been terrible. For all Jo knew I could have been one of the players accused.

That's why I am so grateful for the trust, friendship and love that we've built up

Jo

over such a long period of time. They are the factors that have helped us through and enabled us to sustain such a wonderful relationship.

I FIRST met Jo back in 1986 when her father Doug started working for the same transport company, John Bain Transport, as my stepfather Garry. The job meant that the Tate family — Jo, her sister Peta, brother Brent and mother Carly — had to move to Toowoomba from Roma and they ended up living just up the road from our house.

Because of the family link between Garry and Doug I was given the job of introducing Jo to all the girls at Harristown Primary School. The problem was that we had started to hang out a bit and become good mates, but when she got to know the other girls at school she brushed me!

Jo was always quite tall for her age and was a very good swimmer, volleyballer and netballer. She was very athletic and a bit of a tomboy so she was great fun to hang out with.

When we went to high school nothing changed — we remained close friends. When the Year 12 formal was approaching I asked Mum who I should invite and she said, 'Why don't you take Bubby Jo?' which was her nickname at the time. Her Aunty's name was Jo, so she became 'Bubby Jo' by default.

I was a bit slow off the mark and by the time I invited Jo to the formal she had already said yes to someone else which put her in a bit of a dilemma, but I guess she decided that she would rather go along with me because she told the other guy that she had changed her mind. She was also seeing a friend of mine, Nick, at the time but that came to an end about three weeks before the formal. A day later Jo and I started going out and in hindsight we probably should have waited at least a little while longer. Needless to say, Nick and I haven't really spoken or seen each other since.

The timing wasn't good for me and Jo. She had been seeing Nick for a few years and was on the rebound a little bit when we first got together. She didn't really know what she wanted. My grandfather Trevor died a week later and Jo decided that it wasn't the ideal time to start a relationship. I had to go to Dalby with my family for the funeral and Jo needed some time to herself. We still went to the formal together and still spent time with each other but it took a while before we could officially be called a couple.

At the end of Year 12, Jo's mother Carly told her to move down to Redcliffe with her where she and Brent had moved two years earlier. So Jo moved to Redcliffe and would shoot back up to Toowoomba on weekends to catch up with her mates. It wasn't until the following year, when I ended up staying in Toowoomba and repeating Year 12, that we started going out again.

It was a great year and everything was going well but when I signed with the Bulldogs and moved to Sydney, Jo wasn't in a position to come down and join me straight away. She was enjoying Brisbane and was with her family so it was a tough decision for her to make. I was heading down for my footy whereas the only reason Jo could follow was to be with me. She had nothing else in Sydney.

I was at the Bulldogs for two years before Jo moved down and it was one of the toughest times of my entire life. I told her: 'It's killing me, it's really tough — I'm homesick and a lot of that is because of you'. We would be on the phone doing the old 'You hang up', 'No, you hang up' routine. I would look for any chance to go back to Toowoomba to visit. By that stage Jo was in Toowoomba every single weekend with her friends so if I had a weekend off I would fly up, Mum would pick me up at the airport, we'd get to Toowoomba and I'd say, 'Oh Mum, do you think it would be okay if I went out to catch up with Joey now?' Eventually I said to Jo, 'We're either going to get serious about this and you're going to move down or we're going to have to split up because it's too hard being apart'.

I was on the phone all the time wanting to know what she was up to and I was lonely. In 1995 she finally bit the bullet and moved down. Those early days were probably the toughest time for Jo. We moved into a unit at Kirrawee and had barely been there a week when her little red Daihatsu Charade was broken into and her precious stereo stolen. Jo hated the place.

She was doing temp work for a while before she found a job at AMP in the city working in their medical department and, although she enjoyed it, it meant long hours. We moved to Liverpool where we bought a duplex and that meant an hour on the train each way. I guess it was all too much for both of us and I suggested that it might be best for us to break up. I don't know what I was thinking but Jo certainly wasn't enjoying living in Sydney. When we went back to Toowoomba to celebrate my 21st birthday she had already started planning the move home.

That's when a little light switched on in my head telling me Jo was the one. She

Jo

came back to Sydney for no other reason than to pick up her gear but I said to her, 'No, I want you to stay. You can't go — I'm making a mistake'. Two weeks later we found out Jo was pregnant with Jamie and I proposed in October that year.

I had asked Jo a long time ago: 'If you were ever going to get a ring, which ring would you want?' — and of course she picked the most expensive one she could find — but that's the one I bought. I called her on the way home one Saturday after training and said, 'I want you to have your eyes closed when I walk through the door, I'm nearly home'. I had organised a huge bunch of flowers and had tied a little monkey around the bottom of the bouquet with the ring in a bag hanging from his arms.

I walked in the house, Jo was sitting down with her eyes closed and I got down on one knee in front of her. I said, 'You can open your eyes now . . . will you marry me?' She started bawling and to my relief said that magic word, 'Yes'.

It was a great time for us. The Bulldogs were going great guns and won the premiership in 1995, Jamie was born in January of 1996 and Jo and I were married the following November.

We didn't have a lot of money and Jo was working hard but we survived and we started to enjoy what we had. After everything we had already been through, at least we had each other — it's the most important thing that has happened to both of us.

5 A Change of Scenery

IF IT wasn't for another promising young footballer by the name of Darren Smith, Steven Price could well have been road-kill rather than a future Bulldogs captain.

I didn't actually finish Year 12 the second time around because the Bulldogs wanted me in Sydney by October, so as soon as the footy season was over I began making plans for the big move south. Ironically, Mum, Gaz, Wendy and Dan happened to be moving back to Toowoomba at the same time as I was leaving and they helped me out too. Still, I didn't have a lot back then.

The Bulldogs had arranged for me to stay with a lady named Colleen Prentice who was a long-time member of Canterbury Leagues Club. Apparently Peter just walked up to her one day and said, 'I've got this young boy coming down and I'd like you to look after him. He needs someone like you — a mother-type role model who can cook and clean and make sure he settles into life in Sydney'. She had said no initially but eventually changed her mind — Peter always got his way in the end.

Peter had also arranged for this guy called Darren Smith to pick me up from the airport when I arrived. I had no idea what he looked like or anything else about him so I said to Mum, 'If I turn up and no-one is there I'm jumping straight on the next plane and coming back! I'm not hanging around'. Sure enough, I got off the plane, grabbed my bags and stood there looking around for this Darren Smith guy. There were people everywhere and I didn't know what to do so I just stood there at the side of the room as the crowd thinned. Obviously Darren didn't know what

A Change of Scenery

I looked like either so there were these two blokes standing on either side of the room until we were almost the last two left. He eventually walked over and said, 'Are you Steve Price?'

That's when he saved my life. We were walking out of the airport to a zebra crossing and I just kept going, because in Toowoomba drivers stop and let you cross. I quickly learnt that the same rules don't apply in Sydney — Darren grabbed my shirt and pulled me back as a taxi flew past at about 70 km/h.

'Mate, you can't do that down here,' he told me. I just looked at him and said, 'Oh, okay, no worries.'

AS IT turned out, there was a bit of a misunderstanding between Peter and Colleen. I had been told that everything was organised and I would be moving straight into Colleen's place when I landed in Sydney, but she thought I was just stopping by to have a look and see if I wanted to live there.

Darren and I jumped in the car and he said, 'Alright, we're going to go to Colleen's now where you're going to live and what I'll do is I'll drop you off there and I'll be back to pick you up in the morning'. We arrived at Colleen's, Darren knocked on the door and it was all very pleasant. Darren said, 'G'day Colleen, this is Steven, the guy we were telling you about,' and she said, 'Oh okay, hi Steven, how are you going? Come in, come in.' We walked in and straight away Darren told her: 'Alright Colleen, I'm going now, I'll be back tomorrow'.

'Okay, no worries Darren,' she replied, but then I just walked over to her couch and sat down. Colleen looked at me and said, 'Oh, are you staying are you?' I said, 'I don't know, I think so. I've got my bag and I thought this was where I was staying.'

Luckily Colleen was great about it. She said to me, 'Alright then, no worries, that's something I can deal with . . . are you hungry?' And that was my first day in Sydney.

It wasn't an easy transition so I was pleased to start training with the Bulldogs almost straight away — but my first day was terrifying. All three grades were there at Belmore Oval that afternoon and we were being introduced around.

I was standing out the front of the ground in Terry Lamb Reserve when Terry himself walked up to me and said, 'G'day mate, how are you going? I'm Terry Lamb. I just want to let you know that anything you want, any time, don't be scared to come up and ask me. I'll point you in the right direction and help you out. Don't feel intimidated or anything like that because I'll be really pissed off if you are'. I was amazed that such a legend of the game was so friendly to this young kid from Toowoomba.

Steve Folkes was the same. He was a trainer with the club at the time and was one of the first to come up and say hello. Martin Bella didn't do too much for my self-esteem that day though. Just after the introductions, about 50 of us started a game of touch football in Terry Lamb Reserve. Marty was on my team and I was thrilled because he was a Queenslander and I loved watching him play.

The next minute he throws this cut-out pass to me and I just let it go. The ball hits the ground and Marty yells, 'Jesus Christ, where did we get *this* kid from?' I'm looking at him thinking, 'Are you talking to me?' and he says, 'Yeah you kid, why don't you catch it? What have I got to do, put it in your hands?'

I was shattered. Here was a guy that I had idolised as a Queenslander just ripping into me. I found out later that it was just Marty's way — he is quite a sarcastic person — but being new to the club I had no idea at the time. I had just met two club legends in Terry Lamb and Steve who had said everything I needed to hear and then Marty gave it to me. I'll never forget it.

The worst part was that he and Mum became friends! She drove down when we played Cronulla early in the season and popped in to their club after the game. Marty was sitting down having a feed by himself, they started talking and he gave her some directions to avoid the traffic on her way back to the freeway the next morning. Mum thought he was the greatest from that moment onwards and I'd always say to her, 'You're kidding aren't you?'

Every time we played in Brisbane, Mum would see him and say, 'Oh hi Marty, how are you going?' All of the boys would be watching and asking who this woman was and I'd have to say, 'Oh that's just my mum'. It was all pretty hard, particularly after my initial ordeal.

I STRUGGLED with life in Sydney for a while and at one stage even walked into Peter's office to tell him I wanted to go home. The first thing he did was remind me of a conversation we had when I first arrived at the club. Peter had said to me, 'What is the number one thing you want to get out of coming to the Bulldogs?' and I told him, 'I don't want to go back to Toowoomba a loser'.

A Change of Scenery

It wasn't so much a case of whether or not I made it but I wanted, at the very least, to have given it my best shot, so when I walked into Peter's office he asked me to repeat what I had said. When I told him he said, 'Well then, what do you think you're going to be if you go back home now?' He also said, 'If you stay and you do go as well in your career as you hope, it's a very small period of your life. After that you can go and live wherever you want if you do well enough. If you want to go back and live in Toowoomba you can, because your football career will only last for 10 or 11 years if you're lucky — when you think about it it's not a huge chunk of your life'.

Dean Pay and Mark Brokenshire came and had a talk to me too because Dean actually *did* go home at one point before coming back. They said a similar thing. My main problem was that I didn't *want* to like Sydney. I had this idea in my head that the world began and ended in Toowoomba — that nowhere else was anywhere near as good.

When I decided to actually give Sydney a chance my whole perception changed. All of a sudden it wasn't a place that was over-crowded and dirty, it was a city where you could go to hundreds of different places and have a heap of fun with the boys.

Our Under-21s manager Les Bateman played a huge role in helping me out. Every week he got all of the guys from out of town together and would take us to Chester Hill RSL to watch Friday Night Football and eat a pepper steak. There was Brett Dallas, Scotty Gardner, Justin Ribot, Michael Ellimore and a few others — we were all Queenslanders — and those nights pretty much kept me going in those early days.

The club also helped me get a job. When I missed out on my original goal of being a policeman back in Toowoomba, I had applied for a job as a bank teller at Westpac. I didn't make it through but they did send me a letter saying that although they had filled their quota they would contact me straight away the next time they were recruiting. When I arrived in Sydney I gave that letter to Peter, he met with a few people and the next thing I knew I was working for Westpac at Beverley Hills. I was still lonely because Jo was back in Queensland and I'd wonder what my mates were doing, but it kept me busy and enabled me to meet people outside of football.

I must admit, I'm not sure that I would have made it if I had gone to a club other than the Bulldogs. I wouldn't have had that support as well as the knowledge and persistence from the likes of Peter Moore. Even when I wasn't producing every week, the club could see that I had something and they never gave up on me. If I had gone to the Gold Coast back then they probably would have thrown me away and bought someone else because that was their psychology at the time.

The Bulldogs were willing to put a lot of time and money into you because they were confident you would come through in the end. I will be eternally grateful that the club stuck by me for all of those years.

6 Learning the Hard Way

THE FIRST thought I had once I started training with the Bulldogs was: 'Oh my God, there is no way I'm ever going to get big and strong enough to play first grade'. I would sit there watching these guys lifting 130–140 kg and here I was struggling with 80! I wasn't used to how hard we were asked to train either. During the pre-season we would train about four times a week and every session was tough.

But it was a great club and I loved being part of it. Scott Tronc was our Under-21s coach that year with Ian Schubert coaching reserve grade and Chris Anderson first grade.

I'll never forget my first game — against Balmain at Leichhardt Oval. It was a boiling hot day and, being Under-21s, we kicked-off at around 11 a.m. which made it even worse. We lost that day but I wasn't too concerned. I loved the fact that I was playing in the Sydney competition against the best in my age group. I was actually the youngest in the squad and it was a huge step up from the schoolboys football I was used to. There was also a real excitement around the club that we had a strong group of players ready to make their mark.

Jo came down for the game too and we sat in the stands to watch the other grades after my game. Even reserve grade seemed unbelievably fast compared to what I had just played, and when first grade kicked off I was again thinking: 'My God, I'll never be able to play at that level'. Balmain was still a strong side back then and had guys like Paul Sironen and Tim Brasher playing for them. We had Terry Lamb, Craig

Polla-Mounter and Jarrod McCracken so you can imagine it was an amazing game to watch. We ended up winning that day too, 19–14, and then all three grades went back to the Leagues Club. That's what used to happen back then — you would all go to the club and meet up with the boys in a more relaxed environment.

That's the night that I started up my own little routine after each game of having a banana split with whipped cream, nuts and either caramel or strawberry topping. Over time Scott Tronc and the boys would say to me, 'You can't do that, you can't be eating that', but it was my little reward every week.

'Troncy' did teach me a lot about the importance of eating well though. Being a young guy I tended to eat whatever I felt like which usually included pizza for lunch a few times a week because there was a Pizza Hut next to the bank I worked at. 'Troncy' worked for Rothmans at the time which kept him out and about most of the time. One day he decided to drop in out of the blue and he caught me walking into Pizza Hut to grab my lunch.

He said to me, 'Mate, you can't be eating this sort of stuff all the time'. I thought I was fit enough and played enough game time to be able to handle it but Troncy said, 'It's just like having a Ferrari and filling it up with water — it's not going to perform at its best. You've got to put the best fuel in it and keep it at its peak to get the best performance out of it. Your body is exactly the same — you've got to start eating well because when you're younger your body burns it up pretty quick but as you get older you'll start to pack it on'.

Coming from Troncy, it was quite obvious that he'd had that issue when he was younger and had learnt from it. He said, 'You've got the potential to achieve what you want to but it's going to depend on things like this whether you actually do or not.'

It was a bit unusual that I was letting myself eat so badly because I had always been very conscious of what I ate when I was younger and Colleen cooked me some great meals each night too but, for some reason, I was letting myself go during the day.

It was a good learning experience for me. I even had to cook for myself every Saturday night. Saturday was Colleen's night to go out so I had to 'catch and kill' my own feed. One night she came home and there I was devouring a whole BBQ chicken and a loaf of bread! She couldn't believe it, but I was burning a lot of energy with all the training I was doing and at that age I couldn't seem to keep the weight on anyway.

Learning the Hard Way

It was important that I ate well though. When you're playing country footy you can get away with drifting in and out of games but when you get to Winfield Cup level it's a whole new ball-game. It was similar with our Under-21s side — we had a team that struggled a bit in that first season and a few mistakes would often mean the difference between winning and losing.

There were some fantastic players in the Under-21s competition that year. We played Canberra and they had Ken Nagas, Mark Corvo and Simon Woolford; Cronulla had Dean Treister, Sean Ryan, David Peachey and Adam Ritson; the Roosters had Clinton O'Brien and Robbie Mears. You were playing against quality opposition every week and we didn't end up going too well — we finished last!

The last game of the year was a real highlight though. It was a huge day for the club because we needed to win two of our three games across the grades to win the club championship and we were up against Canberra. In the Under-21s the Raiders were playing for a semi-final spot and they needed to beat us to finish fifth. Somehow we drew the game and Canberra had to turn up again for a mid-week play-off against Manly to see who would claim that last finals spot.

For some reason we were a thorn in Canberra's side that season. Earlier in the year they had touched us up in Canberra but they had used an illegal interchange and lost their points. Needless to say they weren't too thrilled with us by the end of the season. We ended up being club champions after both reserve grade and first grade won, which was a huge feat in such a tough comp and with an Under-21 side that finished last.

I was lucky enough to play a few reserve grade games that year too. I had been made captain of the Under-21s towards the end of the year which was a great honour and hugely unexpected as the youngest guy in the team, so naturally I was in line to step up if the opportunity arose. But it wasn't easy.

Back in 1993, reserve grade was used to give first graders coming back from injury a bit of a run, while teams that didn't look as if they could make the finals would sometimes stack their reserve grade side to try and win it. We had Craig Smith sitting on the reserve grade bench because he couldn't get a start! It was a great way to build your confidence though, to be playing alongside guys like Dean Pay and Craig.

In those days, you would play Under-21s and would sit there with your fingers crossed that Garry Hughes would walk up and give you a jersey to sit on the bench in reserve grade. We used to play bench lotto. You would have about 10 reserve-grade regulars on the bench and maybe another five who had played Under-21s and we would all put $5 in the kitty. Whoever was called into the game first would win bench lotto and get all of the money.

I probably should have played reserve grade a bit earlier that year but it took me a while to realise what was needed. I was running around like crazy in my first few weeks of Under-21s and it took at least five or six games before I started to realise what I was doing. I was lost for a while but eventually I started to understand my role and began playing some decent football.

IT WAS during the 1994 pre-season that I came down with glandular fever. We had our end-of-year break so Jo and I met on the Gold Coast for a short holiday together, because at this stage she was still living in Queensland.

During that week I started to experience intense moments of hot and cold — I would either be freezing cold or boiling hot and it could change in a matter of seconds. Jo kept telling me to stop being a sook because we would be at the beach and all I wanted to do was go back to the room and lie down. One minute I would have the fan up full blast, the next I would have all of the blankets pulled up to my chin.

I went to the doctor and he said, 'You've got the flu', but I wasn't getting any better and felt tired all the time. When I returned to Sydney I went to see our club doctor Hugh Hazard, who sent me off for some tests and found out that I had glandular fever.

Colleen had been through it all before and had been quite sick apparently so she was really careful with me and basically locked me in my room for the next three weeks. I wasn't allowed to go to training, wasn't allowed to see anybody and didn't leave the unit. But I needed the rest. It got to the stage where I'd get up to answer the phone — which was only about eight metres away — and by the time I got there I would be exhausted. Once I'd hung up and walked back to bed I would collapse and pass out. It was unbelievable.

I'd managed to build myself up from 90 kg to 96 kg but after being sick for three weeks I had dropped straight back down to 88 kg! That put a spanner in the works and when I returned to training it took me a while to get back to where I was. It was hard to put the weight back on but I gradually fought my way back to the mid 90s —

then I picked up a stress fracture in my pubic ramus. I had gone through a similar thing the year before with pain in my groin but this was particularly frustrating because I had wanted to have a big pre-season. Instead, everything that could go wrong, had gone wrong.

Again I had to cut right back on my training. The injury usually afflicts joggers and we were doing the Bay Run and the Coogee Run a lot back then as well as a lot of 400-, 800- and 1500-metre runs. There was a lot of road running and a lot of long distance work for endurance but I couldn't do much of it. I'm amazed that I ended up having quite a good season despite the early setbacks.

OUR BIGGEST days of the year back then were the multicultural days we held at Belmore Oval. They always attracted massive crowds and the atmosphere there was unbelievable. It must have been intimidating for the opposition teams that played us there.

I remember playing St George when Scott Gardner was sent off early in the game and we nearly came back and won. Then again, their side had guys like Gorden Tallis and Nathan Brown so it was never going to be easy. The highlight for me that day was driving a Hyundai — Hyundai were our major sponsors — around the sideline before first grade with about 27,000 people there going mad. There were people sitting on the roof, others hanging out of trees — it was crazy.

That year I played one or two games in Under-21s and then moved up to reserve grade for the rest of the year. I began on the bench and then began starting games so my confidence really started to build as my consistency improved.

That was also the year that I made my first grade debut — which for the life of me I can't remember! The record books say that I debuted against Balmain but the first game I can remember was against Manly at Belmore Oval on a Friday night. I had played reserve grade earlier and was sitting on the bench in first grade with my fingers crossed that Billy Johnstone would call my name. Sure enough, with about 15 minutes to go he turned around and told me to warm up.

We were winning pretty comfortably by that stage so on I went — only for Ian Roberts to come flying out of the line and put a massive hit on me. I thought to myself: 'Oh shit, so this is what first grade is all about'. I stood up to play the ball, Ian gave me a bit of a push and the next thing I know Dean Pay is in there sizing him up and telling him to back off, saying, 'What are you going to do?' I felt bulletproof then, sort of like 'Yeah, leave me alone'.

Everyone knew that Ian could fight but having 'Deano' there to stick up for his team-mates like that was brilliant. I loved playing alongside Dean Pay. It's a shame that I didn't have more time with him once he left to join Parramatta but he was a fantastic bloke, as tough as they come. He had also been in a similar situation to me in that he had been homesick and in his case actually went home for a while before realising that being back home wasn't all that he thought it would be.

Dean, Jim Dymock and Terry Lamb are three guys that I think of when I look back on those days and I consider myself extremely lucky to have played alongside them. Terry gave me some great advice over the years.

I remember learning one lesson the hard way. I had a lot of problems with my ankle when I first arrived at the club. I don't know if it was my boots or if I was just unlucky but for some reason I was always spraining my ankle or doing ligaments — it must have happened three times in my first season alone.

I was at training one Saturday before our Sunday afternoon clash with Penrith and I did it again. Hugh had a look and said to me, 'It's no good mate, you're not playing this week'.

That same day Scotty Gardner, Justin Ribot and Chris Cheung were driving back home to Chester Hill from Belmore and were playing chicken with another car on The Boulevarde between Wiley Park and Lakemba. Apparently they shot out from behind one car but misjudged where another car was and ran straight into it head-on. It took the three of them out of the game and they were all shaken up. One of them had a broken arm, another had a shoulder injury.

It was pretty stupid and the club wasn't thrilled but I had this great idea that, because of all the late changes we had to make to our Under-21s side, I was going to play. I was all dressed for the game when Hugh turns up just before I'm about to run on and says to the coach, 'What is *he* doing here?' I thought I was doing the right thing but it turned out to be a huge mistake — I played like a busted arse. I was hobbling around and offered absolutely nothing.

A year later I was struggling a bit with another injury when I started having a chat with Terry in the gym. I said to him, 'All I want to do is play a game with you. I just want to get out there and have one game with you.' He said, 'Don't worry about that, you've just got to get yourself right. You've got plenty of days in front of you to play footy and if you don't look after yourself you won't have to worry about playing with me because you're going to stuff yourself.'

I had been desperate to play alongside him and this was around the time where there was speculation every year that it would be his last. The fact that he was so good to me in those early days, only made me want to play with him even more.

When Jo moved down from Brisbane we lived at Liverpool and Terry lived just over the hill so I would always end up being his cab driver home. He would have a couple of beers and Jo would have a few drinks as well so I would always be their taxi.

I must admit, I wasn't a fan of his when I was a Parramatta supporter because he was the one who was always offside and scoring tries to beat us! But once I arrived at the Bulldogs, my focus was to play a game alongside Terry Lamb. What he taught me was not to focus on the things that I couldn't control but to concentrate on getting everything else right because if I did that it would all work out.

Those were tough days because I was working for Westpac, so I would have to arrive at the physio's at 6 a.m. in order to get to work by nine. I learned a lot about professionalism from those experiences because in Toowoomba you just kept playing with injury and didn't really worry about it. I'm glad that I did all of the work I needed to. I look at a guy like Matt Utai, who didn't do the rehab he should have in the early days, and now he has to have his ankle cleaned out every year.

It's why Terry was so inspirational. He had no cartilage left in his knees and couldn't do all of the training that we did yet he would still get himself on the field of a weekend and go flat out. I can't even begin to imagine the pain that he went through before every game, but at least it taught me the value of putting in the hard work from day one because, just like a tradesman, your greatest assets are your tools. In our case, the tool is our body.

7 A Grand, Grand Final

I HADN'T played in any of the semi-finals in 1994 so I didn't expect to take part in the grand final against Canberra. The boys had won a thriller against the Raiders 19–18 to qualify for the decider and there was a great vibe around the club but I had played only four or five games off the bench that season and didn't think too much about it.

We had our own mini-squad of about 15 players that would be sitting on the bench in the grand final and to be honest we felt like extras. The main squad would be going through their drills and we would just be kicking the footy around and hanging out together! We didn't even go to the grand final breakfast — that was reserved for the guys that were likely to get a run.

Darren Smith was one of the players that went along to the breakfast and he had played in the semi-final win against Canberra, but he had fallen slightly out of favour with the club that season after signing with Brisbane for 1995. It was a shame because he was just trying to do the best for his family and had been looking around at some of the new clubs that were entering the competition that following year — the Western Reds and South Queensland Crushers. When he signed with Brisbane, the Bulldogs were far from thrilled.

The fact that I wasn't expected to play in the grand final didn't take the shine off the day for me with Mum and Garry both coming down to watch. There was always something special about the Sydney Football Stadium come finals time. I'll never forget that feeling of September in Sydney because every game is serious, the weather is just starting to warm up and the grass is starting to seed — it always makes my sinuses go crazy! The whole atmosphere is electric and to be pulling on a jersey on grand final day, even if it was just to be sitting on the bench, had me all pumped up.

The game itself didn't start too well for us — Marty Bella dropped the ball from the kick-off — and it all went downhill from there. As the match went on it was pretty obvious that Canberra were a class above us on the day.

So there I was, sitting on the bench and watching the clock tick down inside the final five minutes when I hear Billy Johnstone call out, 'Pricey, you're on'. I don't think it even clicked straight away — it went straight through me — but then I heard it again: 'C'mon Pricey, you're on'. I bolted up, took my jacket off and ran straight onto the field which was an amazing experience.

After the game I was on a massive high despite the fact that Canberra smashed us 36–12. When I arrived at the Warriors in 2005 I was reminiscing with Ruben Wiki — who played for Canberra that day — and I said to him, 'I'm pretty sure I did the lap of honour with you', because I was running around the ground looking for Mum. There I was running around in my blue and white jersey and the Canberra boys were only a few feet behind me! I'm sure it was a long, hard celebration for the Raiders after sending big Mal Meninga out a winner in his last game.

All of my team-mates were sitting down in the middle of the field devastated and I was so thrilled to have been given a run it didn't hit me until I got back to the dressing rooms what it really meant. You would see Terry Lamb sitting there with his head in his hands looking shattered and suddenly think: 'Oh jeez, it's not as exciting as I think it is'.

'Bullfrog' walked up to me and said, 'Mate, you never want to feel like that again'. I said, 'Actually, I feel pretty damn good.' He looked at me and said, 'Yeah I know that you might, but look around the room. You make a grand final — you want to win it. You don't want to lose a grand final, you don't ever want to feel like this again.'

I appreciated what he was saying but it wasn't until the following year, when we won the competition, that I realised what he was talking about. I actually thought back in time in 1995 and saw the dressing room from 1994 as vividly as if it had been five minutes earlier.

Still, I was buzzing on the bus back to the club even though everyone else looked like there had been a death in the family. That's when it occurred to me that Darren

Smith hadn't been given a run. Chris had decided that he would rather give someone that was part of the future of the club some experience. I still believe that Chris' decision cost Darren a spot on the Kangaroo tour that year. He was playing well enough to play in the grand final and be on the tour but he wasn't picked. I felt terrible for him because we were close friends and even though it wasn't my fault, a part of me felt like it was.

Darren was the guy that had picked me up from the airport when I first arrived in Sydney and he would always invite Jo and me over for dinner with him and Kelly. It was a real shame that, of all the people who had to miss out for me to get my chance, it was my good mate Darren Smith.

1995 WAS a huge season for me personally. It was the first time I had enjoyed an entire pre-season without injury — I had no problems with my hips, I didn't have glandular fever and my body was starting to get bigger and stronger as I approached my 21st birthday. I felt a lot more confident in myself.

We had a few changes at the club that year. Darren had moved to Brisbane and Martin Bella had joined one of the four new clubs — North Queensland — who turned out to be our round one opponents. There are a number of games that stand out from 1995 and that Cowboys game is one of them.

Stockland Stadium resembled a speedway back then and the dressing rooms were basically horse stables. There had been a lot of rain in the lead-up to the game and they had tried to cover up all of the mud with hay.

I played reserve grade that night and the thing I remember most is leaving our centre, Brett Patterson, sprawled on the ground injured at halftime because none of us saw what happened! We were awarded a penalty right on halftime and he was our goalkicker. We all started jogging off the ground as the siren went but, as 'Patto' went to kick the ball, he took a chunk of the ground with him and tore his quad. We were all sitting in the dressing room thinking: 'Where's Patto?' Well, he was in absolute agony in the middle of the ground and we had just left him out there!

The other thing I remember from that trip was having big Marty greet us when we first arrived in Townsville. He actually jumped on our team bus and started showing us around just a few days before the Bulldogs were supposed to be playing against him. It obviously didn't help relations between the two sides because my mate Matt

A Grand, Grand Final

Ryan was hit high by Adrian Vowles and broke his cheekbone.

1995 was also the year that I played my first actual starting game in first grade. Jason Smith had played in a test match a few days earlier and wasn't feeling quite right so I was called into the side to play Newcastle. It was a strange day — we felt like we were in the game but at fulltime we looked up at the scoreboard and saw that we had gone down 42–0!

Newcastle was on fire that day. Everything they tried came off and obviously nothing we tried worked at all. It must be a rare feat though for a side to go on and win the comp after being flogged by 42 points.

I roomed with Terry Lamb and Jim Dymock that trip and I probably didn't make the greatest of impressions. We had gone to sleep and one of them had woken up during the night to go to the toilet but didn't flush afterwards. Mum always blew up if I forgot to flush the toilet while growing up so I made a bit of a fuss about it — 'Baa, I can't believe you didn't flush the bloody toilet!' and 'Jimmy, that's disgusting'.

They were just looking at me saying, 'Are you serious?' Terry said, 'Mate, when you have kids you'll understand why.' I said, 'That's rubbish, if I have kids there is no way — I'll be making sure that if I flush the toilet they won't wake up because they'll be used to it. If it's going to wake them up I can handle that.' He goes, 'No you won't. I'm telling you, you won't. If you've got a baby or something you'll be trying not to make them wake up at all.'

I have to say, it wasn't too long afterwards that Jo and I had our first child, Jamie, and I still flushed the toilet! Admittedly I made sure that we had some music playing as she went to sleep so that she wouldn't hear the toilet, but I still flushed!

The other strong memory I have from the 1995 season was losing to Parramatta, who only won three games all year, 22–16. That was a famous day for the Bulldogs because it was the game that Chris Anderson hauled Jarrod McCracken from the field. Jarrod didn't even stick around for the end of the game — he went home at halftime — and the following week he was dumped from the first grade squad. Chris wasn't happy. This all stemmed from Super League. Jarrod was one of four Canterbury players who had originally signed with Super League before winning a court case to defect back to the ARL. The decision didn't sit well with the club, and Chris in particular, but Jarrod was the one who copped most of the heat and didn't play first grade for the Bulldogs again.

I still remember Peter Moore sitting in the dressing room afterwards looking stressed. I was always the positive one and I said to him, 'Don't worry about it Pete, we'll be right'. Pete later said to me, 'I'm looking up at this 21-year-old kid who has been playing reserve grade and I'm thinking: "Yeah, I really appreciate you telling me that but how the hell are you going to make it okay? I love your positivity but I'm not sure that you're going to be able to help make it okay"'. I guess it's ironic that I ended up being in the starting side for the grand final later that year.

WE FINISHED sixth after the regular season which made our task more difficult — no side had ever won a premiership from so far down the finals ladder. Our first game was against St George at the Sydney Football Stadium and we ground out a 12–8 win in horrible conditions. At one point Anthony Mundine had an unbelievable opportunity to score but instead of just diving on the ball he tried to pick it up first in the wet and knocked it on.

There was also a massive fight between Dean Pay and Gorden Tallis — two players that you wouldn't want to take on too often. 'Gordy' roughed up one of our players and 'Deano' rushed in to sort him out. He was such an intimidating and respected figure, 'Deano' — the type that would never take a backward step.

In our next game against Brisbane he put a huge shoulder charge on Glenn Lazarus in the first couple of minutes that left 'Lazo' with a broken rib. It was a terrible way for him to exit the game but was a huge boost for us because he was their main man up front. That's the sort of impact 'Deano' would have.

We ended up winning that game 24–10 which was a great result for us given the team that Brisbane had. Unfortunately Robert Relf suffered a fractured eye socket and was ruled out for the remainder of the season, but it turned out to be the opportunity I had been waiting for.

The preliminary final was against Canberra — the team that had thrashed us in the grand final 12 months earlier — and Mum said to me during the week: 'I've got a funny feeling that you're going to start on the weekend'. I had still only started one game at this point — the Newcastle game — so I wasn't convinced. Then Chris walked up to me while I was doing weights and said, 'I'm going to start with you. Robert is out and Jason Smith still isn't quite right so I'm going to bring him off the bench'. I was stunned — this was Canberra we were talking about! I looked at their

A Grand, Grand Final

side and they had Brad Clyde, a front row with Quentin Pongia and John Lomax plus their star-studded backline.

I just wanted to go out there and do my job, make my tackles, but as it turned out we won quite comfortably and I set up a try right on the fulltime siren. Ricky Stuart threw a pass that I intercepted and made a break before passing inside to Simon Gillies who scored. To this day I still remember the commentary from watching the replay so many times: 'Simon Gillies — he'll run this all the way back to Belmore!'

That put us in the grand final and unlike the year before I knew I was going to be part of the build-up. It was a great week because there was no pressure on us whatsoever. Manly had lost only two games all season and were red-hot favourites. In fact, reading the newspapers you would have thought that we had no chance at all. The talk was about all of the distractions that we had gone through with Super League and the players that were in court during the finals series wanting to switch back to the ARL.

Our supporters thought otherwise. The morning of the game was unbelievable. We boarded the bus at Canterbury Leagues Club and there were people absolutely everywhere cheering us on as we left for the ground. One guy had painted his car blue and white all over, another had a flat-top truck with people on the back singing and dancing and flags hanging out the window.

There was even a Manly fan who had decided to paint up his truck and drive it through the middle of Belmore. To be honest, I'm not sure I've ever seen anything more stupid. Someone pulled him out of his truck and I think he realised pretty quickly that he had made a mistake when they ripped off his jersey and set it on fire!

Mum and Gaz came down to Sydney for the game as did my mates from Toowoomba: Heath Farlow, Tony Crossley and Russell Bussian. Russell actually rang me that morning and said, 'I'm going to put some money on you to score the first try'. I told him, 'Don't be stupid, you're wasting your money', but he said he was going to put $30 on me.

I was surprisingly relaxed before the game — more excited than nervous. The Canberra game had given me a lot of confidence and I just loved the atmosphere at the Sydney Football Stadium at that time of year. I couldn't wait to run out onto the field and get into it. I felt that I belonged and I knew that I had proven myself to my team-mates. I was a wide-running second-rower but I also had the freedom to pop up basically anywhere.

We were fortunate to have so many players that were great with the ball — Jimmy Dymock, Craig Polla-Mounter, Jason Hetherington and of course the man, Terry Lamb — who I would just follow around the field.

About 20 minutes in, Jimmy got an offload away to Simon Gillies. I was running down the side that I'd run down thousands of times all year and suddenly there was an opening, Simon passed the ball to me and I only had to catch it and fall over the tryline for the first try of the game! There was a fair bit of controversy afterwards with people saying it was a forward pass but Eddie Ward gave the try and it was one of those unbelievable moments as all of the boys ran in to celebrate. Even better, Mum and Gaz were sitting right there in that corner so they had the perfect view.

It was a phenomenal performance from our side that day, particularly because we lost Terry Lamb to the sin-bin for five minutes early on. In the end I think it actually ended up working in our favour. We really stepped up in his absence and ended up winning the game 17–4.

I put that premiership win down to our final regular season game at Belmore when we thrashed North Queensland 66–4. 'Baa' was supposed to retire at the end of the season and the build-up to that game at Belmore was bigger than anything I had ever seen before. I'll never forget a train going past alongside the ground with 'Thanks for the memories Terry' written across the side.

I felt sorry for the Cowboys that day — they were in the wrong place at the wrong time. At one stage I set 'Baa' up for a try and I scored one myself when I ran away from my best mate Ian Dunemann, who was playing halfback for the Cowboys that day. Before the game we had been looking quite scratchy but to win so well gave us a lot of confidence heading into the finals. By the time we reached the grand final we knew we had what it takes.

The celebrations were amazing and straight away I knew what 'Bullfrog' had meant the year before when he said there was no comparison between winning and losing. To look around the dressing room and see the joy on the faces of your mates — it's what we all played the game for.

Peter Jackson was one of those guys. He was on our coaching staff and a great guy to have around. I'll never forget him tormenting a guy by the name of Orissi

A Grand, Grand Final

Cavuilati on the training paddock. Orissi was Fijian and had only one eye, so he struggled in night games at times. The Bulldogs had one of those machines that shoots the ball high into the air so that the outside backs could practise catching bombs, and 'Jacko' would stand there sending these things into orbit. Poor Orissi — nearly every single time the ball would come back down and hit him on the head! 'Jacko' was in his element seeing blokes getting belted by this machine.

It is those moments that happen behind the scenes that make it so special to win a premiership. They help create the culture of a club. 'Bullfrog' used to say, 'It's not the four walls around you, it's the people inside those walls that make a great club'.

We used to have a guy at the club nicknamed 'Snooksy' that would give us our massages. He was a bricklayer in his time and when he came in he would still have half of the bricks stuck in his fingers. He'd be there giving you a massage and you would nearly be bleeding from it!

But that's what the Bulldogs were all about. Peter was CEO and he had all of the families — the wives — involved in the club. They were the right people in the right roles and with the right attitude — all working towards the one cause. Times have certainly changed since then.

We used to go to a place called the Roundabout together after a game. All of us. There would be wives and girlfriends — we would start out at the club and then head to the Roundabout and hang out together. No-one would ever get into any trouble because we were all together and nobody was trying to do anything wrong.

Players don't go out together like that anymore because they're together so much during the week, now that the game has gone professional. Those were great times — probably even the best times — before rugby league went professional and the game started to change forever both on and off the field.

8 War-torn

SUPER LEAGUE hit the Bulldogs hard. Although we went on to win the grand final in 1995 — the year that the Super League war first started — we really struggled for the next few seasons after having the heart and soul ripped from our club.

By far the greatest impact on us was having five of our team-mates sign with the ARL. I was never going to leave the Bulldogs. I was a young kid just starting out in his career and all of a sudden there were all of these dollar signs being thrown about, but I didn't want to be the one that left the club because of it.

When the Bulldogs signed with Super League, they basically made my decision for me. The club spoke to us at one point about the financial difficulties that a number of Sydney clubs were facing and explained that joining Super League was the best way to ensure the Bulldogs had a future.

It was different for Jim Dymock, Jason Smith, Jarrod McCracken and Dean Pay. They had signed with Super League initially, like most of us, but later changed their minds and defected to the ARL (Brett Dallas signed with the ARL straight away). I hold no grudges against them for doing that but it broke the heart of our club. We were all so close and there was such a great culture at the Bulldogs that it really did feel like the heart had been ripped out when those guys left. I can't explain how tough it was when they joined Parramatta and returned to play against us at Belmore in 1996. It just didn't seem right.

Although we never spoke about it at training it was well-known what had happened — they felt that they had been let down and misguided by Super League.

They were pretty disappointed with what they had been told and what actually happened. They may even have signed on for a certain amount of money and then found out what some other guys were getting.

To their credit, they didn't let off-field events affect their football. It's hard enough to focus on week-to-week games when there are outside distractions, let alone go on and win the competition. Not one time did Dean, Jimmy, Jarrod or Jason miss training or show any lack of desire to do what they were there to do.

It must have been difficult for them — we were all good friends and they would have felt that they were letting their mates down by leaving the club — but nobody looked sideways at them or blamed them for going to the ARL. The strength within that squad was really quite powerful and was the reason we were able to go on and win the grand final.

Jarrod was the only player that came out and said anything publicly about some discontent and Chris dealt with that directly by dropping him from first grade. But it didn't change the fact that we were all very close and, to be honest, it was no surprise that we struggled in 1996 after losing those guys. It wasn't just the number of players that we lost — Jimmy, Dean, Jason and Jarrod were all internationals!

In the space of 12 months we went from being premiers and looking forward to some great years ahead to having three-quarters of our squad taken away. It left us with a whole heap of young players that were being thrown in and asked to be regular first graders all of a sudden.

I have to pay tribute to Terry Lamb who unselfishly came out of retirement in 1996 to help out. He could have said no — he had already had his fairytale finish just as Ray Price and Michael Cronin did at Parramatta in 1986 and Mal Meninga for Canberra in 1994, but he put his hand up. It was one of the most unselfish acts I have ever seen.

THE FIRST time I heard about Super League was on April Fools Day, 1995, when I opened the newspaper to find that News Ltd. had launched an undercover raid on the ARL. It was surprising enough to read about just how many players had already been signed but more amazing was that five or six of my Bulldogs team-mates had jumped ship without us having any idea.

I actually started to panic. As the days passed I would hear more and more stories about players signing with Super League or staying with the ARL but I hadn't heard anything from either side. I was starting to wonder if I was wanted at all! Obviously they had a pecking order and spent those first few days trying to get as many big name players and as many clubs to sign as possible.

I eventually received a phone call from Chris Anderson telling me to be at the Bass Hill Inn to listen to what Super League had to say. I didn't even have a full-time manager at the time so the whole process was quite daunting. When I arrived, Chris said to me, 'You're going to sign with Super League because that's the way the Bulldogs are going. I think that you're probably worth about $80,000'. That seemed like a lot to me at the time. In 1995 I was on about $30,000 with the Bulldogs — who also paid for my accommodation and medical benefits — as well as earning $24,000 from my job at Westpac. Still, I decided that although $80,000 sounded great I was going to ask for another $10,000–$20,000 on top.

After a while I was called into a room where Michael O'Conner, one of Super League's talent scouts, was waiting. He introduced himself and said, 'Basically you're here because we want to sign you to Super League. This is what's happening with it . . . so how much do you think you're worth? How much should you get?' I said, 'Oh, I think $100,000'.

Michael started going off! He said, 'What have you done in your career that you think you deserve $100,000?' I told him, 'Well I haven't played a lot of first grade games but I played in the grand final last year'. He fired back at me: 'I played for Australia, I played for NSW, I played so many games in first grade and I never got over $100,000! Why should you get $100,000? You haven't done anything like that'.

I was starting to feel really bad — as if I was ripping them off or something! But I thought to myself: 'Nah, don't be stupid, Chris said $80,000 and I'm saying $100,000'. In the end I signed a three-year deal that rose from $90,000 in my first year to $110,000 in my second and $130,000 in my third, as well as a $25,000 sign-on fee.

For a little while at least, I thought I was rich!

I WAS pleased to see so many of my mates do really well out of Super League. There were some tremendous opportunities presented to some of the guys because of how important they were to Super League's plans. It was an exciting time for me too and I was looking forward to setting myself up financially with my new pay-rise. The reality was very different.

Jo and I went through a really tough time financially at the start of the Super League war. We went from both having fulltime jobs and my football payments — which were split into two half-yearly payments — to me becoming a fulltime professional Rugby League player getting paid once a month.

Towards the end of 1995 I quit my job at the bank to train fulltime. Super League was set to kick off in 1996 but couldn't go ahead after losing its court case against the ARL. Although News Limited continued to pay us, our final payment under the old system was in October 1995. Jo was pregnant with our first child Jamie at the time and was our only bread winner, with my first payment under the new Super League system not due until January 1996. I had received a $25,000 sign-on fee from News Limited but I put that into shares. I had also borrowed $25,000 so I was leveraging a $50,000 share portfolio.

Jo's wage alone wasn't enough to pay off the car, our mortgage for a duplex at Green Valley, her travel expenses to get to and from work and our food. I was forced to take a few cash advances on my 1996 contract which, unbeknownst to me at the time, actually lengthened our difficult financial situation.

Jo gave birth to Jamie in early January and by then we were just scraping by. My new Super League deal of $90,000 a season seemed like a huge increase to a young guy like me but once I saw my tax bill I realised it wasn't that much better than what I had previously been on.

I hadn't been taxed anywhere near as much in 1995 whereas now I was in the higher tax threshold. The end result was that my new wage was split into monthly payments with more tax taken out and more commitments to spread it out over as well. Because we had no money, I had to sell my shares which didn't enable me to let them grow as an investment.

The tax office then decided to tax all money that was paid to players as a sign-on fee, too, so the money I had used for my shares was suddenly taxed at 47 cents in the dollar.

To put it bluntly, we were in the shit. We had only $250 a week coming in through Jo's work which had to pay for the mortgage, her travel to the city and day-care for the baby. When the tax bill arrived we almost went belly-up.

Garry Hughes was very supportive during this period and introduced us to a guy by the name of Richard Shaw, a financial advisor for Saxby Bridge who came out to the club to give a presentation to the players. It couldn't have come at a better time for us and I was very interested in whether Richard would be able to help me set my family up financially. He understood the situation Jo and I were in and what we wanted to achieve. Taking into account that I had already taken a couple of advances on my new contract — and with a new baby girl and unexpected tax bill to contend with — Richard put together a simple but effective budget for us. I look back now and I'm very grateful for the support and advice I received from Richard (as well as from Mum and Garry Hughes). Not only did he help us get by as a family but also helped me focus more on my football.

There is no way I would be in the secure situation I am today if it wasn't for Richard. Not all of the advice Richard has given me has worked well for us but most has. At the end of the day it is only advice and you do with it what you will. Every decision has been ours, with Richard just trying to steer us in the right direction.

This sort of advice is too often underestimated in the footballing community — it's important to make the most of your earning capacity during your relatively short time as a professional athlete.

IT WAS also because of Super League that I very nearly joined North Queensland in 1997.

We finished in 10th position in 1996 and missed the finals following the loss of a large number of our star players. It proved to be a frustrating year for me personally too. I had finished the 1995 season as the starting second-rower in a grand final but within a few games in 1996 I was back on the bench and I spent the rest of the year there. I didn't even know what I had done wrong.

I was at a loss to know how I could regain my starting spot and I started to believe that Chris Anderson didn't think too highly of me. I didn't know if it was because he didn't like me personally or that he didn't think I was a very good player, but whatever it was I knew that there was something wrong.

Towards the end of the season I requested a release from the Bulldogs and they told me I was free to negotiate with other clubs. I met with the Cowboys and we basically agreed that I would join North Queensland in 1997. If it hadn't been for the fact that their chief executive at the time, Rabieh Krayem, was on holiday and uncontactable, I would have been a Cowboy. Instead, during that period when we were waiting for Rabieh to finalise the deal, the Bulldogs changed their mind about releasing me.

Once that happened I knew I had to confront Chris. I was growing increasingly frustrated with the different methods he was using at training and how he was treating me. There would be times when he would yell at me — call me every name under the sun — and others where he would seem almost dismissive.

He would say things like, 'You're just going to go through the motions and you will end up a nobody after a season or two'. I would be racking my brain thinking 'What have I done wrong? He hates me'.

At the end of that 1996 season I confronted him. I walked into his office and said, 'I don't know what I've got to do to please you. It seems that nothing I do is ever good enough'. I certainly wasn't expecting the response he gave. Chris said, 'Do you know that in all of my time here there have only been two other players that have had me at a loss as to how to get the best out of them? Those two were Darren and Jason Smith and I don't know whether to leave them alone, talk to them, yell at them or whatever. You're the same. I've given up. I've tried everything. I've yelled at you, I've abused you and none of it has worked'.

I said, 'Oh, well if that's all it's about then we don't have a problem — I thought you hated me'.

I would say to Chris, 'Why aren't I getting a start?' to which he would reply, 'Until you believe you're a first grader, you're not going to start in first grade'. I would say, 'Well I think I'm a first-grader' and he'd go, 'No you don't'.

It was frustrating at the time but as I started to really think about what he was telling me I realised that there were times when I could get a little bit overawed by who I was playing against. Too often I would be out on the field just filling space. Chris was trying to tell me that I had to back myself — that it was up to me to realise that I was just as good, if not better, than the players that were on the field with me. But I didn't realise what he was saying until we had that discussion.

After that happened, Chris began to leave me to my own devices and I responded in the Super League competition in 1997 with the best season I'd had in my time at the Bulldogs. It was also the year that I moved from the back-row to the front-row. I couldn't understand why Chris put me there when it first happened but we had a lot of back-rowers and not so many front-rowers.

Chris felt I was being wasted in the back-row because if the ball didn't come my way I didn't really go looking for it. Having said that, I didn't play like a conventional front-rower that year — I was more like a back-rower that saw the ball more often — but I really enjoyed the change. My form still wasn't brilliant but it was a vast improvement and my relationship with Chris just grew stronger as the year went on.

It was a shame that 1997 was his last season with the Bulldogs. Chris felt that it was time to challenge himself with another team and the opportunity offered by the newly formed Melbourne Storm was too good to resist.

I HAVE vivid memories from that Super League season of a young back-rower by the name of Matua Parkinson. Matua had these dreadlocks that were long and disgusting — he never washed them! There were sticks and rocks and all sorts of things in his hair and we used to call him 'skunk' because of the smell.

I said to him during the season, 'Mate, you've got to get your hair cut, it's terrible'. He said he wouldn't do it so I made him an offer. I said, 'If reserve grade wins the grand final you've got to shave your head', and he goes, 'If we win the grand final I'll shave my head straight away'.

The reserve grade team was mid-table at that point and I don't know if Matua's hair had something to do with it but from that moment they started moving up the ladder! Of course, they ended up winning the grand final and I was in Brisbane for the game so I headed straight down to the dressing room.

Our front-rower Marcus Hohaia didn't play that day because of injury but for some reason he had a pair of clippers in his back-pack. I said, 'Get them out brother', because we all knew what was going on. Matua wouldn't have been off the field for five minutes before we got hold of him and shaved off every single dreadlock on his head.

I must admit, I understand now why he didn't want to shave his hair off because he doesn't have the prettiest skull. Not too many guys have ugly skulls but we are both lucky enough to be blessed with them!

As it turned out, Matua returned to rugby 12 months later anyway. He got into a fight in the 1998 President's Cup grand final and was supposed to front the judiciary but never showed up — he went on holiday with the boys instead!

We didn't make the Super League grand final in first grade in 1997 but it was still a great week. It was the first time a grand final had been held in Brisbane so they sent up two players from each club to promote it. Darren Britt and myself were the lucky two from the Bulldogs and, even though I don't drink, it was one of the greatest weeks I've been involved with.

Word soon got out as to what was going on — free drinks and pub promotions all round. Suddenly there were players all over the place wanting to get to Brisbane to be part of it. We started with about 16 blokes and ended up with more than twice that many. Some of them even cut short their holidays to be there!

THERE WERE both positives and negatives to come out of the Super League war.

Perhaps the greatest result was that rugby league finally went professional. For a long time there it looked as if it was never going to happen, but since 1995 the game has reached astronomical heights. I talk to current players about what the game was like 10 or 15 years ago — even when I started playing in 1994 — and they always tell me how slow and messy it looked back then. At the time it seemed like the greatest product of all but we've come so far from those days in such a short space of time.

It was also phenomenal to be involved in the celebrations Super League put on in 1997. The amount of money they spent on the launch alone was phenomenal. I was supposed to be in an ad campaign at the start of the year but they ended up using some other players instead. They still used me for a few things though — at one stage they sent a few boys to outback Queensland to tape them riding a bull!

It was a totally different environment to the old Winfield Cup. To be honest, I think they might have gone too far with it. Somewhere in the middle would have been perfect. That was one of the problems.

And as much as I enjoyed playing that year, it didn't feel right to turn on the TV and watch ARL games being played at the same time. The standard of both competitions was lowered because of the war. There were a couple of great teams in each and the rest were just filling the numbers. That whole sense of division between the teams and between the competitions was extremely unsettling.

And believe what you will about the amount of money paid to players, it wasn't always what it was cracked up to be. At the time I thought I had come along a few years too early when I found out what some of my team-mates were getting but I don't regret it now — I saw any number of players get paid huge money but end up with nothing.

They would rush out and buy a fancy car and a great house with the money they had signed for over two or three years but, come the end of their contract, they struggled to earn another deal. A lot of them ended up being in so much debt that they finished up worse off than they had been before Super League started. I'm fortunate that, although Jo and I went through some tough times during that period, it never got out of control.

Player managers were some of the biggest winners. Because players were rushed into ARL headquarters or to meetings with Super League, they often didn't have a chance to call their managers. Most of them did the deal themselves — but they would still receive a bill from their manager for a percentage of what they would be earning, even though the manager didn't actually do anything. That was completely wrong but it was typical of the craziness of the war.

Still, even though I wish Super League didn't happen in terms of the disruption it caused, there were so many great things to come out of it. It took a while for the game to get back on its feet but it has improved in so many areas as a result. And I think it's a great advertisement for rugby league. There aren't many products that could go through what our sport went through and bounce back within 10 years to be more popular than ever.

It just goes to show how resilient rugby league is.

9 Back From the Dead

IN ALL of my years playing rugby league, I have never experienced a more remarkable 20 minutes of football than in our 1998 semi-final against Parramatta. We had already battled our way through a series of sudden death matches that we were never expected to win and when we trailed the Eels 18–2 with 11 minutes remaining in the grand-final qualifier there was no way we were going to get out of jail again.

But then the unthinkable happened. First Craig Polla-Mounter crashed over alongside the posts to make it 18–6; next Robert Relf threw the most remarkable no-look pass of his lifetime that somehow hit Rod Silva on the chest for 18–12; and with two minutes remaining Willie Talau scored in the corner to make it 18–16 and give Daryl Halligan the chance to level the scores from the sideline.

Daryl's kick was remarkable in itself. I don't know whether he meant to kick it the way he did but it looked for certain that it was going to curve away and miss to the left and then all of a sudden it just straightened up. When you look at Daryl's kicks throughout his career, nearly every single one curves away, which he wants them to, but this particular one straightened up instead and went straight through.

From that point we were probably always going to go on and win the game but the one moment I'll never forget was Craig Polla-Mounter having a shot at field goal as the siren sounded. Poor old Paul Carige, Parramatta's fullback, didn't have the greatest of games and with the scores locked at 18-all he decided for some reason to chip and chase on his own 20-metre line as the clock wound down. 'Polly' picked the ball up on halfway and launched a brilliant field-goal attempt that to this day I swear went over. Bill Harrigan ruled otherwise but from where I was standing — and even looking at the replays since — I'm certain it went over. That decision could have changed the game but the Eels were shot ducks by then and we ended up winning 32–20 in extra time.

I still can't believe it happened. We were out of that game and I'm sure Parramatta already had one eye on the grand final but suddenly everything just clicked into gear for us. I remember talking to a couple of the Broncos boys — Petero Civoniceva and Shane Webcke — who were at the game and they had given us no chance. To them it was simply a matter of how many points Parramatta was going to win by.

For some reason, though, we believed in ourselves and even when we looked down and out we hung in there. I had supporters tell me afterwards that they had actually left the ground with 10 minutes to go. They were sitting in the car park when they heard what was happening and were then trying to scramble their way back in! It was the most remarkable 20 minutes of any game I've ever been involved in.

In fact, the entire finals series was like that. Only a week earlier we had trailed Newcastle 16–0 midway through the second half and had come back to win 28–16 in extra time. The only difference was that we had started our comeback earlier than we did against Parramatta.

Through that whole finals series no-one gave us a chance in any game and I have to admit that even I was sceptical. Jo and I had planned a holiday to Phuket and I had every intention of booking it but each week something would come up and I wouldn't get around to it. We played St George in the first week of the finals and I thought: 'We probably won't win that game so I'll book the holiday for next week', but for some reason I didn't book it. We won 20–12.

North Sydney was next at North Sydney Oval and I knew we had our work cut out against them but again I ran out of time and never made it to the travel agent and we beat them 23–2 to stay alive. Then it was Newcastle, who had been on fire, and I was certain our luck was about to run out. This time I even made it to the bank and withdrew the money to pay for our holiday but for some reason I still didn't actually do it. It wasn't because I thought we were going to win any of those games, it was just that for whatever reason other things came up and I didn't get around to it!

Maybe we were blessed because it all just kept happening for us. The stars aligned. We needed a whole heap of luck to fall our way just to make the semi-finals in the first place but that's exactly what happened. It could easily have gone the other way. In both the Newcastle and Parramatta games it got to a point where we would either stage a comeback or fall apart completely because we had no option but to chance our arm. I'm sure Robert Relf wouldn't have thrown that pass to Rod Silva under any other circumstances but he had to try something and somehow it stuck. It was amazing to be a part of and remains one of the most memorable experiences of my entire career.

I WAS excited about the year ahead as the 1998 season approached. We hadn't enjoyed a particularly great year during Super League but were gradually rebuilding after losing so many players in 1995. It was also the first season of the new National Rugby League, the code was united once more after the Super League war and there was a new team in Melbourne that was largely made up of the now defunct Western Reds.

At the Bulldogs, Chris Anderson had departed with Steve Folkes taking over as our head coach. I really didn't know how 'Folkesy' would go because he'd been our trainer and I had never really thought of him as a coach even though he had guided the reserve grade side to the premiership the year before.

Having said that, I always got on well with him because of his ethics. 'Folkesy' was a fitness freak and was similar to me in that he didn't drink a lot. We would often go out with the wives in tow — Jo and Karen — and by the end of the night 'Folkesy' and I would be bored to tears while the girls would want to party on! We had a lot of similarities in that respect and when he named me captain a few years later we became even closer.

It was an up and down season for us, even though there were times when you could see the combinations starting to come together. I broke my hand about halfway through the year but kept playing with it because I hated missing games. The problem was that it wasn't getting any better. With four rounds remaining we were in a situation where we needed to win our last four games just to have any chance of making the finals.

'Folkesy' said to me, 'Right, we're playing Western Suburbs this weekend and I want you to take the week off because your hand isn't healing. You still need a needle to play each week and we want you to be right for our last few games. If we're going to have any chance of making the semis we've got to beat Wests with or without you.

It's not going to make any difference — if we can't beat Wests we don't deserve to be there'. So I didn't play, we won 56–14 and I returned for our next game against St George which we managed to win 28–16.

Then came Melbourne in what was one of the toughest games I've ever played in — I've never seen rain like it in my life. Belmore Oval had been redone and the drainage was as good as any ground in the country but the rain came down so hard that it still looked like a lake. There were times when you almost needed a snorkel to pick up the ball and whenever you were tackled you were worried that you were going to drown! Even the best of drainage systems couldn't get the water away quick enough.

Melbourne's halfback was Brett Kimmorley and at one stage he tried to drop Robbie Ross off inside. I was standing right in front and instead of tackling him I gave him a bit of a push . . . straight into Robbie's knee! It didn't really matter what I did but unfortunately for Brett he was knocked out cold. Chris Anderson was furious because Brett was their key playmaker and losing him was a huge blow in such a close game, but these things happen and we scraped home for another win, 8–4.

That left us needing to beat Illawarra in the last round to make the finals. WIN Stadium was always a tough place to play and we didn't have a great record there. It was a scrappy game too and no matter how hard we tried we just couldn't seem to shake them. With 30 seconds remaining scores were locked at 24-all when Craig Polla-Mounter kicked the most important field goal of his life to help us win and sneak into the semi-finals! Even now, thinking back on that season, it just seemed that we could pull a rabbit out of the hat whenever we needed it most.

THERE IS one other incident that sticks in the memory banks from our journey through the semi-finals. We played North Sydney in week two after beating St George for the second time in a month and the Bears had been beaten up a fair bit by Parramatta the week before.

Their halfback, Jason Taylor, had actually broken his nose and 'Folkesy' came out in the media early in the week saying: 'If he plays he's going to risk getting it broken again'.

The NRL responded by telling us that if anyone hit Jason Taylor in the nose they would be cited and suspended. That wasn't good enough for 'Folkesy'. The next day at training he said, 'If any of you have an opportunity and you don't have a go at

Back From the Dead

Taylor I'll haul you off the field myself — you won't have to worry about the judiciary suspending you!'

Sure enough, a charge-down opportunity came up during the game and I was determined to clean him up. I wasn't planning to hit him in the nose or anything but I certainly wanted him to know I was there. Unfortunately 'JT' saw me coming and stepped past but Barry Ward was plodding along behind me and absolutely smashed him — straight in the nose!

Poor old Barry — he had had no intention of doing it but 'JT' stepped straight back into him. I don't even think he hit him that hard but because it had been brought up during the week it was made to look worse than it actually was and the judiciary made an example of him. We won 23–2 but that tackle cost Barry a spot in the grand final.

TO REACH the grand final that season was a proud moment for Peter Moore. The way we never said die, and fought our way back again and again, typified what the Bulldogs were about as far as he was concerned. It's just a shame we couldn't top it all off with a premiership for him. We actually led 12–10 at halftime and it was the first time we had been ahead in any of the semis aside from the North Sydney game, but Brisbane were masters of turning up the intensity and that's exactly what they did in the second half — they really put the blowtorch to us.

Tonie Carroll scored a try three minutes after the break to give Brisbane the lead and from there they raced away to win 38–12. No disrespect to Gorden Tallis, who won the Clive Churchill medal, but I have no idea how Tonie Carroll wasn't man of the match — he absolutely destroyed us. I still believe to this day that Kevin Campion didn't ground the ball when he was awarded a try in the first half — I had my hand under the footy — but Bill Harrigan pointed to the spot and awarded the try anyway. Still, it didn't really matter — the Broncos were unstoppable in the second 40.

We were just proud to have made it that far and played with plenty of spirit. Troy Stone actually broke his arm early on and kept playing after trying to put a shot on Petero's head. He learnt his lesson the hard way.

As courageous as we were, Brisbane was just too strong. Kevin Walters still tells me to this day that we were so excited to be leading at halftime after everything we had been through that we forgot there was a rampant Brisbane team waiting for us across the other side of the tunnel.

10 A Dream is Realised

VERY FEW people have played such an important role in my rugby league career as Wayne Bennett, but for a long time I was convinced that he hated me! It all stemmed from a grand final I had played for Newtown back in 1991. Our Under-18s coach at Newtown, Graham Tucker, was a good friend of Wayne's and had asked him to come to Toowoomba that day to watch this young back-rower called Steven Price.

We were playing against Wattles who had a guy by the name of Shane Webcke in their side. I had no idea that Wayne was there watching but I played well, the game finished 16-all and we headed into overtime. With a few minutes remaining, our hooker dashed over for what would have been the winning try but Shane grabbed him with one arm and lifted him off the ground. He was literally holding him up off the ground one-handed! The referee called held-up and Wattles kicked a field-goal from the next set of six to win the game.

Wayne fell in love with Shane that day and walked away determined to sign him. He loved the fact that Shane was tough and gave his all despite the fact that he was never the flashiest player around. Obviously whatever I did that day wasn't too exciting for him.

When I missed out on the Queensland Tri-Series side in 1997 after a number of people predicted I would be picked, I remembered back to that grand final and decided that Wayne didn't like me as a player. Even the following season, when I was finally named to make my State of Origin debut, I knew that it was only because Brad Thorn had pulled out injured.

A Dream is Realised

And Wayne was an intimidating figure. During one of my first training sessions for Queensland in 1998 I chased someone from marker and Wayne stopped the play straight away and yelled, 'Steven, don't you dare bloody do that. I know you do it at the Bulldogs but you're not doing it in this team. You do that and we'll get torn to bits'. All week Wayne was into me and Jason Hetherington about it because we kept moving up in defence while everyone else was sliding. When he spoke to me alone he said, 'This could either be the first of many games or it could be your first and last, depending on how you play'. Talk about pressure!

It certainly didn't help settle the nerves — nor did Allan Langer vomiting in the dressing room before the game! I had just put my jersey on for the first time and was feeling all proud to finally be representing Queensland when 'Alf' started throwing up in the bin. I said, 'Oh my God, what's going on here? We're gone. Our best player is spewing his guts up'. The other boys told me, 'No, no, he's okay. It's good that he is throwing up'. I said, 'It's not good for me — I was doing okay until now!' It freaked me out.

The call eventually came for us to head up the tunnel, we sang the national anthem and the game kicked off. I was on the bench so I ran up and down the sideline a few times just trying to calm my nerves and take in the atmosphere while copping plenty from the loyal Blues crowd.

When the time came for me to take the field I was going nuts, running around everywhere and trying to tackle everyone. New South Wales was on the attack and it was last tackle so I decided that this was it — my chance to make a name for myself in State of Origin.

I flew out of the line at Andrew Johns who passed wide to Laurie Daley, Laurie turned the ball inside to Tim Brasher as I tried to change direction and he ran straight through the gap that I left to run 40 metres and score. I was walking back to the tryline thinking: 'Oh well, at least I got to play one game for Queensland'. It didn't help that Wayne pulled me straight from the field. The crowd was into me too, yelling, 'You're hopeless Price'. I looked up at Mum in the stands and just mouthed the words 'I'm sorry'.

At halftime I went up to Wayne in the dressing room and said, 'I'm so sorry Wayne, I didn't mean it. I really didn't mean it'. He walked away and I kept chasing him around saying, 'I'm so sorry Wayne, I'm so sorry'. I couldn't apologise enough. All Wayne said was, 'I bloody told you about that!'

I thought, 'That's it. I'm not going to get another chance. It's going to be a long second half and I'm going to be stuck on the bench the whole time.' When my name was called out for me to run on again I was determined to make up for my mistake in the first half, so when Rod Wishart made a break for NSW I started chasing him as hard as I could. Unfortunately Martin Lang — a front-rower — was faster than me and came across to help Matty Sing make the cover tackle, although if you look at the tape I wasn't too far off — that's how hard I was trying!

I ended up scoring a try in the second half which was an unbelievable moment. I had decided during the week that whatever happened I was going to hang around 'Alf' because he was the one that made things happen. The first time he put a kick through I came pretty close to scoring so I decided to stick with it. The next time Adam MacDougall tried to catch it but the ball spilled out and I came flying through to dive on it.

It was an amazing game and we ended up winning with another famous Queensland comeback. We were down by five points with a minute remaining, and in our own 10-metre zone, when Kevin Walters put up a mid-field bomb that Ben Ikin regathered. Two plays later Tonie Carroll raced over to score and Darren Lockyer converted for a 24–23 win.

That try might have saved my Origin career because Wayne wasn't nearly as cranky with me afterwards as he had been at halftime. I still thought I had played my one and only game for Queensland but at least I didn't get yelled at!

THAT OPENING State of Origin game was a landmark occasion for Queensland, with not only myself but also Darren Lockyer and, ironically, Shane Webcke making their debuts. The games were played on a Friday night that year so the teams were picked the previous Sunday.

I'll never forget arriving home after we had been beaten by the Warriors and receiving a phone call telling me to be at the Crowne Plaza in Coogee because I had been selected for Queensland. I couldn't get my bag packed quick enough! When Jo dropped me off I still couldn't believe it was actually happening.

In one of our very first team meetings Wayne asked 'Alf' to tell us about the first time he played State of Origin back in 1987. 'Locky' was the youngest guy in the squad at 20 and Wayne said, 'Locky, what were you doing in 1987?' He replied that

A Dream is Realised

he had barely even been born, which was a bit of an exaggeration but didn't make 'Alf' feel too great!

I would have been 13 and still in school at the time 'Alf' made his debut so I wasn't much older than 'Locky'. The point Wayne was trying to make was that here was this guy who was 18 years old, as tiny as a school kid, in the big time playing Origin — and he blitzed them. If 'Alf' could do it, why couldn't we?

The other thing I remember about that meeting was Gary Larson standing up to make a speech. Gary had a really raspy voice because of damaged vocal chords and halfway through his speech one of the boys said, 'Larso, have you started talking yet?' It was one of those priceless moments that really lightened the mood.

I learnt a lot from Gary that year. He was a different style of player to me but he had achieved so much in the game and was a workaholic — an absolute fitness freak. I remember partnering up with him when we did a weights session and we started with bench presses. I asked, 'What do you normally do?' and Gary said, 'Oh I just do four or five sets depending on how I feel'. I said, 'Of 10?' I was used to doing three sets of eight and he was throwing around 100 or so kilograms.

He finished his first set and I jumped on the bench to do mine — the next minute he is on the ground doing push-ups! I said, 'What are you doing mate?' and he goes, 'I'll just do this while you're doing your set'. He didn't even have a certain number of push-ups he wanted to get through — he would just keep going until it was his turn to do weights again.

I learnt right there and then that this was what you had to do to emulate Gary Larson — he was a freak! I'm not saying that I did what Gary did but I have always been very particular about my weights and fitness ever since. I don't cut corners and I do everything to the best of my ability. When I went back to the Bulldogs after State of Origin some of the boys would tell me to ease up but I thought, 'Nah, for me to get any better I've got to continue to do this'. It has made a huge difference to my game over the years.

COME THE second Origin game, the Queensland selectors had put a process in place in which they would give you a call before the team was announced if you had missed out. In other words, if you had played in game one you certainly didn't want your phone to ring on Sunday night.

I actually missed the call when it came through that night but I could see it was a Queensland number and I thought to myself: 'Oh well there we go, I'm not playing the next game'. I didn't want to phone back. When I did I told Des Morris, the chairman of selectors, that I really didn't want to talk to him. He said, 'Yeah mate, I'm sorry to be the bearer of bad news. You did a fantastic job for us in the first game but we've decided to leave you out this time because Brad Thorn is going to be okay to play'.

At about 1 p.m. on the Monday my phone rang again — this time telling me to jump on a plane and get myself up to Queensland. I thought they were joking around but Des said, 'We're bringing you up on standby but there's a pretty good chance you'll be in the squad. Jason Smith has been charged with a high tackle and he's going to fight it in the judiciary but we're not too confident'.

I arrived in camp that night, Jason lost his case at the judiciary and I was back in the Queensland team. We lost the second game 26–10 but it was my first game as a Maroon at Suncorp Stadium and I was extremely proud to play at the home of Queensland rugby league. Obviously quite a few heads rolled after that performance but I retained my spot and it was the first time I had been named in my own right rather than being called in as a replacement.

I still wasn't sure how long my Origin career would last so I spent most of the week running around getting things signed by my team-mates! It became a running joke. Every time we jumped on the team bus either 'Alf' or Kevin Walters would say, 'Oh boys, by the way, if you've got any kettles or pots or towels — anything in your room at all — just pass them over to Pricey. He wants to get them signed for his mum'.

But I was a lot more relaxed this time around and I really enjoyed the experience. It was the first time I had felt comfortable in a representative side.

THE 1998 season was by far my most successful year on a personal level at that time. Although we lost the grand final against Brisbane, I had lived out a childhood dream by representing Queensland and playing all three games in the series.

We were still at the Leagues Club commiserating our loss to the Broncos when the call came through that I was in the Australian team to play New Zealand at Suncorp Stadium. I couldn't believe it. Wayne was the coach which obviously helped

A Dream is Realised

and we had a lot of Queenslanders in the team. We had actually lost the Anzac Day Test at North Harbour in New Zealand earlier in the year which prompted Bob Fulton to quit as coach.

We were scheduled to play two more games against them which meant that the Kiwis needed to win only one of them to win the series. I didn't realise it at the time but Australia hadn't lost an international series since 1978 and hadn't been beaten by New Zealand twice in one year since 1953.

It was a huge buzz to play my first test in Brisbane in front of my family. The week itself was amazing. It was surreal to be training in the green and gold with so many greats of the game — Andrew Johns, 'Alf', Gorden Tallis and Steve Renouf — all running around alongside me.

I'll never forget the national anthem before the game — I was bawling my eyes out! I could see Mum and my family in the crowd and was so proud to actually achieve something I had dreamt about as a nine-year-old kid. I just lost it and as the camera panned across I was trying to make it look as if I wasn't crying, but it was no use. I was thinking: 'How the hell am I going to play a game of footy now?'

My test debut was similar to my Origin debut in a way. I was jogging up and down the sideline waiting for my chance and when the call came I went crazy again. I wasn't on the field for very long when I took a hit-up and as I was falling in the tackle I saw Joe Vagana come running across with his big arms flying in. He planted one on the side of my head and that's about the last thing I remember. We received a penalty as a result and if you watch the footage you can see me in the background with my headgear slanted. I try to stand up and all of a sudden you see me stumble and fall straight back down again. We watched the video the following week and the whole team was wetting themselves laughing — there is no sympathy in rugby league!

I came back onto the field later in the game and tried to get square with Joe by putting a big shot on him. The first attempt didn't go so well but the second time I hit him pretty hard.

When we were watching the video Wayne said about my first shot: 'What's going on there Steven? That's just a joke, that tackle'. I told him I was still concussed so he fast-forwarded to the next one and said, 'How did you do that then? You obviously didn't go in hard enough the first time!'

My main goal from then on, whenever Wayne was coach, was to stay out of trouble because that year I seemed to get in trouble all the time. After the first couple of camps I decided the best solution was to do everything Wayne said as well as I possibly could so that I wouldn't get yelled at. That actually worked for a few years until Wayne figured out what I was doing — then he started yelling at me for no reason just to put it up me!

11 A Picture Speaks a Thousand Words

IT WAS June 1998 when I walked into a newsagent's and picked up a magazine called *Not Only Sport*.

My eye had been drawn to a series of creative and artistic nude photos of a netballer by the name of Victoria Roberts. I thought they were magnificent — they managed to capture her beauty and athleticism in a new light without coming across as either dirty or degrading. They were sexy rather than smutty.

I was in a good frame of mind at the time. Jo and I had just had our second child, Kasey, the Super League war was over and the financial problems we'd experienced a few years earlier were finally starting to sort themselves out.

I decided that it would be a good idea to capture the moment with some photos of my own. I was at my peak physical fitness and at an age where I really wasn't going to get any better. I thought it would be great to be able to look back one day and say, 'Yeah, that's what I used to look like back in the days when I played footy'.

I rang my manager at the time, Chris Hayes, who made some calls and eventually came back to me with the name of a photographer. He was a creative type and photos such as those I had seen of Victoria Roberts were his specialty. I met him at Chris' house one day and explained to him what I wanted from the photos. I told him I was doing the photos for myself but that if they turned out well I would love for them to be published in *Not Only Sport*.

A few weeks later the photographer called me back and said that he was happy to take the shots and that it would cost me $600 which would cover his expenses and the hiring of a studio. That seemed reasonable. He also said that the editor of *Not Only Sport* was a personal friend of his and that if the photos did turn out well there was a very good chance that they would be published in that magazine.

I don't think I have ever felt as uncomfortable as I did posing for those photos. For starters, the actual studio was located on Oxford Street which is renowned as the centre of Sydney's gay community. I was still young at the time and I was worried that if people saw me hanging around there they might start rumours. I had to tell myself that I was actually there for a reason and there was no need to be so paranoid. I was obviously nude for the photo shoot and doing that in front of another guy was extremely nerve-wracking. Again, I told myself to be professional and get the job done.

The shoot itself started normally enough. The photographer began taking some shots in various poses and after a while I started to relax. He had brought a few props with him that he thought would fit in well with my image as a rugby league player so we began to incorporate them as well. There was a football taped up in black, some headgear and, given that I played for the Bulldogs, he had a dog collar with him too.

Being young and naïve it didn't occur to me at the time how any of that could look if portrayed in the wrong light. Instead I just went along with his ideas and the photos seemed to come up quite well. When we finished up he said he would get back to me after the photos were developed and let me know what was happening.

He eventually called and said, 'Mate, they have come up really well. I've spoken to my friend — I can't get you in *Not Only Sport* because it only comes out every six months but he really likes the photos and he wants to put you in one of his other magazines'. I asked him which one and he said *Blue*. I had never heard of *Blue* so I asked him what it was. He told me, 'The perception is that it's a gay magazine because the people that buy and read it are predominantly gay, but it's not a gay magazine. It's a very similar magazine to *Not Only Sport* but in a different way. It's not about sport, it's about artistic photography'. I said, 'I'll have to talk to Jo about it'. I went home that night and chatted with Jo. She said, 'I can't see it being a problem, you were pretty happy with the photos'.

In hindsight, the biggest mistake I made was having no autonomy over the photos that were used. I didn't get paid either and although I'm only making an assumption here, I'm pretty sure that the photographer would have enjoyed a nice little payday for supplying the photos to the magazine. I'm also quite sure that he had a fair idea from the outset that the photos could be used in *Blue*. I can't help but feel that it was a bit of a set-up. The more time that has passed, the more I've looked back and thought: 'Oh my God, you're an idiot — it was looking you straight in the face!'

He knew what he wanted to photograph. Every photo that he took using props was in the magazine. We took a number of photos without props and not one of them ended up in there.

Still, I agreed to it at the time and when I was interviewed for the story that accompanied the photos we spoke about the fact that I was married with two kids and that I loved my family. I was asked some questions about homosexuality and I explained that I was brought up to respect everyone and to treat them the way I would expect them to treat me. They even showed me the final story before it went to print and I was very pleased with how it came out, although at that stage I had no idea what photos would be printed alongside.

Just before the magazine came out I ducked into the newsagent at Belmore and asked for a *Blue* magazine because, for whatever reason, I still hadn't had a chance to look through one. The guy that worked there said, 'Really? You want to have a look at a *Blue* magazine?' I asked why and he said, 'Well . . . it's a little bit different.'

I was shocked when he showed me. The magazine was completely different to how I had perceived it to be and I knew straight away that my photos weren't going to come across in the way that I had intended. I spoke to Mum and she was pretty upset for the same reason. I told her, 'That's how I was brought up, you told me that — respect everyone', but she said, 'There are other ways to do that — I don't think this is the best way to show how understanding you are'.

When the magazine came out it was the highest selling issue at the time and obviously attracted a fair bit of attention. You can imagine what it must have been like for Darren Britt and Jason Hetherington — two of the straightest guys you are ever likely to meet — to walk into a newsagent and both ask for a *Blue* magazine! It's one of the few funny stories to come out of the whole thing. Apparently Jason was very nonchalant when asking for his copy and then hid it in a brown paper bag as he walked out. The boys had decided to get down to training a bit early and put a whole heap of photos up all over the walls to welcome me when I arrived. The good news is that there were quite a few people in the newsagent at the time so I can only assume it was quite embarrassing for the pair of them.

Unfortunately the pictures came across just as Mum and I had feared. I had gone from being the 'boy next door' to a guy posing nude in a gay magazine. The insinuation was that I had specifically chosen to be photographed for *Blue*. Once that happens there is no point even trying to defend yourself — people will think what they think. I decided to keep quiet.

THERE WAS another unfortunate coincidence at the time that had Peter Moore worried sick. I had started waxing my legs about two years earlier because I figured that, aside from the fact that I kept cutting my ankles when I shaved them so they could be strapped for the game, it also felt cleaner. I thought I might even be able to slip out of a few extra tackles as well!

I said to my sister-in-law one day, 'I'm sick of shaving my ankles, what would it be like if I waxed my legs?' She said, 'Try it and see'. I'm still not sure what inspired me to do it again after that first experience — the wax wasn't hot enough and I was bleeding from the top of my legs all the way down to my ankles! I guess I figured that it couldn't get any worse so I did it again and the second time wasn't nearly as bad. I've done it ever since.

One day, around the time that *Blue* came out in December, 1999, I was leaving my local salon when June — a lady from the club — happened to walk in. She asked the therapist 'Does Steve Price come here?' and she replied, 'Yeah, he comes and gets his legs waxed'. The next day she went straight in and told Peter and he freaked out. He was still trying to deal with the fact that I had posed for a gay magazine and now I was getting my legs waxed! To top it off, his mates at Revesby Bowls Club had told him there were rumours going around that I was gay. That sent all sorts of alarm bells going off in Peter's head — he was horrified.

I didn't think much of it when Peter rang me and asked if we could have a meeting. He would often ask to catch up and I would always go and see him. Luckily he had phoned his daughter, Karen Folkes, before we met. He asked her, 'Karen, if a guy is waxing his legs does that mean he's gay? Is there something going on there?' She said, 'Oh no, no, Steve's (Folkes) friends do it, they're cyclists and tri athletes and it's just a thing that they do these days. It's not anything to do with being gay.'

That made him feel a bit better but he still needed to speak to me to find out what was going on. He was very distressed that all of these people were saying this about me. It was basically his way of letting me know about the rumours.

We cleared the air straight away and he was very happy when he left — I'm sure he went straight back and told his mates the story that I had told him! He also said that we would do a story in the newspapers to clear everything up.

The problem was that by this stage the rumour has really picked up momentum. I had been told by a friend of mine at the Roosters that before training one day in early 2001 a couple of the senior players had called a meeting and told the whole team that I was gay and was leaving my wife to live with my gay lover. That was the buzz around the league community at the time. I didn't make the State of Origin that year and the rumour seemed to spread like wild fire through the Origin camps.

On top of that, a certain person who worked for *The Daily Telegraph* and now works for *Rugby League Week* wrote about it in his rumour column. He didn't name me but he was so detailed in his description of me that it didn't leave any doubt as to who he was talking about.

I couldn't believe that what had begun as an innocent exercise had been taken advantage of to this extent. I don't regret doing the photos because my reasons were valid. Things were going well for me, I was looking at different things to do and that was something that I wanted to tick off. As it turned out, I ticked it off and it backfired.

I was no longer asked to do any promotional work by the NRL and I don't blame them either because it was an unfortunate situation. Once the rumour was printed in *The Daily Telegraph* I approached Garry Hughes and said, 'Mate, this is what has happened and I know that he is talking about me'. It was upsetting for me and I know that it upset Jo too. My mother was horrified.

I can't thank Garry enough — he really went in to bat for me. He called *The Daily Telegraph* and made a huge deal about it because this journalist hadn't called me to ask if it was true.

The rumour still follows me around to this day. I got into an argument with Josh Perry in a pre-season game this year and the first thing he said was: 'Homo'. Then he backed it up with: 'You're a poofter'. This all happened eight years ago — before Josh was even around — but rumours like that don't easily disappear and in the heat of the battle it is easy artillery.

I know I wasn't playing well at the time but I'm pretty sure that the rumours didn't help my representative career too much either.

The hardest thing was to actually come out and say something because it gave credibility to what this journalist had thrown out there. That was one of the concerns that Peter had. He said that once we had done the story and it was out there, that was it — I wasn't to talk about it again. So that's what we did. We stopped talking about it.

Some of the poses I'm not proud of, only because of how they were portrayed in the magazine. It's not Steven Price and it wasn't why I posed for the photos. As Jason Hetherington said in that beautiful country drawl of his, nobody would have been reading the story — they were looking at the photos. Even those that did read the story could have been swayed. As they say, a picture paints a thousand words.

Mum obviously copped plenty as well and that wasn't fair because I was the one that had the photos taken. I'm a big boy and I can handle the criticism but when my family is affected it upsets me. I don't care if someone calls me those names. I know that I'm not gay but even if I was I'd be proud of it because I'm proud of who I am. I wouldn't be scared of it. It's when people say that you're something that you're not in order to gain some sort of leverage that I get frustrated.

I'd have to say it has been a tough battle since then to earn back the respect I had and to get my profile back to where it was before the photos were published. It's taken eight years. I don't hear it too much now. Every now and then you hear about it. Ironically, Awen Guttenbeil was Googling my name when I first came to the Warriors and found a couple of the photos which made their way onto our notice board. Maybe I'll hear more again now that I've recounted the whole situation but I felt that it was time to tell the full story. I didn't have that opportunity eight years ago. Hopefully, once I've retired, people will remember me for the person and the player I was rather than the person that was portrayed in those photos. But, as I have always said, they are now a part of my history and will never be forgotten completely.

A magical moment as I crossed for the opening try of the 1995 grand final against Manly at the Sydney Football Stadium.

My support crew at the 1995 grand final. From left is Gaz, Dan, Mum and my mates Russell Bussian, Tony Crossley and Heath Farlow.

Left: Our wedding day on 9 November 1996. We always forget the exact date but luckily Mum always calls to wish us happy anniversary. Whoever answers the phone is the one who says 'happy anniversary' to the other!

Below: Me, Jamie-Lee and Jo on our wedding day. Jamie is just 10 months old.

Me, Mum and a one-year-old Jamie-Lee in 1996.

Jamie-Lee and myself with a newly born Kasey at the hospital in 1998.

Steve Price Collection/Inset: Action Photographics

I run the ball forward during the 1998 grand final against Brisbane at the SFS. Peter Moore (inset) was extremely ill at the time but still turned up to watch his beloved Bulldogs in action.

I'm tackled by Glenn Lazarus, David Barnhill and Ryan Girdler in the opening game of the 1999 State of Origin series. 'Lazo' was arguably my toughest-ever opponent and a player I had great respect for.

I had only just stopped wearing headgear when I burst a blood vessel during a game against Newcastle in 2001. I came from the field with a lump the size of a golf ball protruding from my head but returned to action soon after.

Jubilation after Hazem El Masri kicks a miracle goal from the sideline against Newcastle in 2002. We had trailed 19-0 but came back to win 22-21 and continued our remarkable winning streak.

Reality set in after going down 38-34 to Canberra in late 2002. Two days earlier we had been stripped of 37 competition points for massive salary cap breaches and had trailed the Raiders 20-0 before mounting a comeback. It was an extremely emotional afternoon for the club.

I'm carried around Sydney Showground by Bulldogs supporters after beating Brisbane 25-18 in our final match of the 2002 season. I've never seen such emotional scenes after a game in my entire life.

Back in State of Origin in 2002.

Kerry Beever/Melba Studios

Above: A Bulldogs training session with a 1970s theme at Cronulla during the 2004 season. There were some outstanding efforts, led by Mark O'Meley in his G-string . . . hopefully it wasn't his own.

Left: I can't help but crack a smile after we demolished Parramatta 48–14 in round one of the 2004 season. After Coffs Harbour had dominated our pre-season, we were relieved to be playing football again.

12 Rock Bottom

I DON'T think I've ever had a worse year than 2000. I probably should have known that it wasn't going to go too well when I broke my ankle in our last game of the 1999 season.

We came within two games of the grand final in '99 but lost to Melbourne in the semi-finals when Ricky Stuart put in a kick that hit Matt Geyer's legs before he raced the length of the field to score.

We didn't have a lot of luck in that game. At one stage I reached out to score but fell a few inches short of the line. It was a huge moment because not only did I break my ankle in the tackle, referee Steve Clark penalised me for a double movement! I was caught in the moment and I was blowing up. I hobbled after Steve shouting, 'I didn't even get the ball over the tryline, why am I being penalised?'

A few days later Jo's sister Peta came down to visit and we all went into the city. My ankle was still really sore so I was having a bit of a whinge. Jo said to me, 'You'll be okay, we're only going to be out for a few hours. Don't be such a wus, it's not that bad'.

The following week I had a golf day with the Queensland State of Origin team, because we didn't have time to celebrate retaining the trophy during the season. Again I was hobbling around in pain the whole time so when I returned to pre-season training with the Bulldogs I told Hugh Hazard and we decided to get a scan. We found out that I actually had two fractured bones in my ankle that I had been carrying around for the past eight weeks!

That really set me back. Instead of getting stuck into the pre-season, I had to wear a boot and stay off my ankle. I was picked for State of Origin in 2000 but was dropped after we lost the first two games. That was the first time it really hit home that things weren't going too well for me. I had gone from playing my best footy in 1998 to having an absolute shocker in less than two years. Steve Folkes dumped me to the bench and I didn't know what was going on. I probably felt that I was playing better than I actually was.

It wasn't until I came back from Origin and 'Folkesy' said to me, 'Mate, I'm really struggling to keep you in the 17 — I might have to drop you back to reserve grade', that I started to see how poorly I was playing. It was a real reality check but sometimes when you're not playing well the people around you are reluctant to tell you the truth. That was the first I had heard of it because for some reason I thought I was going okay.

The year didn't get much better. Peter Moore passed away in July, I did my knee for the first time and we missed the semi-finals — it was horrendous all-round. Everything that could go wrong, did go wrong.

It did prove to be a turning point for me though. After 'Folkesy' relegated me to the bench, I came home one night and asked Jo to be honest in telling me how she thought I was playing. She said, 'If you want honesty then I think you're playing pretty shithouse actually'.

I couldn't believe it. It was like my whole world had been tipped on its head. It had broken my heart when I was dropped from the Origin squad because I loved representing Queensland more than anything else in the world.

What Jo made me realise was that I had started to get my priorities mixed up during that period. I had made the Queensland side because of the hard work I put in at the Bulldogs but once I started being named in these representative sides I let it go to my head. I stopped doing the hard work and let outside influences — such as media commitments — take up too much of my time. I had become complacent and far too comfortable in my success. I had all of the excuses in the world. I was complaining that I wasn't getting the ball when in reality it was up to me to go looking for it.

I was also suffering a little bit at rep level from that lack of self-belief that Chris Anderson had spoken to me about a few years earlier. I didn't totally believe that

Rock Bottom

I deserved to be in the representative arena. I thought I was just making up the numbers and because I was coming off the bench I assumed I was just filling space.

It didn't occur to me at the time just how important the bench is these days. I was trying to be other people and come up with big plays rather than doing what I was actually there to do — the simple things that had earned me selection in the first place. It wasn't until I focused on the core parts of my game that I began to play decent football again.

TO GIVE an insight into where my head space was that season, I was actually contemplating playing for England in the 2000 World Cup. My grandmother was born and bred in England and had often tried to convince me that I was a Pom rather than an Aussie. I hadn't made the Australian team for the Anzac Test earlier that year and I thought that by representing England I could at least play in the World Cup.

Because of the Olympic Games being held in Sydney that year, the NRL season had finished early so I decided that I had plenty of time to get my knee right in time for the tournament. Luckily I spoke to 'Folkesy' about it. He said, 'You need to be concentrating on having a good pre-season and getting over your knee injury. England probably won't win the World Cup so you're only going to go over there to get beaten at some stage and it will upset your pre-season'.

It was good advice, although I wasn't too thrilled with it at the time. In hindsight it was some of the greatest advice I ever received. I ended up having a great pre-season heading into 2001, trained my backside off and spent a lot of time with 'Folkesy' going through reviewing every aspect of my game.

He started by throwing me back into the front row full time, which meant I was immediately more involved again. To be in the game I had to either be touching the ball, supporting the ball or making tackles, and playing up front had me busy with all three.

It was an exciting time in a lot of ways because it felt like a fresh start. The position itself was very different from playing back-row — and not just because I was no longer standing around out wide for 80 minutes. Rather than having one opponent to beat, I now had three or four guys standing in front of me when I hit the ball up. It took a little while to get used to and I didn't necessarily play a typical front-rower's game — I was more like a second-rower playing in the front row — but it suited me.

DARREN BRITT was our other prop and he was more your old fashioned front-rower — tough and hard with a bit of skill to go with it. The balance was quite good between the two of us. From missing the finals altogether in 2000, we finished second in 2001 behind Parramatta and only a few injuries at the end of the year prevented us from going deeper through the finals than we did. We played Newcastle in the last round and it was a meaningless game for us — we were going to finish second no matter what the result was. 'Folkesy' was going to rest a heap of players, including me, but I insisted on playing and ended up doing rib cartilage damage which put me under a lot of pressure for the finals.

Our qualifying final was against St George Illawarra and they beat us 23–22 after Trent Barrett had a blinder. I was already struggling with my ribs but Braith Anasta picked up an injury and two or three other guys were forced off as well.

A week later we were smashed 52–10 by Cronulla and our season was over, but it was a big improvement on where we had been 12 months earlier. More importantly, the Bulldogs were on the verge of great things — even if off-field distractions would come to diminish our achievements.

13 My Mate Matthew

AS HIGH-PROFILE athletes, our occupation provides us with plenty of opportunity to visit hospitals and meet families that are going through a difficult time. To see a young kid lying in a hospital bed really puts life into perspective. There was one boy in particular who had a huge influence on me — my little mate Matthew Mitric.

I first met Matthew in late 1999 at a fundraising luncheon for Child Cancer hosted by Saxbury Bridge — the company that my financial advisor Richard Shaw worked for. I was on crutches at the time — having broken my ankle in our semi-final loss to Melbourne — but I wanted to lend my support so I didn't hesitate in accepting Richard's invitation.

Matthew, who had been diagnosed with a brain tumour, was a sort of 'guest speaker' that day. He actually stood up on stage and answered questions about his cancer, what he had gone through as part of his treatment and his hopes of beating such a terrible illness. He struck me straight away as an incredibly courageous little boy.

I had been attending a lot of schools and promotional events at the time and the back of my car was full of posters, mini-footballs and various Bulldogs paraphernalia. As we were leaving, Jo said to me, 'Why don't you give Matthew one of those mini-footballs?' I couldn't move too well because of the crutches but we called out to Matthew and his mum Kim as they were getting into their car, I signed a football and Jo ran over and gave it to them. It was nothing unusual but they really appreciated the gesture. You could see Matthew's face light up.

About nine months later the club received a letter from Westmead Children's

Hospital asking if a few players could come out and visit. They specifically requested that I head out to see Matthew because he was a huge rugby league fan and he had met me at the Saxbury Bridge fundraiser. His mum thought I could be a positive influence on him. Matthew had been really struggling, things weren't looking too good and she wanted me to head out to try and lift his spirits.

I didn't receive the letter until very late on a Monday afternoon. The State of Origin teams had just been chosen and I knew I was flying up to Queensland early the next morning to join Origin camp. I was trying to figure out how I could find the time to visit Matthew that night with everything that I had to organise but I found a way and it was one of the greatest decisions I have ever made.

Matthew was just like any kid with a big smile on his face but his mum told me what he had been through — the surgery, the sickness and everything that he had to deal with. We had a photo taken together and decided that we were best mates. After about an hour Matthew started to get tired so they both thanked me for coming along and I headed home.

I received another letter not long after thanking me again and telling me that I made a huge difference — that I had inspired and lifted him — but a few months later the hospital called to tell me that Matthew had gone through another rough trot after being in good health for a while. I raced back out to the hospital to see if I could lift his spirits again.

I noticed that Matthew had our photo next to his bed in a small home-made frame. His mum told me that the kids often had craft sessions to fill in time and he had wanted to make a frame for the picture he had of him and me together. Poor old Mum — Matthew had replaced her with Steve Price!

He used to tell everyone — doctors, nurses and friends — that I was his best mate. Whenever I went to see him I would take along some Bulldogs posters or some sort of Bulldogs toy to cheer him up and his family would send me a heartfelt letter thanking me for the visit.

The third time I went to see Matthew in hospital was a lot more serious. He had been operated on three times that week and on two of those occasions they had called for the Reverend to come in because they were going to read him his last rites. He actually died on the operating table. They don't know how or why but he came back both times.

His mum was desperate. The family was devastated to think they had almost lost him twice so they decided to try what had worked before and asked me to go along and cheer him up.

He was in Ronald McDonald House at Westmead by this stage and it was amazing — you could never have guessed that Matthew had experienced two close calls that very week. He was walking around and playing like any normal kid and his mum said he pretty much did that because he knew I was coming and he was so excited. Only 24 hours earlier he had been on the operating table.

I look back at that period of my career and I'm disappointed because the type of football I was playing was certainly no reflection of how much Matthew inspired me. It breaks my heart because he was so proud of me and so proud of telling people that we were best mates. I wasn't representing him the way I should have been.

I WAS sitting at home one day in January 2002, when I heard Matthew's voice coming from the lounge room. I said to Jo, 'That's Matt, I can hear Matt', and raced around to see him on TV. He was talking about everything that he had been through and his hope that they could find a cure. He said that even if it was the last thing that he did in his life, if he could help doctors find a cure for cancer then he would be satisfied that he had made a difference.

I was staring at him in awe and just so proud to see him on TV. Then came the words: 'Unfortunately Matthew lost his battle with cancer on 30/12/01'.

I was devastated — absolutely shattered. I look back and sometimes wonder why it hit me so hard because even though Matthew was a real fighter, you always knew that there was a very good chance that this day would come. I guess there was a part of me that believed he might just beat his cancer. For so long he would fight back from serious situations. He was such a tough little kid.

I was also really upset that it had been almost a month since Matthew had died before I found out. No-one had told me. I certainly didn't expect his mum to call me because she had her own grieving process to go through and it must have been a terrible time for her — I just didn't expect to find out the way that I did.

I waited a while and eventually contacted Kim to tell her how much of an impact Matthew had had on my life. I said to her, 'I hope you don't take this the wrong way but you should be very proud of having had such a wonderful person in your life. He was a special gift that was put here for a special reason. I know that right now you might not be feeling too great about it but to actually have him for 11 years has been something that I know you will cherish for the rest of your life. You shouldn't have any regrets because he lived a lot longer than people expected and I think it was a lot to do with the love and support he got from you and your family'. I thanked her for giving me an opportunity to be part of that as well.

She sent me a letter not long after that and it was one of the most powerful things I had ever read. She told me that my visits were more than any doctor or surgeon could do for Matty. To put that into perspective, I'm Steven Price from Toowoomba — a kid that happened to grow up and do something he really loved to do. I never thought that someone like me could ever have that sort of impact or influence on someone else's life. It's hard to contemplate but it is why I say that meeting Matthew put a lot of things into perspective.

I remember an incident a few years back where my daughter Kasey jammed her finger in a door and it took the whole end of her finger off bar the smallest piece of skin. We were terrified that she might lose the end of her finger and raced to Bankstown Hospital. They told us we would have to take her to Westmead for specialist analysis. We were freaking out. Eventually we got her in, she had microsurgery and they managed to save the end of her finger. You wouldn't even know it had happened to look at her finger now.

She was one of the lucky ones but the girl lying next to her in hospital was three years old and out of that three years she had been home for a total of four-and-a-half months because of cancer. Now that was a reality check! Obviously Jo and I had been worried about our daughter but it made us realise how blessed we are to have three beautiful children that are healthy.

It's why I am so passionate about visiting kids. My experience with Matt has made me realise that a few moments of my time spent visiting these kids can really mean the world. You can't put a value on being in a position to influence these kids.

Certainly Matthew had a huge impact on me. There have been other kids in Australia and New Zealand and I've been lucky enough to have an influence on them too, but Matthew is the one that changed my life.

One of the things that Jo and I try to teach our kids is that when you're feeling down and think that things aren't going too well, have a good look at what it is you're unhappy about and put it into perspective. We all have things in our lives that frustrate us or times when we feel that nothing is going right, but that is nothing compared to what people like Matthew have had to deal with.

Aside from the letter that Matthew's mum sent me, she also sent the photo and frame that Matthew had next to his bed. She thought I should have it because it was special to Matt and she appreciated what our relationship meant to him. The photo now takes pride of place on my mantelpiece.

Matthew was buried in his Bulldogs jersey and other Bulldogs clothes that I had given him. It's hard to accept that he is gone but also that something could mean so much to someone. People say rugby league is only a game but I can assure you that it is much more than that.

A few years ago I sent Matt's sister Danielle a signed Warriors jersey. Earlier this year I received a letter from her saying that there had been terrible storms on the Central Coast where she lives, their house had been flooded and a lot of their belongings had been ruined — the Warriors jersey included. She begged me to send her another one because she cherished the relationship I had with her brother. That jersey meant a lot to her.

Jamie Pandaram from *The Sydney Morning Herald* wrote a story about Matthew last year. I've known Jamie for quite a few years now and we were chatting about Matthew when he decided that it would make a good yarn. I didn't know he was actually going to call Matthew's mum but he did and I think she was blown away by it. I've told her what an inspiration Matty is to me but I'm sure she thought that over time I had slowly forgotten about him. When Jamie called her she was blown away that I was still talking about her son five years after he passed away.

But I'm proud to have known him. It's difficult to put into words but I really do feel honoured.

Helping children with cancer is a passion of mine these days. *The Footy Show* used to have a segment called 'Face Your Fears' and I called them up to say I was willing to do something to raise money for cancer research.

There was a particular microscope with three-dimensional viewing that the Westmead Children's Hospital needed because it could view cancer cells from the top and side as well as cutting them into pieces so that you could see the full shape. The way it was first explained to me was that if you had a tennis ball it would look round from the top and side but when you cut it you could see the real shape. To go any further with their research they had to know about these cells.

I'm terrified of heights but I volunteered to climb the Sydney Harbour Bridge and thank God it was a magnificent day because I was shitting myself! I was walking under the bridge — the bit directly under the road — and I could see straight down to the ground. It was only 80 metres away but to me it may as well have been five kilometres.

As you keep walking along you go up some stairs that are hanging off the side and over the water and by this stage I wasn't in a good state of mind. There are these little clips that you have to keep clipping and unclipping as you go and I said to the guide, 'I'm sorry mate but I really don't want to be clipping this thing on all the time'. He said to me, 'Why? That's your safety, it's going to save you'.

I said, 'Yeah but if I fall over I don't want to be hanging from the side of the Sydney Harbour Bridge waiting for someone to pull me back over. I'm pretty much resigned to the fact that I'm gone if I go over the side. I will definitely have a heart attack if I'm hanging 50 stories above the water. I'd rather be gone and have my heart attack on the way down!'

The microscope cost about $500,000 and for each fear that was faced a sponsor would donate $10,000. In the end the segment raised around $200,000. I went to the launch when they finally took ownership and I felt so proud that I was able to help. I'm not sure that my fear of heights has been cured but it was something I had to do and I'm glad I did it.

When I moved to New Zealand I was waiting to do a radio interview and was reading a few brochures they had lying around in reception. One of them was for a fundraiser called 'Shave your Lid for a Kid' which involved people donating money for you to shave your head. The money would go to the Child Cancer Foundation.

I had only about two weeks to do so but I whipped up as many people as I could — mostly sponsors of the Warriors — and we managed to raise $20,000 in those two weeks. I asked the boys at the Warriors to do it too and about 13 of us went down on the day, as well as our media manager Richard Becht, and our chief executive Wayne Scurrah. Wayne just happened to be there on the day and thought it was a good cause but, thank God, he hasn't done it since because it's not a good look for him!

Still, my theory was that I was more than happy to look stupid for a few weeks if it could help make a difference. I've done the same thing each year since and raised almost $30,000 last year so we're getting better all the time.

Since then I've been asked to be the ambassador for the Child Cancer Foundation in New Zealand. They've never had an ambassador before, and I've never been one for any foundation, but it was always going to be for the Child Cancer Foundation if it happened. That's all thanks to Matthew. I'll never, ever forget him even though it was only a short time we had together. He has changed my life for the better.

I have come across cancer a few times in my life and it's never fun. Cancer is a nasty, nasty disease that eats away at a person and takes their dignity. Towards the end they are rarely the person that people remember them to be and there have been a couple of occasions where I haven't gone and visited people because I didn't want to see them in that state.

I *did* visit Peter Moore and I saw him in some terrible states but he needed you to see him to show that you still loved him. I needed it too because there were things I needed to speak to him about. That gave me some experience of what cancer does.

When you visit hospitals as a rugby league player it can be easy to look straight past what's actually happening and just see it as some sort of promotion or time spent at a place to try and make a few people happy. The hard thing is when you grow attached to these people — it hurts when they don't make it.

But I'm privileged that I have had that type of influence in my life because it has changed my thought processes. Our time is precious and we are lucky to have our body, health and mind. You have to make the most of that.

Ever since my experience with Matthew I get really frustrated when I see someone with talent failing to give their best at whatever it might be. They waste the opportunities that are there for them.

It's not fair that someone like Matthew was struck down with cancer, but everyone is dealt a hand and at the end of the day it comes down to how you play it.

That's why Matthew was so inspirational. He has driven me forward. I'm 34 years old but is there any reason why I shouldn't still be playing in the NRL or for Queensland or Australia? Who says I'm too old to do that? As long as I put in the hard work there is no reason why I can't. I won't let my age become an excuse.

It frustrates me when people come up with excuses because there are little boys like Matthew who never had a choice. His mum and his sister were affected by it and they didn't have a choice either.

Sometimes people need to realise how lucky they really are. I know that I am lucky that my little mate Matthew Mitric is a part of my life.

14 Top Dog

I HAD always wanted to captain the Bulldogs, but when the opportunity arose in 2002 (after Darren Britt announced he was headed to England) I was pretty certain that neither Steve Folkes nor my team-mates thought I was the right man for the job.

Midway through the 2001 season I went to see our club sports psychologist, Alex Gilandas, and spoke about my aspirations. I told him that I wanted to be more consistent and, more importantly, that I wanted to be captain when Darren left. Alex said, 'Alright — and how are you going to do that?' I told him, 'For the rest of this season I want to prove to the coach, my team-mates and myself that, one: I'm a leader and two: I've got the consistency to be a leader'.

I knew that consistency was my main downfall. I would play a good game one week and then have three games that were only solid. It wasn't good enough for a captain so it became my primary focus. At training I worked harder on the little things such as jogging on my way to get a drink. I started talking more than I used to — not necessarily in open play but certainly behind the in-goal or in certain situations. I was wary of not stepping on Darren's toes because I didn't want it to look as if I was trying to take his job, but I did want to act more like a senior player.

At the end of the season 'Folkesy' came up to me and said that the captaincy would come down to a choice between myself, Braith Anasta and Darren Smith. He said, 'I've got a few things with Darren and Braith that I need to talk to them about too — things they have to prove to me — and it is the same with you. There are no more games to play so it will be about attitude during the pre-season.

Obviously the biggest concern 'Folkesy' had with me was my consistency. He told me, 'I don't want to name you captain and then find that you're not playing as well as a leader should be playing. I don't want to have to drop our captain back to the bench or reserve grade and I don't want the team performing poorly because their leader isn't leading'. It was a big risk for 'Folkesy' to take but I wanted to prove by my efforts that the captaincy was actually going to help *me* as much as it helped the team.

The announcement was to be made at our season launch in early 2002 at Luna Park. For any of those who know 'Folkesy', he is a master at keeping things very close to his chest and he didn't let me down on this occasion. Braith had probably dropped out of the running to a fair extent because he was still quite young, so it came down to a choice between me and Darren. Darren was at the other end of the spectrum to Braith. He was the oldest of the three and the concern must have been how much longer he was going to be at the club. I fell right in the middle.

I was as nervous as hell on the night of the launch. I had no idea that 'Folkesy' had actually called Darren a few days earlier and told him that he was going to name me the Bulldogs' new captain.

When the announcement was finally made I was blown away. It was very emotional and I thought straight back to 'Bullfrog' — the influence he had on me and the fact that he had told me I would one day lead the Bulldogs into battle. I'm pretty sure I actually shed a few tears on stage — I'm pretty good at that — but it was a huge moment for me. I had finally achieved one of my greatest dreams. Believe it or not, through the whole thing I hadn't even prepared a speech in case I was chosen! Luckily I was still able to utter a few words about how honoured I was to lead such a great club.

BEING NAMED captain was one thing — backing it up on the field was another. I was quite nervous because I needed to earn my team-mates' respect as their new captain and I was worried about how to prove I was a good leader. I wanted to be given as much respect as Darren Britt or Terry Lamb but I had no idea how to achieve it. I knew that I had to remain the same person I always had been because if I tried too hard to change, the boys would see straight through it.

My main focus became making sure I did my own job to the absolute best of my ability so that my team-mates could have no excuses as to why they weren't doing the same. From there it came down to earning respect by making decisions and being confident that those decisions were the right ones. It was something that could only be achieved out in the middle, under pressure. Talking wasn't going to get the job done, my actions had to speak for me.

In our first game of the season against Wests Tigers a couple of guys questioned my decisions at the time and I let them know in no uncertain terms that I was the captain and I needed their support in what I was deciding. I told them that even if they didn't agree, it was my decision and it was therefore up to the whole team to make sure it proved correct. I think they started to understand very quickly that I was serious about what I was trying to do and what I wanted to achieve.

That first game was a great learning curve for me. Even though we lost, it really tested me. There were a few decisions that went against us but I didn't carry on like an idiot and that was something I had thought about during the pre-season — I wanted to be a cool-headed captain. I didn't want to show my emotions and all of the pressures that a captain can be under. If things went against us I wanted to be controlled about it and stay positive so that my team-mates wouldn't let negative thoughts creep into their minds.

I also wanted to build a relationship and an understanding with referees that they had my absolute respect. I would question some of their decisions but I would do so in a respectful manner. I wanted them to return the favour by explaining their decisions with similar respect towards me. I've seen captains and even played under some in the lower grades that are very emotional and far too disrespectful of referees. Those captains never get anywhere. Refereeing is a tough job and they're only human. If you rip into them they'll just come back to haunt you — whether they mean it or not.

I spent a lot of time with 'Folkesy'. I wanted to ensure that the decisions I made fitted in with what he was trying to achieve each game. If, for example, I took the two points when we received a penalty rather than going for the try I would approach him after the game and say: 'What do you reckon about that, do you reckon it was the right decision?' He would give me his feedback but no matter what decision I made he was always very supportive. That in itself helped my confidence and it grew and grew as the season went on.

I took the responsibility of being Bulldogs captain very seriously and that extended beyond the club itself. When I was speaking to the media I would always be as truthful as possible. I would consider who was listening — be it supporters of my club, supporters of other clubs, people from outside the code or sponsors — as well as family and friends of the players. I knew that my team-mates and opponents would hear what I had to say and I wanted them to be proud.

As the season went on, and the Bulldogs started to have some success, my confidence went through the roof and it made the job a whole lot easier because my team-mates started taking real ownership over their own performances. It also helped me get to know the boys as individuals. When you are trying to get the best out of the team it is vital that you know each individual and what makes them tick. If something is wrong you need to know how to communicate with them.

I learnt, for example, that if I yelled at Braith he would just yell back and it would quickly end up becoming an argument. That was no good for any of us. I've been in sides where that has happened and thought: 'Well this is just great — we've got two blokes ripping into each other verbally'.

Brent Sherwin was the opposite. If he put in a bad kick or took a poor option I would raise my voice straight away to tell him it wasn't what we wanted and he understood straight away. These are the little things that you can only learn from experience and I was always very mindful of taking everything on board.

The Bulldogs captaincy is a bit like royalty and you've got to be in the right place at the right time. Before me was Darren Britt, before him was Simon Gillies, before Simon was Terry Lamb and before that was Steve Mortimer. Provided that you proved yourself to be a good leader, the opportunity was there to captain the club for a very long time.

TAKING ON the captaincy — and all that comes with it — took my own game to a new level. I'm a person that tends to stress a lot but it's hard to stress when you're busy, so I quickly learned to love all of the media and sponsorship commitments that are part of a captain's day-to-day duties.

My biggest struggle through the early stages of my career as an NRL player was putting together the right preparation each week and being able to duplicate it. I remember an important chat I had with Terry Lamb at Campbelltown Stadium one day. I would always arrive at the ground early, and an hour before the game I would already be dressed and sitting around waiting.

On this particular day Terry said to me, 'Today I want you to go out and watch the lower grades for a while — just give yourself about 15 or 20 minutes to get strapped. Do that and see how you go because I think you're sitting in here wasting too much energy'. I actually cut it a bit too close that day so I was rushed but I could see what he was saying.

By taking over as captain it added to the things I could distract myself with before each game: 'Is Hazem going to play well today? He's been a little bit crook. Sonny Bill Williams has a bit of a groin injury. Andrew Ryan has a thumb problem, hopefully he's going to be alright'.

Some people would tell me that I should be concentrating more on my own game but it actually helped me to have those distractions. It's still something I do today. I think about how the boys have been going, if they're in form, if they're out of form, how they are going to play themselves back into form and what type of impact the opposition is going to have on them on the day.

The other thing I think about is the opponents that I'm playing against and if there is anything that I can do to make it hard for their key players. I used to love playing against Andrew Johns because I would always try to put pressure on his kick. I knew he hated it and he would call me every name under the sun but I knew that if I was successful it would upset him. I figured that if I gave 'Joey' time to kick the ball he would put it exactly where he wanted, so by applying some pressure I was going a long way towards helping my team. It's probably why I was never one of his favourite people.

Little things like that can be the difference between winning and losing. In Joey's case, I would try to watch him every week so that as soon as I played against him there would be things about his game that would trigger in my mind.

It's obviously a lot easier to do that these days with Pay TV but I still try to watch every game, every weekend. People tell me I'm a footy nut but the reason is that teams and players go through different ebbs and flows throughout the season and I always like to keep up to date — even if we're not playing them for another eight weeks. You store it in the memory bank for future reference.

Aside from that, I just love the sport of rugby league so I watch games because I'm a fan. Jo and the kids love rugby league too so we can all happily spend hours in front of the TV of a weekend.

By the time we get to our video sessions I've already got my own ideas about how players are going and what their strengths or weaknesses are. The coach takes us through footage and gives us tips on their strengths and weaknesses which I add to my own thoughts. Something that has really developed in my preparation is visualising players and running positive footage through my head of particular players when I am playing them — whether it be in attack or in defence. It is amazing how many times I have visualised something and it has come true during a game.

DESPITE ALL of that, my initiation as captain during that first year was a tough one. We had enjoyed a tremendous pre-season but were scheduled to play Wests Tigers in the opening round. Nobody rated the Tigers as a premiership threat but they had a pretty decent squad and we always seemed to struggle against them. True to form, they battled away and ended up beating us 28–22.

Our second game was aginst the Broncos away and we had a terrible record playing up there. I had never won a game in Brisbane playing for the Bulldogs — we always seemed to get close and then they would run away with it at the death. It was a big game for us and we nearly got home but the match ended up finishing 20-all.

It meant that after the first two weeks of my captaincy we were on one point while all of the top sides were on four points. It was hardly the perfect start I had been looking for but I could never have expected what happened next.

We claimed our first win of the season against St George Illawarra in round three and from then on we just kept winning. By the time our streak was halted we had won 17 games in a row and pulled off some of the most memorable victories in all of my years at the club. People ask me what it was like during that period and all I can say is we felt that nobody could beat us no matter what the situation — and we were certainly in some tricky ones.

In round 20 we were down 19–0 at halftime in Newcastle but came back to win 22–21 in amazing circumstances. We were behind 21–16 in the final minute when Luke Patten scored in the corner and Hazem El Masri nailed the conversion from the sideline.

Our final win of the streak was against the Cowboys in Townsville in a game where absolutely nothing went our way. It felt like the referee was doing everything he could to help them beat us — which I'm sure he wasn't — but it was one of those frustrating games when all of the close calls go against you. Somehow we finished over the top of them to win 34–26 and make it 17 in a row.

We were finally beaten by the Warriors, who were still a bit unpredictable but on their day could put 40 points past you. I don't know if it was because we had a lot of Kiwi players in our team but the Warriors seemed to love playing the Bulldogs and they really put it to us that day to win 22–14.

In some ways it was almost a relief to finally lose a game. There had been so much pressure building through the media to keep the streak going, so, even though we tried not to focus on it, it was hard to escape the attention.

A week later we beat Parramatta 28–10 on the Friday night and our season seemed to be right back on track. Little did we know the devastating news that was about to destroy our season.

15 Crushed

FOUR DAYS after *The Sydney Morning Herald* reported that the Bulldogs were guilty of deliberately breaching the NRL salary cap by more than $1.5 million over the previous two years, I came face to face with the journalist who broke the story.

I was scheduled to appear on *NRL on Fox* that Wednesday night and turned up expecting to sit down with Warren Smith, Laurie Daley and David Gallop. I had no idea that journalist Kate McClymont would be there too. As soon as I arrived Kate came up to me all chirpy and said, 'Hi Steve, I'm Kate McClymont. You probably don't want to know me. I wouldn't be one of your favourite people at the moment'. I asked her, 'Oh, why would that be Kate?' and she replied, 'Well I was the person that unveiled the story'. I said to her, 'Yep, you're pretty much right Kate. I'm not much of a fan of yours at the moment. You've changed my world just a little bit'.

As soon as she started speaking before we went on air I was thinking: 'Oh, here we go'. She said to me, 'Steven, you wouldn't believe it but ever since that story came out I've had nothing but death threats and all of this terrible mail from Bulldogs supporters. I don't understand it'.

I kept my mouth shut at the time but I felt like saying: 'Kate, I don't know whether you understand what you've done. You wanted to break a big story and you've done so but didn't you realise how it was going to affect innocent people? We have some of the most passionate supporters in rugby league and now there is a chance that the team that made them so proud all year could be out of the competition. We've had one of the greatest seasons of all time and you're telling me that you don't understand this?'

When we hit the air she asked me what impact the story had had on the team and on my life. I answered truthfully and held in my emotions but I was furious that she had asked me that question. I can understand that she was proud — as a journalist there can be nothing better than breaking a massive story — but it was the way she went about it that made me so angry. She was smug and because she wasn't a rugby league person I'm quite certain that she had no idea what she had done. Here I was sitting next to the person that had just turned my whole world upside down and she was ecstatic about it.

I'm surprised I managed to control myself and apparently so was everyone else — when we got off the air my phone rang about 30 times with people telling me they were stunned that I didn't lose the plot.

I was particularly angry that *The Sydney Morning Herald* had printed photos of individual players with their salaries splashed alongside. I told Kate there was no need to present those stories the way they did. Her response was that the story couldn't have been reported in any other way. I told her, 'Kate, if you're as talented a journalist as you say you are then there are plenty of ways to get your message across without having to put a photo of a guy with his salary listed alongside'.

Braith Anasta was only 20 years old but copped the brunt of criticism when his salary was published. I was disgusted by how that was done. They could have printed all the details of how far over the cap the Bulldogs were and that players received a certain amount but the stories were directed squarely at individual players. It was typical of how the blame for the entire situation was constantly directed towards the wrong people.

I HAD no idea just how serious the salary cap scandal was when I first heard the rumour on Friday 16 August 2002. We had beaten Parramatta 28–10 that night, I attended the press conference and then I drove home as usual.

About an hour later I received a phone call from the Bulldogs' media officer Polly McCardell, who said, 'Steve, I just want to let you know that there is going to be a story in *The Sydney Morning Herald* tomorrow and it's about a salary cap breach. Apparently it's going to be a pretty big story. I just wanted to warn you'.

I mentioned it to Jo but didn't think too much more about it. I didn't think it could be anything to worry about. Even when I woke up the next day, read the story and listened to the radio I still didn't grasp it. I went to rehab and there were reporters everywhere but I had no idea what to say to them because I had no idea what was going on. The club told us that day not to speak with the media but they needn't have bothered — there was nothing we could have said of any consequence anyway.

The players knew no more than what the public knew through what was printed in the newspaper. Each day *The Sydney Morning Herald* would drip-feed a little bit more information and we would learn as much through them as through the club itself.

We started having regular meetings that week and one of the very first, on the Monday, was when Gary McIntyre and his son came to us with the idea of players taking an eight-percent pay cut. The Bulldogs felt that we needed to show the NRL we were doing everything possible to be under the cap, that they had made a mistake and that everyone was truly sorry.

They wanted to make sure there were no issues moving forward. From a player's perspective, we just wanted the NRL to dish out a fine and let us get on with the season because we felt that any mistakes that had been made were the responsibility of the administration.

Gary's son David showed us the figures involved and talked us through the benefits of taking a pay cut. They were basically trying to convince us to say yes on the spot but I asked if I could have some time to speak to the players. When Gary and David walked out, I said to my team-mates, 'Guys, I'm only going to tell you how I feel and I hope that you feel the same. There are people in my life that are very important to me. I've got kids, I've got a wife and I need to know within myself that I'm making the right decision for me and my family. You have all made your way to this club through your talents and the decisions you have made and you will either stay or leave based on the same thing. I'm not going to be bullied into making a decision right here and now because the club has made the error and we're the ones that are going to pay the price. Even if we do take a pay cut it might not make a difference in the end. I believe we need at least one night to go home and talk to our families and the people we trust before making a decision'.

The players agreed with me. Gary and David came back into the room and we told them we wanted 24 hours. They weren't too thrilled because they had wanted to issue a press release that afternoon. Steve Folkes asked me afterwards what I had said to the boys and when I told him he was filthy — he felt that it was jeopardising any opportunity we might have had.

The problem, from my perspective, was that at no stage had the NRL come out and said that by doing so we could avoid any serious punishment. At the end of the day, the Bulldogs had been over the salary cap for the past two years and by massive amounts each time. There was no escaping that fact.

I'LL NEVER forget the day that the NRL announced the punishment handed out to the club. It was late on a Friday that we received a call to head over to the club because the NRL had called a press conference for that afternoon. Tony Grimaldi was the only player not present because he didn't have a mobile and wasn't at home.

It was a terrible day. We were all sitting together in one room while Garry Hughes was waiting for the call in his office. His door was closed but he had glass walls so we could see him when the phone rang. It was only minutes before the NRL's press conference was due to start so we knew that this was the phone call that would determine our fate. Straight away you could see that it wasn't good news. We were looking for some sort of body language from Garry that might give us an indication of the verdict, and his head just dropped.

We had already endured an awful week while we awaited our fate. Jo and I spent the previous weekend listening to 2GB and almost every caller wanted us kicked out of the competition. From being unbeatable and sitting on top of the table we were suddenly being labelled cheats and it was hard to take. Jo actually wanted me to call 2GB and defend the players but I knew that it wouldn't help — we just had to sit tight and wait for the NRL to make a decision.

When that decision finally came through we were shattered: the club was fined $500,000 and we were docked 37 competition points — every point we had won up to that point — which relegated us to the bottom of the NRL ladder.

When Garry walked in after taking the phone call he said, 'Guys, that was David Gallop on the phone — he has advised us of the penalty being imposed for breaches of the salary cap', and proceeded to read through each point one by one.

It was like a bomb had gone off. We all sat there for about 15 minutes without saying a word, just looking out into space. What could you say? We didn't know what to do and didn't know how to react. Our whole season had just been ripped to pieces.

When I started hearing details of the club's salary cap breaches earlier in the week I realised that it might be more serious than I had first thought but I didn't think we would ever be kicked out of the comp. I kept running through the possibilities and I just didn't think that could happen. To be stripped of 37 points amounted to the same as being booted out. The only difference was that we still played our final three games of the year.

BY DEFAULT I became the official spokesperson for the club throughout the salary cap saga and if you had told me that would have been the case when I took on the captaincy at the start of the season I would have laughed my head off. I wasn't someone that spoke with any great confidence to the media because I was a pretty emotional person and I tended to start crying whenever I spoke about something that meant a lot to me. To suddenly stand in front of the cameras and the print media every day and talk about how I was feeling was anything but easy. The benefit was that it kept me busy.

We made a decision early on that I was going to be the spokesperson because having 25 players and 25 staff members all giving their opinions wasn't going to help anyone. We held a series of meetings in the week leading up to the NRL's decision to get updates from the board and where we stood on certain issues, because there was more information coming out every single day. Afterwards I would front the media and say whatever needed to be said as a result. I could be wrong, but I believe the media respected that. I never tried to avoid them. Whenever I was asked to front up, or someone called, I would do my duty.

My phone would go flat by 11 a.m. every day. It would start ringing at 6.30 a.m. or seven and wouldn't stop. If I was on the phone to someone I would hang up and find two more messages waiting for me. When I charged my phone I would have to sit beside the charger while it was charging because the phone would still be ringing. It wouldn't stop until about 6.30 p.m. when the newspapers began hitting their deadlines.

In a strange way I think we actually garnered some respect from people within the game — be it the media or referees or whoever — for the way in which we handled it. I don't think anyone felt sorry for us but they quietly applauded the way we went about handling everything. We didn't sulk because of what had happened, we just got on with what we did best and that was playing footy.

I wouldn't say that I was building great relationships with the media but they weren't trying to dig up dirt on us because we weren't trying to hide anything. It was all out there in the open. We answered any questions that were thrown at us. I understood that the media needed stories and I would rather be fronting up than letting them say what they wanted without my presence. If I was asked to appear on TV I wanted to be there when they ripped into us. In fact, they very rarely ripped in when I was sitting there because they actually had someone to talk to about the whole situation.

I have to give credit to our media manager at the time, Polly McCardell. She never threw me into a situation she didn't think I could handle but she also knew that if anyone could field the tough questions, I was the man for the job. Polly has a real passion for sport and she showed during that period just how talented she is. It was quite ironic that, not long after the salary cap scandal, the NRL recognised those talents and poached her.

I spoke to Polly long and hard about working for the NRL's media department. I said, 'It's going to be different to the Bulldogs because you've got the whole NRL to worry about rather than just one team, but it's something I know that you can handle and I think you've earned it'. Not surprisingly, she did an unbelievable job at the NRL too.

For a woman to come into an environment that is dominated by men must have been difficult but she was a professional and the players understood immediately how to deal with her and how she dealt with them. There were times when the boys would try to rattle her — I called her Bridget Jones because she reminded me of the character in the movie (in a good way) — but we respected her because she was up-front and honest.

During the salary cap saga she would update me with any information that I needed and then let me be myself. It was largely thanks to Polly's help that the club and the players were so comfortable with me representing them. There wasn't one person that said to me that I had said the wrong thing or didn't do the right thing by the club or an individual.

And it wasn't easy. I was always aware of how my words could be viewed, be it from a Bulldogs supporter or sponsor, a Roosters supporter or even an AFL supporter. I wanted to be honest and up-front because people can see straight through insincerity.

Crushed

The salary cap saga was pretty powerful and I don't know how I dealt with the things I dealt with, but I do know that having to deal with it made me a far stronger person. It galvanised my leadership qualities. I wouldn't be the captain or even the person I am today if it hadn't happened. I've become stronger and a lot more understanding of situations — I'm more open minded than I once was. I still don't know how I made it through, but as the saying goes — what doesn't kill you only makes you stronger.

THE GREAT tragedy of the salary cap crisis was that it was the innocent parties — the players and fans — who were punished most for the mistakes of others.

Kate McClymont was already doing some research into the Oasis development at Liverpool, which was supposed to become the future home of the Bulldogs, and along the way she obtained some highly confidential information regarding player payments and other club interests. Kate didn't fully understand the implications because she had no history in rugby league so she showed Roy Masters and his eyes lit up.

From that point onwards *The Sydney Morning Herald* began drip-feeding information. Every day I would come home and say to Jo, 'This came out today. Surely it can't get any worse from here', and of course the next day there would be even more. This went on for three weeks.

Meanwhile the players — having enjoyed an unbelievable season in which we won 17 games in a row and looked unstoppable — suddenly had all of our hopes and dreams shattered in an instant. For that to happen was heartbreaking. Why was it that when we went to Canberra to play, it was the players that people called cheats?

I'm not angry with anyone for what they did, just that the wrong people suffered. I understand their reasoning. At the end of the day they were just trying to do their very best for a club that they loved and unfortunately they went about it the wrong way.

I felt sorry for Barry Nelson. He had been at the club for so long but when he left he felt that he had let everybody down. Barry had been great mates with Peter Moore and he would have been thinking about Peter when he was forced out. I ran into Barry a few years later and he still seemed embarrassed that he had tarnished the great name of the Canterbury Bulldogs. I was actually concerned that he was going to shut down and drop into a deep depression because he just didn't seem like the person he used to be. He was always so proud in his time at the Bulldogs — an ex-policeman who was one of the toughest guys you would ever meet. Almost overnight he appeared to be a man who felt like a failure and that was anything but true. It was devastating to see.

I have to give a lot of credit to Steve Mortimer though for the work that he did under difficult circumstances as CEO. This was a unique situation for a club like the Bulldogs. Most of the guys on the board had been there for years and worked side by side with 'Bullfrog'. Very little had changed. Even when Peter left and Bob took over, very few changes were made. That was the culture of the club. It was 'The Family Club'. When Chris Anderson left and Steve Folkes took over from him, most of the staff stayed.

One of the great strengths of the Bulldogs was solidarity and consistency, but through this period there were so many changes — it was like a revolving door. I believe that's why 'Turvey' was so successful during his 18 months in charge. Whether or not he was the ideal person to take us forward in the long-term I don't know but he was passionate and he was a Bulldogs person through and through. That's what we needed at the time. Any deficiencies he might have had business wise, he had the right people around him to help out. He was the main reason that the supporters became so close to the players again. He was the people's CEO. He would sit on the hill with the fans and really try to get them behind the team. I don't know that anyone else could have done it as well as he did.

Even when 'Turvey' asked me to take an eight-percent pay cut he was only trying to do the best for the club. He wanted to get stuck into contract negotiations with me as soon as he came in because he wanted to show that the captain had re-signed and the Bulldogs were ready to move forward again. It certainly wasn't his fault that I decided it was time to head elsewhere two years later.

The worst part about the salary cap — and Coffs Harbour later on — was that it destroyed 'The Family Club' ideal. Once Steve and Garry Hughes were forced out, there really wasn't much left. Instead, infighting began to surface and factions appeared. It's sad that these guys don't feel too welcome these days because that should never be the case. They are club legends and should be allowed to return whenever they want.

Crushed

The Bulldogs seem to finally be on the right track again with a new board and that can only be a positive but I doubt they can ever regain the great culture that existed at the club for so long. They used to be the benchmark of the competition in every way — on and off the field — but that's not the case at the moment. There is a lot of hard work required to earn it back.

I WAS proud of the way both our players and supporters handled the devastation of having 37 competition points stripped from us. The day after the announcement we were due to board the team bus and travel down to Canberra for our Sunday afternoon clash with Canberra. When we arrived at Canterbury Leagues Club there were people everywhere and as we walked to the bus our fans formed a guard of honour.

They say a picture paints a thousand words — well I was photographed just as I started to bawl my eyes out yet again and it pretty much summed up my emotions at the time. I was stunned that our fans could give us such great support at a time when they must have felt as devastated as we did. Even when we arrived at Canberra Stadium the next day the crowd must have comprised of three-quarters Bulldogs fans.

It was a tough game for us. Twenty minutes in we were behind 20–0 and were walking around like zombies after the emotional turmoil of the previous week. I couldn't even bring myself to yell at anyone because I was exactly the same. It was a wonder that we played at all. But we didn't give up.

I give Canberra's hooker Simon Woolford some of the credit for that. He had come out in the media earlier in the week saying that they shouldn't have to play against us — that we had been caught cheating and Canberra shouldn't have to risk injury by facing us. Once the game started we had 17 blokes running around wanting to let Simon know exactly what we thought of his comments. Funnily enough, he kept apologising all game and insisting that he didn't say it. I was disappointed in Simon. We're all players playing in the same competition and there are certain things that you just don't say.

As it was we ended up fighting back and went down by four points, 38–34. I had said to the boys before the game, 'This has been one of the greatest seasons I've ever been a part of, not only at this club but in all the time I've played rugby league. I've never seen a team with such a strong bond and I'll be really disappointed if we don't finish the season the way we have played it throughout the year. That's our greatest challenge now'. I don't blame anyone for our poor start to that Canberra game but the way we fought back showed me how much we meant to each other.

We beat Melbourne 24–16 the following week and then had our final game of the season against Brisbane at the Sydney Showground. With us now relegated to the bottom of the NRL ladder, Brisbane had a chance to claim the minor premiership by beating us while a loss would give the Warriors a chance to finish on top if they could beat Wests Tigers. We had nothing to play for but pride.

I saw Wayne Bennett before the game and said to him, 'I'm really sorry mate but tonight isn't going to be your night'. He was looking confident and told me the Broncos were up for it but I said, 'No, after the game I think you'll understand why tonight's not going to be your night'.

There was something about the build-up to that game that felt like a grand final week. A huge crowd had turned out and we needed to show our fans that we appreciated their support over the past few weeks.

We had accepted the NRL's ruling and were ready to move on but we wanted to finish strongly to cap off what had been a remarkable season the way it deserved to finish.

And we did. We played superbly and didn't give Brisbane a chance in a 25–18 win. You talk about grand finals and State of Origin but that Brisbane game goes down in my book as the most emotionally satisfying win of my career.

When the game finished the crowd ran onto the ground like they used to 25 years ago and hoisted us up onto their shoulders. Fans aren't supposed to enter the playing arena these days but they weren't out of control — they were just so proud of their players.

The officials couldn't even get anyone to leave. We returned to the dressing rooms and not one supporter had gone home. We were sitting there for about five minutes when Todd Greenberg, the Bulldogs' operations manager at the time and now CEO, came in and said, 'Okay guys, this is the situation. We've still got the whole crowd out there and they're not going to leave until they see you again. It's up to you Steve but I think it would be a good idea'. We went back out and actually did a lap of honour. It was probably the slowest, most satisfying lap of honour I've ever done. The Showground has pretty high fences but that didn't stop people jumping down and hugging us.

Crushed

Steve Folkes, Steve Price and team,

Just wanted to pass on my support to you all in this extremely tough time.

It's a test of character that surely no one could have seen coming, but all I can figure you guys can do is see it as that — just a test.

You've overcome every other obstacle that's confronted you this year, and I bet every one of you believes, deep down, that if you want to, you can treat this rubbish with the disregard it deserves. The whole community fully realises that you blokes are the innocent party in all this.

I can't say I know enough to understand what happens next year with the team set-up, but stick together over the next few weeks. Continue to be the champions you've been all year and sit back after the last match whenever that may be and you blokes will be able to reflect on an unbelievable period of time in your careers with pride. I'm sure life-long bonds will arise from this setback, and the inspiration you have and will provide to the supporters will be talked about for years to come.

All the best guys, do what you do best.
Gilly

Adam Gilchrist sent the boys this note of support after we were stripped of our points.

In a lot of ways that was the day that the Bulldogs fans came back to the players. When Super League took place there was a real rift between the players and the supporters. They felt alienated and weren't as close to the players as they once were. It meant a lot to them that they could come up to us again and pat us on the back or say what they wanted to say. When you look at the ramifications of everything that happened, regaining our supporters was one of the few truly positive outcomes.

At the height of it, the salary cap saga was one of the worst things that has ever happened in my life. Watching the Sydney Roosters beat the Warriors in the grand final was really tough. But the positive was that we actually gained supporters from other sports and other teams because of the way we handled it. We handled it graciously. They say that sometimes you have to go through some pain to achieve a positive outcome and this was certainly one of those occasions.

A LOT of people asked me in the lead-up to the grand final whether I was going to watch the game. My reply was: 'Of course I will. I'm a part of the NRL and I love the NRL, why wouldn't I? We might not be in it but there are 13 other teams that aren't in it either and I guarantee they'll be watching it'.

The week after the regular season finished I was named Dally M Captain of the Year and I was so proud to receive the award. When I gave my speech I wished the eight teams in the semi-finals all the very best and said that whoever won the competition would fully deserve their title. I didn't want any side to have that honour discredited just because they didn't have a chance to beat the Bulldogs. At the end of the day it wasn't to be.

David Gallop called me after the NRL had made their decision to strip us of 37 competition points to make sure that the players were okay. He was sorry that such a decision had come to pass but mistakes had been made and he had to act. The NRL felt terrible for the players but they also had a duty of care to the whole competition — it would have been unfair to the other teams, to the sponsors and to their supporters if we were standing there on grand final day holding the trophy aloft.

Whether I agree with David or not is a different story but I totally understand what he was saying and I appreciated his phone call. It would have been a tough call to make. He had just made a decision that had ripped my heart out and he phoned me. He had no idea how I was going to react. I respect him for being up front and honest about it. He told me that if anyone needed to talk to him about anything — even if they needed to vent some anger — then by all means give him a call because he would much rather them do it to his face than via the media.

David called me again a few weeks later to thank me for the way the club and I had handled the situation. He said, 'I know it wouldn't have been easy but you're a credit to your team, to the game and to your fans. It's what makes our game so great'. It was a nice touch and it reminded me again that sometimes from adversity comes hope.

16 Leading Light

AS I have progressed through my rugby league career I have constantly been reminded that there is a lot more for me to learn. In particular, there have been a couple of moments that have stood out to me as lessons to apply to my personal life — whether they be goals or words that I stick by in order to help simplify things.

The first came via a guy called Stu Rutherford who was the boss at Carlton United Breweries in Sydney. We were sponsored by CUB when I was at the Bulldogs and I often attended functions or promos that the company held. I was talking to Stu at one of these promos and he was thrilled that I had turned up with a very positive attitude and willing to meet a whole range of different people. He said to me, 'You will do well in life because of your attitude'.

I asked him what he meant and he said, 'I'm a big believer that every person is a brand. When you go to the shops to buy something you will always sort through the options and make a decision based on either the colour, the price or the quality. It might be because you have had a good or bad experience with that brand before. Whatever it is, you're going to make your decision based on that reason. Think about when you go to buy shares and why you are going to buy shares in a certain company — is it because of the solidity, the performance, the type of ethics or the quality? It's the same in your situation — you go to a promotion and you might not feel like it. You might have had a blue with your missus or you might want to play ten-pin bowling with your friends instead so you turn up with a negative attitude. It's the first time some people are going to come into contact with you and it will probably be the only time that they're going to have a perception of you as a person. That will be their perception of you for the rest of your life. Who knows where, when, how or why but that person may or may not influence you in the future. Depending on your attitude it could be a positive influence or a negative influence and it could make a huge difference to your life'.

Stu mentioned a few examples of guys he knew that had made a couple of poor decisions or made a bad impression and had found themselves in trouble. He said to me, 'If you were looking to buy some shares in that brand, would you after that?' I said, 'No', and he told me: 'The equity in that brand has just depreciated by a certain amount of money and I'm not sure that the guy even realises it. I don't think he ever will and that's unfortunate for him. I'm an outsider who's looking in and I wouldn't touch that brand with *your* money — so what type of message does that send to a lot of other people?'

I started to put Stu's words into context and I certainly had plenty of opportunities to apply them. The salary cap and sex scandals were examples of that — when you say that you're a role model you've got to be conscious of that 24 hours a day. Players always make excuses that it's not fair, that 'I'm just a normal bloke'. Well, the fact is that each player is a brand and they should be wanting to make that brand as valuable as they can every single minute of the day.

When I go and speak to companies I say to the employees: 'If you haven't become the vice president or the manager of the company when you think you should have, look at yourself and ask why. Is it the boss's fault because he was having an affair with the person that got the job or is it actually because of you? Is it that you're not turning up to work on time every day or that you look a bit scraggly? Do you smell bad or cut corners in your work sometimes? Is it that you whinge all the time or that your personality is too aggressive and upsets other people in the business? Whatever it might be, it could be you that is the issue rather than anyone else'.

A similar sort of thing can happen with football players. You see a player that moves around to a lot of different clubs and at the end of it he is too busy blaming the club that just released him rather than the fact that he didn't perform. If you perform, it's not too often that a club will want to get rid of you.

Stu couldn't have told me this at a better time. In 2000 and 2001 I was having a great time in some ways but I was looking at my brand and it wasn't very strong compared to where it had been. I had experienced a drop in equity and off the field there were things that were also hindering that — decisions that I had made.

Stu's words didn't change who I was as a person but they did make me a lot more conscious whenever I was in the public eye of where I was and what I was doing. Whenever I went to a promo I always made sure that I shook hands with people.

I've already spoken about no excuses, no regrets and it applies again here. In 2000 I had been going through a bit of a form slump and Queensland had appointed Wayne Bennett as coach for the 2001 series after we were humiliated. Wayne is a person who doesn't have much time for false people. He is similar to me in that he will give every person every opportunity as long as they are respectful. If they treat him the way he expects to be treated, and vice versa, there is no issue. If they don't deserve that respect their brand loses some value.

That year, in the pre-series camp, Wayne said to us, 'We're going to find out from you guys everything that needs to be done leading up to Wednesday night. Whatever you need done, we'll do it for you as a staff so all you've got to do is make sure your preparation is spot on and turn up on Wednesday night ready to play the game of your life. If you don't, you've only got yourself to blame for letting yourself down because we've given you every opportunity to perform well. We'll give you the great food, the great bed, we'll make sure you go to bed early, we'll make sure you train in a great facility — everything so that you can have no excuses and no regrets come Wednesday'.

That was something I took into my personal life as well. I thought of all the times that I hadn't achieved something because I had an excuse. On top of brand value, this outlook really helped me with the captaincy and leadership role I took on at the Bulldogs in 2002. It's all about honesty and leading by example — to make sure you don't give anyone any excuses that they can lean on.

There is always that fight between the two little men on your shoulder — one telling you to stop and the other telling you to keep going. It's a lot easier to keep going when the person you look up to keeps going as well. These are the key factors that have motivated me over the years.

I've also been very mindful, particularly as I've grown older, of what I can control. I'm not going to stress too much about anything that's out of my control and it's something that is very prevalent in games. If something happens in a game such as a bad call by the referee, you can't dwell on it and blow the rest of the game. Those two points could be very costly at the end of the season.

I KNOW now that whenever I didn't achieve the things I was hoping to achieve during my career, it was because I wasn't putting the work in that was required. You know when you're cutting corners, you don't need people to tell you. Others might not be aware of it but you certainly know within yourself.

I get really down on myself at times because, being in rugby league for as long as I have, you develop a feel for your body and a feel for the game — you understand what you should be doing and what you aren't doing to get the best out of yourself. You have to make sure that you keep working hard because there is always an 18 year old that is bigger, stronger, faster and more skilful than you waiting to take your spot.

That's another thing that drives me each week. People often talk about a player's age but I remember how hard it was 12 or 13 years ago when I came up against an older guy. I also remember how easy it was coming up against an old guy who wasn't putting in the hard work. A lot of it is mental. I'm very passionate about what I represent, both as an individual and what I stand for in general. At the moment it's the Warriors and before that it was the Bulldogs.

When I first came to New Zealand it was something I was very concerned about because the public weren't really that proud of the Warriors. They *had* been, a few years earlier, but that had waned. The players weren't as proud of what they represented as they used to be and that could be seen quite clearly. It is something we have worked extremely hard on since.

When I was at the Bulldogs you very quickly gained an appreciation of what you were representing and what was expected of you. Whether that was from the supporters, from the sponsors or from the administration, you understood by the culture, the atmosphere, the environment and the body language that the people around you displayed. At the end of it you're not going to associate yourself with something that you're not proud of.

In general society, I believe a lot more people need to look at themselves with more honesty and actually see how they are viewed by other people. Think about when you get yourself into trouble or have a fight with your partner. It mightn't always be the other person's fault. It may never be the other person's fault but you're always blaming that other person. You could end up destroying some great friendships or bonds that you have with people, companies or clubs over nothing.

These are the key factors for me: you've got to be proud and passionate about what you do. Have no regrets and no excuses. Understand your brand, where it's at and where you want it to be at. When you're the boss of a company, you're aware of where the company is at, where you want it to go and what you've got to do to get it there. You could be exactly the same with an individual.

I relate this to Jo and me. We went through a period at one stage where she would come to bed in a foul mood. Everything had been fine all day and into the night but she would come to bed upset and I would wonder what I was doing wrong. One day I decided that I was going to find out what the problem was and fix it. It turned out to be the washing up! Jo would cook dinner, we would eat, we would watch TV and then I would just jump into bed because I'd had a tough day at training. Well, Jo had a tough day at work too. She had been working hard, she had come home and cooked dinner and the next morning the washing up still hadn't been done. It wasn't going to do itself and I wasn't doing it because I had been training. Jo hated having dirty dishes there in the morning so she would end up doing them every night before she went to bed and it would give her the shits.

I said to myself, 'Right, that's it. I'm going to do the washing up. I'll see if that's what it is and if I'm right it will make a big difference to our lives'. I went and did the washing up one night and didn't say anything to Jo. She said, 'No, no, I'll do that', but I wouldn't let her. She went to bed a lot happier and woke up in the morning a lot happier and all of a sudden things changed dramatically — all because of a small issue we had that could have gotten way out of hand.

I told this story to a group of people at Hill & Stewart — a company in Auckland that sells electrical goods. It was their awards night and one of the salesmen said, 'I'll fix that, I'll send you a dishwasher. It will solve your problems and her problems just like that'. I told him, 'That's nice, unfortunately someone has to pack and unpack the dishwasher and that's one of the issues we have now'.

Again, it all goes back to excuses, regrets, your brand and consciously working very hard in all parts of your life to continue to improve. It is these things that have given me the knowledge and confidence to be where I am now.

17 Coffs Harbour

IN FEBRUARY 2004, the Bulldogs played a trial match against Canberra in Coffs Harbour. We had spent the best part of a week there preparing for the game and were staying at the Novotel — a first class facility better known as Camp Wallaby.

The set-up was very professional and the club used our time there to work through aspects of our individual games that needed improvement. We actually had our eyes checked at one point and they discovered that my eyesight, particularly at night, wasn't great. I started wearing contact lenses as a result.

We had played in Coffs Harbour 12 months earlier and a complaint had been made about one of our players so we put rules in place to ensure that nothing happened this time around. Number one on the list was that no girls were to be brought back to the hotel. We accepted that young men will be young men but we also wanted to make sure that nobody was going to put their team-mates in any difficult situations. Because some players were single while others were married or had a partner, we agreed that if a player met somebody they were *not* to bring them back to the team hotel.

We played Canberra on the Saturday night and went out to The Plantation Hotel for a few hours afterwards. At around 2 a.m. I jumped in a cab and headed back to my room. My room-mate, Ben Harris, was already back because his girlfriend — now his wife — was an air hostess who was overseas at the time and he had arranged to call her. He was sleeping when I walked into the room but woke up, so we stayed awake talking for a while before we eventually fell asleep.

We had rehab at 8 a.m. the following day and I was just finishing up when I noticed a girl standing nearby looking for someone. She was talking with one of the boys and I walked over to see if everything was okay. She told me that a friend of hers was upset so I called Garry Hughes over to talk to her. I told Garry and our club chaplain Ken Clendinning what she had told me, then went back to my room to pack my things.

When it came time to return to Sydney a few of the guys were asked to stay back in order to give a police statement, but I didn't know the details of what had happened at that stage so I didn't give it too much thought.

When I arrived home Jo asked me how the trip was and I replied, 'Good, why?' She said, 'Oh I was just wondering. It was just like any normal trip was it? Nothing unusual?' I said, 'No, no, everything went alright'.

I didn't know this at the time but Jo had a friend who knew people involved in the police who had actually called to let her know something had happened. It was the next day when Jo actually asked me about it. I told her, 'I don't think there is anything to worry about. There was a girl that was upset but that's about it as far as I know'.

That perception changed when the next day's headlines read '*Woman accuses Bulldogs of sexual assault*'.

IT WAS reported that in the days following the Coffs Harbour story the Bulldogs staff and players got together for a 'truth meeting' in which we supposedly told each other what had happened and correlated our stories before meeting with police. That wasn't the case at all. The real story is that 'Folkesy' walked in and asked us straight out if anything had happened that matched the accusations. Every single player told him straight to his face that nothing had happened. He said, 'Okay then, I respect and trust that what you say to me is the truth and I will back you guys.' It was important to us that we had the support of our coach because at that early stage it felt as if we were being attacked from all sides.

It was in this 'truth meeting' that we decided the best thing to do was co-operate with police as much as possible in order to have the matter resolved. We decided that every single player would go through the whole process, we would all be questioned and we would all be DNA tested. The club's lawyers told us that we were under no obligation to comply unless police requested a particular individual. By co-operating as a group we figured it would speed up the whole process.

Coffs Harbour

I have to say, I wasn't exactly thrilled with any of this. I knew that I had done nothing wrong so why did I have to be questioned by police? Why did I have to give a DNA test? The only reason I agreed was because if it was just the six players accused of raping this girl that turned up for police questioning then the media would know exactly who these individuals were. Even if those players were innocent their reputations would be tarnished for life.

Hazem El Masri was the one player that refused to be DNA tested. Hazem told *The Sydney Morning Herald* at the time: 'I have built up a reputation that I'm proud of and I felt sick in the stomach when I had to go to a police station over something I had nothing to do with. It was a humiliating and degrading experience just to walk up the stairs'.

None of us had a problem with Haz making that decision. We said in the meeting that although we would co-operate as a team, we weren't going to force anyone to do so. I felt similar to Hazem. One of my biggest fears was that because I was at the same hotel on the same night that the sexual assault was alleged to have occurred, there was absolutely no reason why Jo wouldn't think that it could have been me. No-one was named and we were all going in to be tested, so for the wives and girlfriends and families — even for the fans that idolised certain players — there was nothing to say that they weren't one of the ones being accused.

But the salary cap scandal two years earlier had made us a very tight-knit group so when everyone said that they didn't do it we trusted that. There was massive media interest in the case, as there should have been, because it was a very serious allegation. We were as curious as the media were as to what the processes would be and how they would be dealt with by all parties.

WEDNESDAY 3 March 2004 was to be a sad day in the history of the Bulldogs. I turned up to training that morning and found half a dozen players missing — they were the first batch to be interviewed by police. The players were taken into the city to talk to the club's lawyers and then to Surry Hills police station to be interviewed individually.

The following morning there was a photo in *The Daily Telegraph* showing players turning up to their interviews wearing T-shirts, shorts and thongs and we were accused of being disrespectful to what was a very serious accusation. The truth was that none of the players interviewed that day knew they would be going to the police station when they turned up at training that morning. Every other group that went in over the following week or two wore suits but it wasn't because of the criticism — it was because they were told in advance when to expect their interviews.

I was upset that the media pounced on that the way they did but I was even more pissed off at the club when they fined Willie Mason $10,000 and Brent Sherwin $5000 for wearing 'inappropriate attire'. They were fined because of the media outcry when we all knew it wasn't their fault.

In the end it was the clothing issue that saw Garry Hughes sacked as Bulldogs football manager. It was deemed that the players' attire that day was Garry's responsibility and because of the pressure being applied by the media, sponsors and the public he became the scapegoat to make it look like the club was actively doing something about the accusation.

It was terribly unfair. Garry was doing his best under duress to be as co-operative as he could and to ensure that everything ran as smoothly as possible for the players and the police. When Garry was sacked I started to realise just how much the club had changed over the past few years.

There was a time when an issue such as this would have been dealt with internally but instead the Bulldogs succumbed to external influences and Garry was shown the door. He was a victim of circumstance because all eyes were fixed on our every move. Never mind that there was a world happening around us — for the best part of two months the Bulldogs were on the front six and back six pages of the newspapers every single day.

IT WAS about a week after police interviews began that I was called upon to head to Surry Hills. Because the whole process was taking so long the police had become backlogged so it was a long week with players putting in some very, very late nights while being questioned.

The day that I was finally called in was hectic because I was also scheduled to appear on *A Current Affair* that night.

I went to see the lawyers first, they wrote down everything I said and then I went to the police station where I waited to be interviewed. Eventually, after waiting around for hours, I shot off to be interviewed by Ray Martin on Channel 9. Ray was actually quite gentle on me but he ripped into George Peponis who was on the show with me. I thought George handled himself quite well under the circumstances. Afterwards, I rushed back to the police station to go through the full process and it was one of the scariest moments of my life.

I met with the lawyers again and we walked in to meet the interviewing officers. There were cells all along the wall full of people that had been locked up for whatever reason and they were going off their nut calling me names. They didn't care who I was, they just wanted to get out of there and were yelling all sorts of things that scared the living daylights out of me.

The interview room itself was a tiny little box with myself, the lawyer and three police officers crammed in there. They also had a video camera and three voice recorders. It was all very intimidating. The officers started asking me questions and the procedure I had been advised on was that with each question I would look at the lawyer. If he nodded I would give my answer, otherwise I would answer: 'No, under the legal advice that I've been given I can't answer that question'.

But it was an interrogation and the three officers had an obvious game plan to extract information. There were times when I would answer a question and they would say: 'That's not what your mate said. He said that you were out until after 3 a.m.'. I would tell them: 'No, I wasn't out that late at all. I went back to the hotel and this person saw me, then I went to my hotel room.'

They were trying to scare me. As far as they were concerned there was no reason to suggest I wasn't one of the players accused. My job was to prove to them that I was innocent. They took a DNA swab from my mouth and the whole time they were hammering me with questions. It was just like you see in a movie — one playing good cop and the other playing bad cop — the only difference being that this was for real.

I don't ever want to experience something like that again. It scared the life out of me — and I was innocent! I'd hate to think how you would feel if you had actually done something wrong.

I was exhausted by the time it was over. The interview lasted for about an hour — it could have been two — but it felt like days. I've never felt so uncomfortable. The officers would watch your body language so that if you answered a question a certain way they would say: 'Why did you just move your hand when you said that?' You constantly felt that you were doing something wrong and with the video camera there you didn't know if other people were watching as well. It was terrible but that's their job, it's what they are paid to do.

One thing I didn't agree with was being asked to stand in a police line-up. Apparently the girl was having trouble identifying the players allegedly involved but the problem I had was that it would be easy to mistake someone's identity when they are a high-profile NRL player. After all, we're on television all the time so no doubt she had seen a lot of us before. In my case, I had become the club's spokesman again. Even if she had seen me on TV for two seconds, seeing my face in a line-up could have been enough to trigger some sort of mistaken recollection in her head. I was more than happy to tell my story but the line-up was way above what I should have been expected to do.

Throughout the whole process, none of the Bulldogs players spoke with one another about what they told police — it was all personal and confidential — and no-one spoke about what they had told the lawyers either.

Despite that, by the time all interviews were completed every one of the players' stories matched up to exactly what we had been saying all along and that proved crucial to the club being cleared. The fact is that you don't find 25 players with identical stories if they have something to hide.

Unfortunately, while we were all looking forward to the case being closed, the manner in which the officer in charge of the investigation conducted his media conference suggested that the police simply hadn't been able to find enough evidence to charge us.

Although no charges were laid, we didn't come away feeling that we had been cleared of any wrongdoing. It left doubt in the public's mind.

Once the dust settled from the investigation it was found that the case had actually been conducted in an unsatisfactory manner. There was vital information leaked to the media throughout the case and in one particular incident a confidential police report was read out to 2GB's Ray Hadley on air. A number of officers who worked on the case have now left the police force due to the stress and disillusionment that came with the Bulldogs rape allegations. Malcolm Noad, who took over from Steve Mortimer as chief executive while investigations were ongoing, has since shown me letters sent by officers saying how sorry they were and how poorly the investigation was conducted.

Coffs Harbour

THE SUPPORT we received both publicly and privately from 'Folkesy' and the football staff was great, but I felt the Bulldogs' board as well as the NRL considered us guilty until proven innocent. We held a meeting with the board to voice our disappointment at their lack of support but things didn't improve a great deal. Too often we felt isolated with only our families and one another there for support.

I would go to pick my kids up from school and could sense the other parents looking at me. I can just imagine what they were thinking: 'I wonder if it was him involved?' I'm just thankful that my kids were too young to understand what was happening. Jamie's school was very compassionate about it — they promised that if anything was said or any trouble brewed they would nip it in the bud — so I was devastated that NSW Education Minister Andrew Refshauge publicly stated that no Bulldogs players or anyone from the club would be allowed on any school grounds for promotions while the investigation was continuing. That *told* me that people considered us guilty.

I can understand that with all the media coverage there would have been parents saying, 'I don't want rapists at my child's school', but it was an ill-informed train of thought. People often assume the worst but it's a shame when they treat you as a criminal without knowing all of the facts.

One minor miracle was that no rival players said anything to us during games about Coffs Harbour, but we copped plenty on the streets and our fans were ridiculed at away games.

We played the Sydney Roosters at Aussie Stadium in round three and there was a huge fight in the stands. Bulldogs supporters are very passionate, loyal people so when rival fans started abusing us it was just like someone was abusing their own brother or sister. I was told by one of our fans afterwards that a Roosters supporter was actually urinating off the top balcony onto some Bulldogs supporters. Another young girl had her head scarf pulled off which was extremely disrespectful.

We were thrashed 35–0 that night with Roosters fans calling us 'rapists' and telling our fans that they were exactly the same. The whole debacle was a terrible look for the game and there was nothing we could do about it at the time. Hazem and I started filming messages to be shown on the big screen at our home games saying, 'Please, if there is trouble, go and see a security guard rather than trying to sort it out yourself'. That was one of the tragedies of Coffs Harbour and to a certain extent the salary cap as well — not only did people judge the players but they also started judging our supporters.

The club felt a lot of that pain too. Bing Lee was supposed to be the Bulldogs' sleeve sponsor that season in a deal worth quite a bit of money to the club but they pulled out. I was talking to a member of their marketing team one day and he told me that they had received more than 10,000 emails from customers refusing to shop there if they continued their association with the Bulldogs. He was very apologetic but they had to look at it from a business perspective.

BlueScope steel pulled the pin as well. They were supposed to be our shorts sponsor and a similar thing happened. The clothing had already been produced and was ready to go but they couldn't afford to be associated with us.

I was extremely appreciative of Mitsubishi Electric for sticking to their guns. Keith Allen was managing director at the time and was under a lot of pressure from their head office in Japan. They had heard about the investigation and it wasn't something they were keen to be associated with but Keith was level-headed about it. He was one of the few people that recognised that no charges had been laid and he kept his bosses in Japan updated on events as they happened. If Mitsubishi Electric had pulled out, the club would have been in trouble. There would have been no income coming in and I don't know if the Bulldogs could have survived.

BEING SPOKESMAN for the club again was far more difficult this time around than it had been during the salary cap crisis. It was crucial to be selective in the words I used whenever I spoke to the media because this was no longer a rugby league issue — this impacted upon the whole community. News of the investigation reached as far as the United States. There were certain things I could and couldn't talk about. It was important that I worded everything correctly.

Our opening game of the season was against Parramatta in a double header at Telstra Stadium — the game where Sonny Bill Williams debuted and tore them apart. We held a press conference in the lead-up to promote the game which I knew would be difficult because of everything that was going on. You usually go to a press conference and you know all the media guys — Andy Raymond, Tony Peters, Greg Pritchard, Steve Mascord — they're your rugby league reporters that are always at the games. This one was always going to be different but I didn't realise just how different. We walked into the room and I didn't know a single journalist — they were all criminal journalists that report on the Courts. Straight away I thought: 'Oh no, here we go'.

It was basically their only chance to speak to a player because we had been told to stop talking as the investigation gained momentum.

We were there to talk up the game and the first question went to Parramatta captain Nathan Cayless. That was the only one aimed at Nathan — for the next half an hour the media were pumping me about the investigation. I had no choice but to offer the same line every time: 'Unfortunately I can't say anything because it is a police investigation'.

When we were leaving we were heading out to the lift and two reporters followed me. I've always hated that sort of footage — with the person walking off looking like they're trying to escape — but there wasn't much I could do. They made it look as if I was running away from them as they were asking questions. We had just been in a press conference for 30 minutes and they didn't ask me a single question but as soon as I headed for the lift they followed me. They knew what they were there to do. Of course, all they showed on the news that night was the reporter shoving a microphone in my face as I was walking away. All I could say was: 'I'm sorry, I can't make any comment on that'. It looked as if I was trying to get away from them which is so far from how I deal with the media. I've always made myself available and I've always been as honest as possible when I've done so.

I was furious. I made sure I watched the news that night because I had a terrible feeling that they were going to paint me in a certain light and that's exactly what happened.

No doubt the whole thing was a result of us backing away from the media at the time because we weren't allowed to say anything anyway. A few television stations were apparently upset that they didn't have access to us. Channel 10, in particular, felt that we were giving favouritism to Channel 9 because we had done a few things with them including the interview with George and me on *A Current Affair*. Their reaction was to get nasty.

I wasn't happy. I told Brad and Malcolm and they made some phone calls. It all came down to Channel 10 being upset that we were supposedly giving preferential treatment to Channel 9. I eventually called Channel 10 management to let them know how I felt. They said, 'It's your club's fault because of the way they've treated us. I'm sorry you were the one that was portrayed in that way'. I appreciated those sentiments but it was too little, too late by then.

IT WAS terrible to see Garry Hughes and Steve Mortimer sacked because of the Coffs Harbour scandal. I realise that there was pressure from the media, sponsors and even the NRL to hold someone accountable but did those two deserve to go? I don't think so.

'Turvey' wasn't happy with how the whole affair was dealt with by the board and he told them what he thought too. I'm sure it had a lot to do with his decision to 'stand down'. It was sad to see him go. I know how much 'Turvey' loves the club and the board was basically comprised of his former team-mates. To have something like this cause so much friction between them was devastating.

In the space of a few months the once famous 'Family Club' went out the window. That we went on to win the premiership that season is one of the greatest achievements of all time. It was such a difficult year — every time I went to a press conference someone would mention Coffs Harbour. It really plays on the mind but one thing I said to the players at the start of the season was: 'At the end of the day we're rugby league players. We're not politicians, we're not doctors, we're not trying to disillusion anybody. Let's just get out there and do our job.'

The first game of the season against Parramatta couldn't have come soon enough. The time between our trial match against Canberra in Coffs Harbour and the Parramatta game felt like an eternity.

I felt sorry for Parramatta — who had Jamie Lyon walk out on them the following week — but to go out there and unleash on the Eels was one of the best things that could have happened to us. We had a lot of built up frustration and we took it out on Parramatta. By halftime we were ahead 36–0 and although we eased off a little bit in the second half we ended up winning 48–14. It was a great start to the season and it was a relief to have something else to talk about other than Coffs Harbour.

We beat Cronulla the following week, before that thrashing at the hands of the Roosters which gave us a chance to take stock and reassess where we were at. From that point onwards our season began to steadily improve.

18 Guiding Stars

I'VE ALWAYS believed that there is more to life than meets the eye — that when we die it's not necessarily the end of the road. I'm not a religious person and I don't go to church each week but I do believe that there is something else out there.

That belief has only been strengthened by a series of strange but undeniable incidents that have taken place over the past decade or so. And none of them blew me away to quite the same extent as an e-mail I received from Mum in 2002.

Not long after Peter Moore passed away, Mum called to tell me about a conversation she'd had with a friend of hers (who will remain anonymous). He had often spoken to her about his psychic abilities and his ability to communicate with spirits using a wedding ring that had been passed down from his grandmother.

One day he said to Mum, 'I've had an experience that's to do with Steven. Do you want to know about it?' Mum said, 'Yes, I'd like to. Whether it's good or bad I'd like to know'. He went home that night and wrote out the conversation for her and after reading through it she really didn't know whether to tell me about it or not.

Mum e-mailed it through to me the very next day and I must admit I was a little freaked out. This was before the Bulldogs' salary cap drama had hit and I didn't quite know what to make of it but looking back now I'm amazed by what transpired. Mum's friend told us that he had communicated with Peter and had some important messages for both me and the club.

When I read through what he had written I was taken aback — even though I wasn't completely sure what he was referring to at the time. His knowledge of the personal relationships I had with Peter and others was incredible. I couldn't discount it.

He has given us three readings over the years — one shortly after Peter died, another before the salary cap saga and the third before I joined the Warriors — and each have been scary in their accuracy. The following is a transcript of the second reading that he gave us in 2002:

Friend: Is it still possible to speak to 'Bullfrog' Peter Moore?

Response: No he is in too far. I can speak to you.

Friend: Who are you?

Response: Dafid. I am Welsh. I speak as though I am him.

Friend: Okay, is there anything Peter would like to tell me?

Response: He does want to give a message to young Dogs. Is that the right name?

Friend: Yes. What is the message?

Response: Do not despair. Just cop it on the chin. Do that for the team and for yourself. Nothing else matters but the survival of the club. Let this be a lesson to you all. No-one is mightier than the game — no player, no club. From this a greater club will rise. Take a moment to reflect on the consequences of your actions. You almost destroyed the club — my beloved Dogs. Hold on to the principles of being a true Dog. I am saddened that money counted most. You have been led along that path.

Friend: What are the principles to hold onto? Do they know?

Response: The Dogs come first. You must make sacrifices for the survival of the club. I am glad to be able to talk to you. I can't for much longer though, there is no such thing as time here.

Friend: Any message for Steve Price?

Response: Son, you face a far greater test than on the field. I know that you can come through with both your credibility and honour intact. Remember everything we talked about. (Friend), have an hour's rest; you are tired.

That session finished at 7.45 p.m. and started back again an hour later.

Friend: I am back, are you ready?

Response: Yes, hold your energy. I don't know why I said that.

Friend: Can you carry on with your advice for Steve?

Response: Let the players decide if they are just players or Dogs.

Friend: In what way?

Response: Money or honour.

Friend: Anything for anyone else?

Response: There are two Steves. Pricey, I taught you what it means to be a Dog. Everything I taught you will bear fruit now. Separate the grain from the chaff. I don't remember everything and soon there will be nothing, so you remember.

Friend: Who is the other Steve? Steve Folkes?

Response: No, Steve Mortimer. You have taken on a great burden. The path is not easy mate but you are up to the task. Now for the club.

Friend: You have a message for the club?

Response: If they will believe what you're doing, stick with the boys. Remember the Bulldogs spirit. A Bulldog led London from the ashes of near defeat. This is the Bulldogs spirit. You can do the same. Think of what I am saying and rally around the Bulldogs. The chaff will go, Dogs will be left. Take heed of the lessons and go on to victory next year. Be brave my Dogs, I will try to communicate tomorrow — same time, same station. Haha.

The second session finished at 9.30 that night before they began again the following evening at 8.45 p.m.

Friend: Are you ready Peter?

Response: Sure. Pricey son, let go of the past and go forward. Do not forget me but build on what I taught you. First, get rid of the chaff in the team then build on what is left — more than you think. You will still have a mighty team. I can't tell you the future, don't know mine. Go for it son, you are on a winner. Dogs a winner.

Friend: Anything else?

Response: Just build up from the ashes and be great again. Just take your time and be careful who you let in this time. There are people who could not give a stuff about the club other than what they can get out of it — money, prestige or both. Stick to those that stand by your shoulder. Well, that's everyone. Remember me and all I've stood for, the mighty Dogs. They and family were my life on earth.

Friend: Is that it?

Response: No. Thank you (friend). You might be a Dragon but you are a Doggy mate. Thanks for your strength, I've used it and goodbye.

Friend: Glad I could help you Peter, maybe another time soon.

Response: No, I'll be in too deep. Thanks again mate, goodbye.

I've never shown that reading to anyone. I was going to show Karen Folkes as well as Peter's wife Marie but I didn't know how they would deal with it. I know that Marie is quite religious and I didn't know if it would help or hinder her grieving process. I didn't want to unsettle that so I've never shown Marie and I've never shown Karen. I've thought about it since too but I didn't want to open up old wounds. Having said that, I think enough time has passed now and to be honest I'm proud of the reading — it's from somebody and something that we all love so much. It was like a forecast of what was about to happen. Is it real? I don't know. But I can't believe that anyone could know about the personal relationships I had with Peter and the club the way Mum's friend did. It was one of a number of moments in my life that have only served to strengthen the beliefs that I hold close to my heart.

IN 1997 I visited a clairvoyant in Toowoomba named Kara. I had always wondered what a clairvoyant would say to me and I must admit I was a little bit sceptical but Mum told me that Kara was extremely talented. She was certainly right about that — the things Kara told me were mind blowing.

I paid for a half-hour reading but our session ended up lasting three hours. Kara told me afterwards, 'It's people like you that I like to do readings for because of your aura. It's a successful, positive and loving aura that is very unique and special'. I thanked her for that but it was what she predicted that really caught my attention. The first was that I was about to receive a big award that would mean a lot to me.

Our presentation night at the Bulldogs was only a week or two away but there was no way I was going to win the club's Player of the Year award. In fact, there was nothing to suggest I was going to get anything, but the night came and I won the top prize.

Kara told me that Jo and I would have three kids — two girls and a boy — and that the boy would be last.

At this stage we only had Jamie. Now we have three kids — our two girls Jamie-Lee and Kasey and our son Riley. Kara actually said that Jo was pregnant with our second child, Kasey, at the time. I told her, 'No she's not', and Kara fired back: 'Yes she is'. It turned out that she was right.

She also said that she could feel a nagging pain in her right knee. I had no pain but she said, 'I can't get away from it, you've got a sore knee. It's giving you hell, it's not going away. It's there but it just won't go away'. Three years later I did the medial in my right knee. Four years after that, in 2004, I did my other medial. In 2005 I did the right knee again. I've done my medial a total of three times — two on my right knee — and that knee actually cracks and clicks. It's quite sensitive most of the time.

Kara told me that I would be successful but that I would have to deal with some serious issues during my career. She said that some of these issues would be extremely difficult but that they would be the making of me and would eventually take me in an entirely new direction. At the time I had no idea what she was talking about. I was 23 years old, was playing first grade for the Bulldogs and that was about it.

But every single thing she said turned out to be accurate. The salary cap saga of 2002 and Coffs Harbour in 2004 were two of the toughest periods of my life but they made me a stronger person and eventually led me to a new start at the Warriors in 2005.

Kara wasn't alone in what she told me. Two years ago we were in Newcastle preparing to play the Knights and were returning from an afternoon walk before the game. There was a wedding party standing in the foyer of our hotel and as I opened the door to let my team-mates in, one of the girls in the party stopped me.

She said to me, 'Hi, how are you going? Who are you guys?' I told her I played for the Warriors and she said, 'Oh, okay. My boyfriend is into soccer so I don't really follow rugby league.' Her friends were laughing at her because they all knew who I was. I assumed she was just a girl that was a bit drunk.

Then she said, 'I read people's palms and for some reason I have to tell you a few things. I'm pissed but I'm telling you that I've got to tell you these things and you'll know what I'm talking about'.

It hadn't been an easy time for my family. About six months earlier my dad's mother had passed away while Mum had lost her best friend Charmaine to cancer. This girl said to me, 'There is a lady that you're very close to that wants to tell you not to worry anymore, that everything is alright. It's your dad's mum.' I said, 'Oh yeah, she died about six or seven months ago'. The girl said, 'Yeah I know, you were really worried about her because you loved her so much and you were concerned about how she died'.

She was spot on because I couldn't be there when Nan passed away and I was worried whether Dad would make it to see her too. Dad wasn't around when Pop died a few years earlier and that was a big regret for both of us. He didn't even find out until a year after it happened which is a devastating way for a son to find out he has lost his father. He lived in Perth and wasn't easy to contact so it took a while for the news to reach him. I decided that if anything happened to Nan I would make sure he was there because if anything he was probably a little bit closer to Nan than Pop. Dad was the wild child of the family and Pop used to tell him to stop carrying on like a rebel whereas Nan tended to understand where he was coming from.

When Nan was sick and we realised how serious it was I rang Dad and told him I would fly him over. He said, 'Nah it's okay, I'll get myself over and see her'. I gave him a day and he still hadn't flown over so I called him back and said, 'Dad, I'll pay for you to fly over. You can pay me back later but you need to be there now'. I ended up booking a flight for him and my half-sister Georgia and organised for them to stay at Jo's mum's house which was in Redcliffe and close to the hospital.

Dad was the sort of person that hated putting people out so when he landed in Brisbane he rented a car and went straight to a hotel. He ended up spending her last three or four days by her side and was extremely appreciative but I was really worried because I couldn't be there myself.

It hurt when Nan died. There were a couple of times that I probably could have gone to see her but didn't for whatever reason — you become preoccupied with things and tend to believe that people will be around forever. It doesn't work out that way. So I was stressed about that and also about making sure that she could at least have Dad by her side.

That's what this girl was talking about. She said, 'Nan wants you to know that she's looking over you and is making sure that everything is going to be alright. Don't worry about her anymore because she's fine, she's well looked after and she's with Pop'.

The girl moved onto Charmaine next. Charmaine was Mum's best friend but was struck down too early from a melanoma that grew between her toes. Mum was always worried about her and would help make her look as good as she could when she was undergoing chemotherapy. She basically spent the last two weeks of Charmaine's life by her bedside and was devastated when she died.

This girl looked at me and said, 'Tell your mum that Charmaine loves her very much and thanks her so much for everything that she did for her. Charmaine says that she is okay and will see her again one day'.

It was freaky stuff. You couldn't make it up. Admittedly she had downed a few drinks that day but she said that this information was in her head, she had to get it out and she had to get it out to *me*. It wasn't for anyone else.

I'm sure there are some that will think I'm a stubby short of a six pack by printing this but I can't help what I believe. I've seen and heard too much to believe otherwise. It inspires me and gives me hope for the future because I know that not only do I have the support of those around me that are living but also the likes of my grandparents, Matthew, Peter Moore and everyone else that has been so influential in my life.

I WAS in Year 12 when I had my first real experience of losing someone who was close to me. My cousin, James Christie, who was 19 at the time, was driving home one night when he fell asleep, hit a tree and was killed. It was a devastating blow because James was only a few years older than me and we had been very close growing up back in Dalby.

It was around the same time that my grandfather Trevor passed away as well. I was at school when I received a phone call from my aunty down in Redcliffe to say that Pop wasn't looking too good and I should try to see him as soon as possible. He survived the night against all expectations but died two weeks later.

What struck me as being a little strange was that I was at peace with their passing. I had always believed that there is something after you die. I don't go to church and I'm not religious but I do believe in God. For some reason I felt that Pop was in control, that he was at peace. It was the same with James.

After they died I started up a new pre-game ritual that I've continued to this day. After my warm-up I go into the shower, put my head under the water, close my eyes and say, 'Please God, give me the confidence and enthusiasm to play to the best of my ability, injury free. Can you please send my love to James, Pop etc.' The list started out with those two and over time it has grown as I've lost people who have been important to me. Mum's best friend Charmaine was added to the list, then Peter Jackson; Dan Ryan — the father of a friend of mine from school, Sean — who died of cancer; our former first grade manager at the Bulldogs Alan Nelson who died of a heart attack at one of our player reunions; 'Snooksy' the former massager; Peter

Guiding Stars

Moore of course; and former Canterbury Leagues Club president Kevin Stewart who passed away in 2006. My little mate Matty Mitric is always there, as well as my grandmother who died just before the Anzac Test in 2005. I also mention Lady Di, who was a beautiful person, and Mother Teresa. I never knew Pop's father but I've heard stories about him. He had an injured leg and used to hop around everywhere so he was known as Hoppy Price.

The other person is Jo's great uncle Lee Walton, who was always up front with me. He didn't pull any punches and when I was playing like a busted arse he told me so. It was a real shock to hear but he was right. No-one was more honest with me than Lee.

I say all of these people's names and then I say, 'Thank you God for everything that you've given me, I love you. Amen'. When I'm finished I turn the tap off and then I'm ready to run onto the field. It gives me confidence every time I play that I don't just have the fans and my family supporting me but those who have influenced me and are no longer with us.

It's a small thing that I believe has helped my rugby league career. It has helped my life in general. I feel that a lot of the things that I've achieved are to do with those people giving me the strength and enthusiasm to be the person that I am. People say that you make your own luck but I believe there are certain things that happen that are a bit more than luck. They are meant to be. Who is to say that when I injured my knee before the 2004 grand final it wasn't Peter Moore telling me he was upset that I was leaving the Bulldogs? If that's the case I fully understand. He gave me a follow-up injury in 2005 as if to say: 'You're not going to play against the Bulldogs this year Steve'.

If people think I'm cuckoo, so be it. I've never told this to anyone — not my mother, not Jo, or anybody else — but it's my little routine that I do before each game and it's something I've been doing since I was a teenager.

I don't know if any of my team-mates do anything similar and I've never asked them just as I don't want anyone to ask me what I do. It's not easy to make this public for the first time but I have done so because it's part of who I am and I'm proud of what I do.

It's not a superstition. I just want to thank whoever it is that might be helping me at the time. Everyone makes mistakes and we learn our lessons in whatever way

— be it through injury or something that is taken away from us. It could be these people saying: 'We are still around and we're not going to allow you to make the same mistake twice' or 'We're going to make sure you learn a lesson from it', whatever it might be. I've had plenty of lessons to learn. I'm no angel by any means but I've learned from the mistakes that I've made. It's why I want to thank the people I've lost for everything they have done for me in my life.

19 Falling Short

I CAN'T help but feel that I was never meant to play in the 2004 grand final. I had already enjoyed one lucky escape during the finals that season. In our first semi against North Queensland I was placed on report for striking Cowboys forward Glenn Morrison and was facing a week's rest after being charged by the NRL's match review committee.

Very little went right for us that night — I was sin-binned for 10 minutes by referee Tim Mander for lying on Matt Sing too long after he made a break and we lost the game 30–22.

Fortunately I beat the charge and took the field against Melbourne the following weekend in a game we won comfortably 30–0.

The week leading into our grand final qualifier against Penrith was an exciting one for the Bulldogs. We had put the disappointment of the Cowboys loss behind us and gained a lot of confidence from our win over the Storm — now we were just one win away from the biggest game of the year. I couldn't wait to get into it, but things didn't quite work out as planned.

Most sides tended to kick off to my side of the field, so I would usually take the first hit-up and then Mark O'Meley would come in and take the second. On this particular night Penrith kicked off to Mark's side instead so he took the first hit-up and I did the next one.

I still remember the tackle. I ran into the two Hair Bears — Joe Galuvao and Tony Puletua — as well as Martin Lang, and was flung to the ground. I felt a whip in my knee but I played the ball, tried to run and could barely move. I tried everything to get going again and stayed on the field for about two minutes, but I knew what the problem was. When Larry Britton, our trainer, came on to see how I was I told him straight away I had done my medial ligament. He said, 'Are you sure?' He couldn't believe it. He said, 'See how you go for a little while', and I tried again but it was no good and I hobbled off.

Deep down I knew exactly what had happened because I'd done it before and this had the same sound and the same feeling. When I tried to run it felt like my knee cap was wedged inside my knee joint.

The club doctor Hugh Hazard had a look and told me to get it strapped up. I went for a jog but couldn't move too well so I sat down and didn't give it much more thought because it was such an important game. I was more worried about the team. I hadn't missed a game all year apart from when I was in State of Origin camp and now in our most important game we had lost a starting front-rower in the first minute, our bench was under pressure and I was really stressing.

It was only when we won that it started to sink in — we had made the grand final and I might not be there to take part. I was trying to stay positive though. When the media came in I said, 'Hopefully it will be fine. We'll have a scan but it doesn't feel too bad'.

The next morning, Pat Molihan from Channel 7 called me to ask if he could come to my house to do a story. We lived out at Picton on an acre block, which was lucky because Pat turned up by car with his cameraman but had to be picked up in the Channel 7 helicopter. Apparently the traffic was shocking and Pat had to head straight back to Aussie Stadium to cover the Sydney Roosters-North Queensland game afterwards so the helicopter became his mode of transport! He was talking to the pilot while he was flying out to our place because we had to give directions then wave him in. I must admit there aren't too many times you can say that you had a helicopter land in your back yard!

I was still upbeat when speaking to Pat. I told him I was looking forward to the grand final, that I was hopeful the scans would clear me and I would be okay to play on Sunday night.

On the Monday morning we had the team photo and I sat in the middle where I was supposed to as captain, then I headed straight to the specialist who happened to be based in Randwick — right in the middle of Roosters territory! I basically tried to sneak in so that nobody would recognise me.

The news wasn't good that day — the specialist told me that there was no way I could play in the grand final. I sat there in his office looking at my knee and I said to him, 'Is there anything at all that you can do to my knee to get me out on the field on Sunday, some operation where you can put some sort of band in there to make up for the medial that I'm missing?' He said, 'Mate, there is nothing on this planet that I know of that can do that for you in seven days. That's it, it's no good'.

It was hard to take. When I walked out I was still thinking: 'He is just saying that so I don't get my hopes up because not playing is only the worst possible scenario. I'll still be okay to play'. Steve Folkes wasn't surprised when I told him the news — I was probably the only one in denial — but he told me to keep it quiet and we would continue on as if I was playing until he could make a decision on who would replace me as captain.

That decision turned out to be quite ironic. A few weeks earlier Andrew Ryan had called to ask if he could come over and talk to me about something, so he and his now-wife Olivia came around for dinner. It turned out he wanted to know about the club captaincy for 2005. We spoke about my beliefs as a captain and how I tried to lead as well as how I approach my own game.

I had already had a conversation with 'Folkesy' about this same topic and had suggested that Andrew would make a great captain once I was gone. Braith Anasta was the other player in contention and had captained the team well on other occasions when I was in Origin but I just felt at that stage of his career he was too emotional and could let things get to him — I felt that his mood on the field was too easily influenced and that he needed a bit more time. Having said that, it's not something 'Folkesy' and I discussed in grand final week — I had as much insight as anyone else as to who would be named captain and who else would be brought into the squad.

On the Tuesday morning I broke the news to the team that I wouldn't be playing in the grand final but we still kept it quiet from the media. I even took my knee brace off, walked out onto the training paddock and kicked a footy around for a few minutes to throw them off track! I told the media afterwards that I was resting the knee for a few days before resuming full training later in the week.

It seemed to work because I even fooled Willie Mason. He came up to me the next morning and said, 'Wow, that's great news Pricey, you're actually playing now!' I said, 'No mate, I told you yesterday that I was out' and he replied, 'Yeah, but I saw you on TV last night and you said you were going to be right to play. You said your scans came back and they were a lot better than what you had expected'. That wasn't completely off the mark — I had completely ruptured my medial ligament so I knew that I couldn't play. If it had been a partial tear I might have tried too hard to play when in reality I shouldn't have.

I'm grateful to 'Folkesy' for helping me feel a part of the team that week. On Thursday morning we had the traditional grand final breakfast and I was recognised as captain because the media still hadn't been told. That was Steve's way of giving himself time to make the right decision but it was also hugely beneficial to me on a personal level. Emotionally, being involved with the team kept me busy and helped mask the disappointment I felt about missing the biggest game of the year. It was also a bonus for the team to be able to prepare for the game without the media constantly distracting Andrew or the boys — most of the focus was on me instead.

The whole thing was quite surreal and it didn't actually hit me until the Thursday night when Andrew and I appeared on *The Footy Show*. That's where we finally announced the truth and as I started speaking the words, the emotion began to hit me. It was such a hard thing to do because there was a huge crowd present and they gave us an unbelievable applause as we walked out. I started thinking about the fact that my final game for the Bulldogs had only lasted two minutes. I could have had a fairytale farewell but instead I lasted two minutes and then missed the grand final.

As it turned out we won the game, I did a victory lap, was given the honour of making a victory speech and have another premiership ring to show for my efforts thanks to the generosity of one Johnathan Thurston.

EVEN THOUGH I wasn't playing, I was extremely nervous when I woke up on grand final day. Mum, Gaz and Dan had come down for the game (Mum cooked my favourite dish of risotto with garlic prawns for dinner the night before — as she did before every big game) and we went to the Leagues Club early to have lunch at the Chinese restaurant.

Even at 1 p.m. the place was packed. The fans started cheering as soon as I walked in and I started bawling. I couldn't help it. There were people everywhere and I stood there for about an hour-and-a-half signing autographs and having photos taken. After that we had our lunch together and then the boys started turning up one by one.

I had been conscious all week of staying positive and refusing to dwell on my own misfortune, particularly around the boys, and I made sure I maintained that on the big day. I was one of the lucky ones that had already experienced a grand final but a lot of the players hadn't so I made sure I was there to offer my support or advice to anyone that needed it.

Andrew Ryan was shitting himself — you could tell he was nervous. 'Bobcat' is usually quite talkative and jokes around a lot but now he was barely saying a thing. When we arrived at Telstra Stadium I pulled him aside and said, 'Mate, you've got to be yourself. You're not yourself today, you're not Andy Ryan and I noticed it straight away. If I noticed it I know that the other boys will have too. You're the captain today and you're there because of who you are and what you can do'.

Andrew took that on board which really helped the team. He said, 'Yeah you're right, I'm a bit nervous.' I told him, 'There is no use being nervous. You should be excited because this is what you live for, this is why you've done all of this training — this is the moment. This is what you want, but you're making yourself all tight and wasting so much energy'. He relaxed after that and the minute he did the whole room changed.

I started walking around and joking with the boys, trying to take their minds off just how big this day was. The club had put e-mails from supporters up all around the dressing room walls and I couldn't help shedding a few tears as I read them. Quite a few had been sent to me and they were absolutely brilliant. I actually had to go back to Andrew and tell him that I didn't want anyone running onto the field thinking that they were going to win the game for me.

Having said that, I nearly ran out onto the field by accident when it was time to head down the tunnel. I had my jersey on and the crowd went crazy — there was blue and white everywhere — and they basically had to pull me back!

One of the great memories I have is of the ground manager Eric Cox — who passed away in 2006 — walking up to us as we sat on the team bench. Each club was only supposed to have 10 people sitting on the bench including officials but with me there we had 11. He told us that we had one too many and when I looked around I noticed that Luke Ricketson was sitting in the pen for the Roosters rather than on the bench as I was. I said to Eric, 'It's okay mate, I'll go and sit back where I'm supposed to be'. Eric walked over to me and said 'No Steven, you stay there. I'll accept this one for once'.

THERE WAS one other amazing gesture from Eric that night — he gave me one of the balls used in the grand final. A few weeks earlier he had actually told me he was going to do that because he thought we were going to be there. He said, 'You've been so great for the Bulldogs so it would be a gift from me. I want to give you the footy from the grand final'. Eric kept his word.

It was a strange experience watching the grand final from the bench. At one stage, about 20 minutes into the game, the crowd let out a huge cheer and I assumed they were trying to keep themselves amused because there wasn't a real lot happening on the field. Then I looked up at the big screen and saw my own smiling face up there. It was a real thrill to hear the reception of the fans and I had to choke back a tear once again.

Not long after that, Mark O'Meley was given a rest and at the same time our physio Albert Alonso told him to go for a walk up the sideline and come back again. I thought: 'I'll go and have a chat to Mark as he's walking back to the bench'. So there I am having a yak and when we get back, Eric Cox is waving his arms at me and going nuts with this bright red face, veins popping out everywhere. He was pointing at me and blowing up. I didn't know what was going on! Our football manager Brad Clyde walked up and said, 'You've got to sit down. You're not supposed to be here at all but you damn well can't be walking up the sidelines talking to the players!'

I hadn't even thought about that — I was lost in the moment. I thought I would see what Mark's thoughts were on how the game was going and offer some tips on what he was and wasn't doing well. Obviously I could have done that when he sat down but for some reason I did it while he was walking back and nearly lost my spot on the bench!

We ended up winning the grand final 16–13 and Andrew Ryan had an unbelievable game. It's incredible that his first game as captain was a grand final win! He pulled off the play of the game right near the end when the Roosters made a break and he managed to ankle-tap Mick Crocker to save an almost certain try.

I was humbled by the manner in which 'Folkesy' and the team looked after me

Falling Short

once the game was over. They made me feel a part of it and I'll never, ever forget that. I may not have played but it was the second best thing that could have happened.

I can't even remember what I said but to be able to go up on stage and give a speech was amazing. I didn't think I would get that opportunity and I didn't really think that I deserved it either. I wasn't the captain on the day but people said, 'You were captain through the year and this was just one game'.

The whole thing has hit me more in the years since. I always wanted to captain a Bulldogs premiership-winning team and that was my chance — I was 78 minutes away from doing it.

The last four years have been the hardest in trying to cop that. At the time I was really proud of the boys and proud to be a part of it but as the years have gone by it has hurt me more and more because of the fact that I was so close. It breaks my heart. The history books will always say that Andrew Ryan was captain and that I didn't play. It breaks my heart because it was something I spoke to 'Bullfrog' about through the whole time he was CEO and he had a real faith and real belief that I would one day achieve it.

Maybe I'm being selfish in thinking that way because I'm still honoured by what happened. It also gave me a whole new perspective on what it means to win a premiership and the people involved. It's not only the people that run out onto the field on that particular night — there are 20 or 30 blokes involved in that whole season of highs and lows, of winning games and losing games. All of that has an impact on what happens at the end of the year. They all have an influence.

I'm not sure I would have had the same appreciation of that if I had been holding the trophy up as captain. When you're not playing you don't feel like you're a part of it — you feel like you're a hanger-on. You're not, but you feel like it because you didn't actually do the work on the day.

The truth is that it takes more than 80 minutes of footy to win a premiership. There were a couple of guys — Dennis Scott and Jamie Feeney — who had a real impact throughout the year but didn't get to play in the grand final. The other side of it is Johnathan Thurston, who was handed an opportunity he will never forget when I was ruled out.

But it was nice to take part in the celebrations even though I didn't play. Our CEO, Malcolm Noad, had spoken to the NRL earlier in the week and said that if we did win the comp, he wanted to make sure that I received a premiership ring on the night. I thank Malcolm for that. I told him that I didn't want to go up on stage to receive it because it didn't seem right but he said, 'No, no, it's been organised for you to do so'.

After the speeches, the players were awarded their premiership rings and to this day I'm amazed at what happened next. Each ring has a number on it to represent the jersey number but because they are handed out randomly the players all get together and swap them over afterwards so that they each have the right number.

My place in the team had been taken by Johnathan. Can you believe that of all the numbers he could have been handed, Johnathan was handed No 10? He walked straight up to me and said, 'I want you to have this, you deserve it'.

I was very embarrassed, very proud and very honoured all at the same time. I also thought that if I didn't take it I was going to disrespect what he was trying to do. He was very sincere in what he was saying and it meant a lot to him that I take the ring — so I accepted it.

As it turned out, Malcolm had the spare ring on him so Johnathan received his on the night anyway but that doesn't change the sentiment in what he did. He wasn't swapping rings, he was *giving* it to me — that's how much it meant to him. I guess it was meant to be.

THE POST-MATCH celebrations were amazing. Once the media had cleared out of the dressing room and things had settled down we all jumped on the team bus and drove to Yagoona, just off King Georges Road, where there was an open-top double-decker bus waiting for us. We pulled down a side street, swapped over and continued driving down King Georges Road.

The traffic basically stopped going the other way with Bulldogs supporters going nuts and we had a convoy of cars and supporters following us. We turned left down Canterbury Road and the whole right lane had come to a standstill. If anyone else was trying to drive somewhere it was bad luck because our supporters were out of their cars and dancing on the street! We had music blaring and were cruising down the street slowly with thousands of people behind — it felt like the whole of Sydney was following us. Two guys even tried to jump on the bus with us before the cops dragged them away!

I give the boys a stern talking to during our round six match against Newcastle in my first season at the Warriors in 2005.

Playing for Australia at Suncorp Stadium in 2005. We beat the Kiwis 32–16.

Wairangi Koopu and Ruben Wiki congratulate me after the test match. I had attended Nana Christie's funeral earlier that day so it was an emotional win.

Right: I was devastated after picking up another knee injury midway through the 2005 season. I was attempting a charge-down on Wests Tigers halfback Scott Prince, but he fell on top of me and I snapped my medial ligament.

Below: After waiting more than 12 months, I finally scored my first try for the Warriors against South Sydney in 2006.

A powerful fend on NSW halfback Brett Finch during the second State of Origin game of the 2006 season at Suncorp Stadium.

I celebrate our 2006 State of Origin series win with teammates after game three in Melbourne. Pictured alongside (left to right) are Adam Mogg, Chris Flannery, my brother-in-law Brent Tate and Cameron Smith.

Above: I push off my former teammate Hazem El Masri while playing the Bulldogs in 2006. We actually led that game 16–0 before losing 22–18 in golden-point extra time.

Right: We're awarded a much-needed penalty during Awen Guttenbeil's testimonial v Cronulla in 2006.

My face tells the story after going down to the Eels at Parramatta Stadium in 2007 on a night where nothing went right for us. Warriors fans would remember it as Manu Vatuvei's nightmare outing.

Referee Jason Robinson doesn't give me the answer I expected after I asked him to explain a penalty during our match against South Sydney in round seven, 2007.

I plant an enormous fend on Willie Mason and brush off Jamie Lyon at Suncorp Stadium in game one of the 2007 State of Origin series.

I celebrate our first-ever victory at Telstra Stadium in game two of the 2007 State of Origin series with Johnathan Thurston and Petero Civoniceva.

Game two of the 2008 State of Origin series at Suncorp Stadium. I missed game one with injury and was under intense pressure heading into the return clash.

I cross for a rare State of Origin try in game one of the 2007 series after beating Brett White and Andrew Ryan to the line.

Action Photographics

The Queensland side celebrates our third consecutive series win after game three of the 2008 series at ANZ Stadium in Sydney. It was a very special moment shared with a wonderful group of guys.

Falling Short

When we pulled up in front of the Leagues Club there was just a sea of blue and white. We had a microphone with us and I stood up to say a few words to them. They went ballistic and I lost it again. I said something along the lines of: 'Be careful and look after each other because we don't want anyone hurt. It's great and it's exciting — we're celebrating but make sure you don't hurt each other because things could get pretty nasty'.

When we went into the club we had two sections cordoned off that had room for only a limited number of people for safety reasons. We had half the group in one area and half in the other, then we swapped so that we could see as many fans as possible. These are the people who turn up every week and it meant so much to them — as much as it did to us really.

Afterwards we all headed upstairs to see our families which is always a special moment. They know what you've gone through and now they get to celebrate your achievements with you. It was a huge moment for Jo, Mum, Gaz and Dan. It was basically my last night with the club because once the celebrations are over that's it — the year is over.

The only disappointing thing for me was that after what felt like about 45 minutes a lot of the younger boys shot off into the city, leaving guys like myself, Hazem El Masri, Tony Grimaldi, Adam Perry, Benny Harris and 'Bobcat' to stay with all of the families. I remember after the grand finals in 1994 and 1995 we stayed together — all of us — for days. Obviously it was an indication of the way that the club is going and that I was from the old school. It's not all about that old-school bond where you stay together as a team anymore — that doesn't mean as much to these young guys.

I didn't have a problem with the young guys heading into the city but after all the club had been through, from the salary cap two years earlier to the sex scandal in January that ripped the place to bits, I would have thought the whole team would have wanted to celebrate our achievement together.

THAT LAST week at the Bulldogs taught me a lot about myself. For one, it was a final reminder of how lucky I had been to be involved with the club — mainly because of the people who were there and the culture they created.

When I first arrived at the Bulldogs, Billy Johnstone wouldn't talk to me for 12 months because he had wanted me to join the Gold Coast. When he came to the club a few years later I walked up to him, albeit a little bit scared, and he said to me 'Well, you made the best decision didn't you. If you had been at the Gold Coast you wouldn't be where you are now'.

I've often wondered throughout my career if I've been making the right decision — be it to leave the Bulldogs for the Warriors or to leave my mates and family behind in Queensland to join the Bulldogs — but I know now, you've just got to have faith and back your gut feeling.

When I did my knee a week before the grand final, I was trying to find some sort of reason for why it had happened and I couldn't think of one at the time, but since then I've realised that perhaps it was so I could get a whole new level of respect for those players that miss out on a grand final after playing such a huge role all season. It taught me that things don't always go your way.

The majority of my life has been like that — getting so close that I can almost smell it. I'll never forget the try I almost scored in State of Origin in 2003 when I ran 50 metres but overbalanced in the final few strides and was tackled half a metre short. People say that would have been one of the great Origin tries, but it wasn't to be — I was half a metre short of the line.

But I've achieved so many fantastic things and I don't regret anything that I've done. I'm so proud of what I've achieved and even if I had scored that try in State of Origin it wouldn't have made me more or less of an Origin player — the same as captaining the Bulldogs in the 2004 grand final wouldn't have made me a better or worse person.

And I'm thankful for being so involved in grand final week. I had no time to feel sorry for myself or to think about what I was missing out on because I was right in the middle of it.

The same thing happened with the salary cap and again with Coffs Harbour. People say to me: 'I don't know how you were able to do what you did', but I was so busy that I had no time to think about the ramifications of the punishment we received. When we had 37 competition points deducted, it wasn't until the season was over that I actually sat down and thought about all that had taken place. There is no way that I would have been able to do what I did and be the face of the club if I had realised what I was doing. It's unusual how it all works out.

20 A Terrible Loss
— *By Marie Moore*

I CLEARLY remember the day that Steve Price announced he was leaving the Bulldogs after 11 seasons in first grade — I hated it.

I was terribly upset to see Steven leave. It wasn't that I thought he should have stayed but I remember very strongly my disappointment that we were losing him.

The Bulldogs were always known as 'The Family Club' and Steve fitted right into that. I know for a fact that he considered the Bulldogs to be his family and he wanted to be a one-club man. But life doesn't always work out the way you want or hope it will.

My late husband, Peter Moore, always said that once someone has given all of their years to a club and is ready to sign the final contract of their careers they should make that decision based upon family. He encouraged his players to make the best decisions for their families because family is the most important thing that you have.

Steve called me shortly before he signed for the Warriors in 2004 and asked me what I thought about him leaving the Bulldogs. He and Peter had been extremely close and I was sad to see him go but I said to him, 'Remember what Peter used to say — if it's better than what Canterbury can do for you then don't hesitate. Family is most important'.

That was Peter's philosophy for all top players during his time at the Bulldogs. Sure, there were a few players that Peter was upset with during the Super League war because they left for different reasons — the club had looked after them and it didn't turn out right — but in Steve's case I said, 'If it's the best thing for your family you should go . . . but we will miss you'. And we *have* missed him.

Steve comes from a lovely family and to this day I remain close friends with his mother Margaret. Only recently I said to her, 'He just keeps getting better with age — I wish he could come back and play for us again because we could really do with him!' I'm sure that Peter would have felt the same.

Peter and former Bulldogs president Barry Nelson used to go to all of the big Schoolboys carnivals and Steve was one that particularly caught his eye from an early age. They couldn't be in Queensland all the time of course but Peter would watch Steve play and kept a close eye on him for quite some time before he eventually signed him to the Bulldogs. He was impressed by the fact that Steve always gave everything he had. He often played 80 minutes and not many front-row forwards do that kind of work. At an early stage he showed that he had the right stuff and he just loved playing footy.

When he came down to Sydney he made the Bulldogs his home and everyone loved him because he gave his all in every game that he played. From that moment onwards Peter was like a proxy grandfather to Steve. Our door was always open if Steve wanted to have a word with Peter about any sort of problem.

I didn't have too much to do with him myself in those early days but he would come around to visit and I would leave them on their own to talk about their business. I've been a football person for a long while so I know when to listen and when to walk away!

What I did know was that Steve was only very young when he first came down to Sydney and sometimes these young kids get very lost. But he stood up to it very well and Peter saw quite quickly the leadership potential that he possessed. In those early days Steve liked to go out, do as he was told and focus on his own game but I think the leadership role was something that was constantly developing in him. He was such a reliable young man that when he eventually became captain you knew he would always do the right thing for himself, his family and his club. That's the sort of person you want to have in mind when you're thinking of a captain.

There were some nervous moments though. I remember when Peter heard a rumour that Steve was gay and he just yelled, 'Get out of here Steve, forget it!' Peter had read something in the newspaper about it and said, 'My goodness, what's going on here?' He was very quickly onto Steve to have a little word. I mean, Steve is a good-looking young man and a lot of people take notice of that don't they? Peter often thought that less is best when it came to publicity because sometimes you can get caught up in the wrong thing. He always thought it was best to play it cool and do just as much as was necessary.

But Steve meant the world to him — they were very close. When Peter was sick in hospital Steve would often visit. He was always there for Peter and I still have a couple of lovely photos of the two of them together, one of them from when Peter wasn't very well. He gave us some wonderful memories both on and off the field.

Peter didn't like long visits when he was in hospital and although he wouldn't exactly send you home, he let you know when he was tired and needed a rest. But he loved to see people too. Steve was his link to the Bulldogs because Peter liked to know what was going on. He was a real Bulldogs man through and through.

Peter may be gone now but Steve has always stayed in touch throughout my own poor health of late. That's one of his most impressive attributes — he cares about people — and it's why I was so sad to see him go.

One of the great travesties was that Steve was injured before the 2004 grand final and didn't get the opportunity to leave the way he would have liked. He didn't deserve that but, as always, he learnt from the experience. You can see that the Steven Price I first met just grew and grew to become a very special young man and now a very mature young man.

But Steve and Jo both know that even though they live across the Tasman these days, we're still with them and always will be. I just hated losing a very special friend.

21 Once Were Warriors

I WENT out of my way to give Mick Watson and the Warriors the benefit of the doubt, but it didn't take long to realise that something was amiss after I arrived in 2005. George Mimis had had his concerns from the moment he first met with them the previous season and told me straight out, but, me being me, I said, 'No, give them a chance. I'm sure they can't be as bad as you think'.

Still, I was wary from day one and as time went by I began to piece a worrying puzzle together. Mick would often invite me to his house in those early days to discuss the Warriors and I was far from impressed by the way he would speak about individuals at the club.

The one that stands out clearly was when he asked me, 'What do you think about your brother-in-law coming over to play for us? I'm thinking of swapping Francis Meli for Brent. I think he could give us more value and I could pay your brother-in-law what I'm paying Francis which is really good money for him'. I told him, 'I don't really know if that's going to be possible. I don't think Brent will leave the Broncos and I don't think Wayne will let him go'.

Mick may have been ambitious but I didn't like the way he was talking about some of the players that were already at the club. I had seen him talk to Francis acting as if they were good mates and I couldn't help but wonder: 'If you're saying that to me about Francis, what are you saying to the other guys about me?'

I had heard a number of things about PJ Marsh and how he was sent packing from the club when he really didn't want to be. Mick would tell me that PJ was causing problems, but the players said otherwise. Then there was Vinnie Anderson. He had just returned from the Kiwi tour of Great Britain when all of a sudden he started being called out of training to meet with Mick. Low and behold, two weeks later he was off to St Helens in England. Before he left he was quoted in the media saying, 'I'll never play for the Warriors while Mick Watson is in charge'. Mick would tell me that there were a number of issues with Vinnie — one being that he was told not to tour with the Kiwis in 2004 so he could get over an injury and have a full pre-season for the club — and that he didn't have the right attitude, but that didn't make sense to me. I had started to become good friends with Vinnie and he loved being at the Warriors, he loved living in New Zealand and he loved his team-mates. Here was Mick telling me otherwise and it didn't add up.

Eventually Mick stopped talking to *me* as well. I made a point to say hello whenever we crossed paths but our relationship went from being quite open to suddenly being shut off completely. Rumours started circling through the media about how I was homesick and wanted to return to the Bulldogs. People would call me to ask if the rumours were true and I had to tell them they were way off the mark.

It was exactly the same cycle that had taken place time and time again. I had heard similar stories about Ali Lauiti'iti and even Stacey Jones. Once the rumours began about me I knew I was next on the chopping block.

But I didn't let it affect me and I didn't change anything I did. I made sure I said hello whenever I saw him because I didn't want the perception that I had any problem with him. And at the end of the day I didn't have a problem — not personally at least. I just didn't like the way he went about his business. There was no trust in the place and I could understand why. Mick had guys he would talk to all the time and that he got on well with. It was a strange situation and another issue that we didn't need to be dealing with.

I don't know how you can be expected to run a successful business in those circumstances. Even the front office staff were frightened of him. Mick is quite an intimidating guy when you look at the size of him and he can be quite aggressive.

And Mick always had some strange ideas. He said to me once, completely out of the blue: 'What do you think about Tim Sheens?' I said, 'I think he's a very good coach'. Mick asked, 'What do you reckon about us getting Tim Sheens as our coach?' I told him, 'That's fine, but I think he's signed with Wests Tigers'. Wayne Bennett was next. Mick said, 'What about Wayne Bennett? He's a good coach — we'll get Wayne Bennett'.

That was Mick's thinking process. If something wasn't working he thought he could just snap his fingers and bring in the best. The other candidate he threw up for the coaching position was Brian Noble, now head coach of Wigan. I spoke to Brian when I toured with the Kangaroos during the 2005 Tri-Nations and he told me: 'I had some phone calls from Mick to start with and all of a sudden they just stopped. I don't know what happened'. All I could say was, 'I'm not surprised buddy'.

They were strange times but what really started to ring alarm bells was watching Mick go about his daily business. Having captained the Bulldogs and been through some difficult times with the salary cap and Coffs Harbour, I knew what a difficult job it was to be CEO and how much time it takes up, but when I arrived at the Warriors, Mick was training with the players — nearly full-time!

When the Warriors were trying to convince me to sign with them in 2004 they sent me a DVD, part of which had various players saying what it would mean to have Steven Price play for the Warriors. The other part was a documentary on Mick and what a great job he had done at the club. It had originally been on *60 Minutes* in New Zealand and was all about how far the club had come. I was really impressed by it at the time but once I had been there for a while I thought: 'Here is this documentary on how great things are, I'd love for them to come in and see how great the Warriors really are'.

I realise that it was from a time when the Warriors were playing very well in 2002–03 but it goes to show that publicity and success can easily go to your head and you then start to change the things that you had been doing. I experienced that very same thing in my own career. When you aspire to reach a certain level, it's easy to let yourself get comfortable and even a little arrogant once you achieve your goals and once that happens it all starts to fall down around you.

That's what happened with Mick. He was great for the club when he first arrived. He was a breath of fresh air and he helped the club rise from also-rans to grand finalists in the space of two years. But it all spiralled out of control from there and he started to believe all of the positive press he was reading. He wanted the publicity when the going was good but when it started going downhill he didn't want to know about it. The fact is that you have to front up no matter what the situation.

Once Were Warriors

THREE YEARS after my dreams were shattered when the Bulldogs had 37 points deducted, the salary cap struck yet again. The 2005 season was a tough one for the Warriors and resulted in some major changes off the field after we finished 11th. Our coach Tony Kemp was sacked and replaced by Ivan Cleary while Mick Watson also resigned after two disruptive seasons that had seen the Warriors fail to reach the finals, more than 20 players leave, and Kempy's predecessor Daniel Anderson forced out despite having led the club to its maiden grand final less than two years earlier.

In February 2006, we were on the Gold Coast to play a trial match against the Bulldogs and had gathered together for a seminar with a financial planning company. Instead, our new CEO Wayne Scurrah and head of football John Hart walked in and said they had some bad news. We were all handed a press release stating that the Warriors had been found to be in breach of the salary cap by almost $1 million in 2004–05. I couldn't believe it. I was devastated. It was like a bad recurring nightmare that would follow me wherever I went.

Worst of all, the NRL began focusing their investigations on me because of some irregularities in my contract and the fact that Ruben and I had been the latest big recruits to the club. Their primary concern was that there were some differences between the letter of intent I signed in July 2004 and the actual contract that we finalised the following February.

I actually ended up signing two contracts with the Warriors — the first being my playing contract and the second relating to a radio show I had been doing on Radio Sport each week. I spend an hour every week with host D'Arcy Waldegrave taking calls from fans about the Warriors and rugby league in general and I have continued to do so ever since my first season at the club in 2005.

Although I was assured that everything was above board, the fact that there were two separate contracts was enough for the NRL to accuse me of trying to help the club get around the salary cap. Wayne said to me, 'They've really come down hard on you because you were involved with the Bulldogs and there were some changes made to your contract'.

The fact that there was an eight-month gap between signing the letter of intent and my actual contract didn't help, but that was out of my control and wasn't something I was particularly pleased with. I was calling George every single week asking where the contract was because I had been in that situation before with the

Bulldogs and ended up signing for less money than had been originally agreed.

Perhaps Mick had intended that to be the case because he never expected to secure both Ruben and me and was shitting himself when we both said yes. By the end I was calling George almost every single day because I needed the reassurance of a legally binding NRL registered contract. It might have been what got me into trouble because I just wanted to get something signed and know that I was receiving what had been agreed upon.

I found out that the NRL was actually considering deregistering me because they felt that I had an involvement in the club trying to evade the salary cap and were trying to make an example of me. Apparently they were sick of players saying: 'Oh I didn't know anything about it, I just signed a contract with my manager and the CEO'. Their thinking was that the player has to take some responsibility — it's your livelihood and you know how much money you're being paid. They wanted to make a statement to all other players and clubs that it wouldn't be tolerated.

When I heard that I called David Gallop straight away and said, 'Are you serious? With what I've just been through with the Bulldogs, do you honestly think that I'd go to the Warriors and try and break the salary cap?' He told me, 'Steven, we did speak about it — I won't deny that — and it's something we were contemplating but in the end we didn't feel that we had enough evidence to support it'. I was disgusted. I couldn't believe they would ever think about doing that to me. For my livelihood to be taken away when I had absolutely nothing to do with what happened was a terrifying thought.

Nobody even bothered to mention that the club had also been over the cap in 2004 before Ruben and I even arrived! I thought the Warriors had a CEO who was out of control and I was the one who very nearly copped the brunt of it. As it was, we had four points deducted and became the first team in premiership history to start a season on negative competition points.

It felt just like what had happened at the Bulldogs where the players, the fans and the sponsors were the ones that were punished while management walked away scot-free. Bob Hagan was paid out to leave the Bulldogs in 2002 and I hold no grudges against him for that, but it was the players who had their dreams shattered when we were leading the competition by a country mile. Now we were the ones suffering again despite the fact that we were under the cap by the time the 2006 season kicked off.

It was something we had to deal with for the entire season, the irony being that we missed the finals by exactly four points. I understand that there has to be tough punishment for breaking the salary cap but I've been involved twice now and it's broken my heart on both occasions. I'm sure that every supporter of the Bulldogs and Warriors has been broken hearted too.

OFF-FIELD DRAMAS aside, it was a tough initiation for me at the Warriors. For starters, I spent my first two months in Auckland by myself while Jo and the kids stayed behind in Sydney to finish up the school year and finalise the sale of our house in Picton. Jo and I went to the Melbourne Cup and then I headed straight across for pre-season training.

The Warriors boys had actually started training two weeks earlier but because of my knee injury I couldn't join them straight away. I had been receiving treatment from the Bulldogs physio Albert Alonso ever since the Penrith game and I basically continued that on once I moved to New Zealand.

So not only was I by myself, I couldn't even get to know the Warriors players properly because I couldn't train with them. It's one thing to talk to the boys off the field but as captain I wanted to know what they were capable of as well as showing them what I could offer other than what they had witnessed as an opponent.

One of the great advantages I had when I took on the captaincy at the Bulldogs was my knowledge of the players because I had been there for so long and had seen them all arrive at the club. Now I was the new guy. There had been quite a few changes at the Warriors and because a lot of the guys were away on tour with the Kiwis we actually began training with quite a small squad.

The first training session I turned up to was terrifying. It was a bit like my first day at school — I didn't know what to expect. I didn't know how I would be received by the boys and I didn't know what the culture was like. I was very wary of stepping on people's toes. I was basically just sitting there, very vulnerable, hoping I would be accepted. I didn't know what perception the boys had of me and it was a really tough time. It was the one thing I hadn't thought of when making the decision to join the Warriors.

And I wasn't prepared for just how low the morale of both the players and staff was when I arrived. Everyone was depressed. We were training hard because it was

Tony Kemp's first pre-season as head coach and he wanted to get them back on track but it was also the hardest they had trained for years so there were a few of the guys breaking down and others just finding it tough to handle in general.

To be honest, I didn't know how I was going to pull us out of this one. The fact that I was injured meant I couldn't get out there and do anything with the players. Even though I was there for the whole pre-season, I didn't get to do many of the things I would have liked to have done to get to know the players better and for them to get to know me better.

Being invited to be captain was a great honour but again I was worried because I hadn't played with the boys and I didn't know if they would enjoy being captained by me. I didn't know if I should continue to captain the way I had at the Bulldogs either — was I supposed to change? All of these things were going through my head.

If it hadn't been for a few people — particularly Bruce Sharrock who was the Warriors' football manager at the time — I would have really struggled with the transition. There were plenty of times when I questioned if I had made the right decision. I was in New Zealand by myself, I couldn't train and although we had bought our new house, I didn't have any furniture. The club had hired me a TV, a washing machine, a fridge, a bed and a lounge suite, but that's all I had in a four bedroom house!

That's where Bruce really helped me. He manages around 100 rugby union players so he has been dealing with that sort of thing for a long time. He was the perfect person to help me out and he bent over backwards to make sure everything was as smooth as it possibly could have been. Awen Guttenbeil and Stacey Jones were also very welcoming and could sense that I was apprehensive.

We began our pre-season training at Waitakere in west Auckland because Ericsson Stadium was being renovated at the time. All I could do at the time was some light running which wasn't the most enjoyable way to start my Warriors career. I would jog around the field in the wind and the cold with rain hitting me at 90 degrees and it was a real shock to the system. I was lonely too with my family still in Australia.

Just above the ground was a gymnasium and on one particular day early on they had some sort of school sports carnival. As I was doing my laps around the oval these two little Maori kids were standing near the gymnasium watching me and obviously trying to figure out if I was Steven Price. I see people all the time when they think they recognise someone — they call out their name just loud enough for the person to hear it so that if you turn around they know that it's you; if not, they don't get embarrassed.

The boys called out my name and I looked up and said, 'Hey boys, how are you going?' They called back, 'Yeah good, good. You played for the Bulldogs, ay?' I said, 'Yeah, I was the captain'. They asked me, 'You played with Sonny Bill Williams, right?' I said, 'Yep, I played with Sonny Bill Williams'. 'You just signed with the Warriors didn't ya?' I told them, 'Yeah I've signed with the Warriors so I'm really excited'. Then one of them shouts out, 'Damn, I wish the Warriors had signed Sonny Bill Williams instead of you!'

When you come to a new club, let alone a new country, one of your biggest fears is whether or not you are going to be accepted — and here I was with two kids telling me they wanted Sonny Bill instead of me! I didn't know whether to laugh or cry but at the end of the day I had to laugh. It was one of those priceless moments that become quite funny over time. That was my first experience as a Warriors player and it's something that I look back on with a huge smile these days.

The other challenge for me early on was trying to get the whole Bulldogs mindset out of my head. I was constantly referring to what we did at the Bulldogs and I probably sounded like a broken record. I wasn't meaning to do it but it was all that I knew. I had to make a conscious effort to stop when I realised how often it was happening.

At the same time, I was aware that my experience at the Bulldogs was one of the reasons that the club brought me to New Zealand so I didn't want to ignore that completely. In the end, it might have hurt my relationship with Mick Watson a little bit. I think he felt slightly insecure, as if I was trying to take his job.

All I was trying to do was pass on my knowledge because I felt that my role was to help the club get back to where it should be. I had been at a club that was very successful and I just wanted the Warriors to be the same.

22 Rolling the Dice

IN 2005, *The Daily Telegraph* ran a story about a gambling addiction that had supposedly taken over my life. According to the story, I developed a serious problem with poker machines that saw me lose thousands of dollars and very nearly my family with it. Fortunately the story was a long way from the truth.

Although there were plenty of times when I sat down in front of a poker machine, only once did I feel that it could spiral out of control if I continued. It certainly didn't put my family at risk, although the rumours that followed certainly did cause them plenty of stress. I was angry at the way my 'gambling' was portrayed because it wasn't an accurate reflection of who I am or what I had done, so I will set the record straight.

I had never played a poker machine when I first arrived in Sydney as an 18-year-old. Queensland didn't have poker machines so you had to travel to Tweed Heads to play. Sydney offered a very different lifestyle to what I was used to and going to the pub or club with a few mates usually involved throwing a few bucks in the pokies.

I still remember going along with a few of the Bulldogs boys once to have dinner at the club and afterwards we went and played the pokies. It was my first time so I only put $5 in and pulled out $50. I thought: 'How good is this?' From then on I would play them every now and then as something to fill in the time. That's how it started and that's how it ended — it was never anything other than that.

One of the great things that I found as I got older and my career started to take off was that the poker machines provided an opportunity to get away from the public eye. I'll be out to dinner and have people come up for an autograph or I'll walk down the street and be recognised — all of that is fine — but sometimes you need some time to yourself. When I was playing the poker machines no-one seemed to bother me — it was like my own little world. I was never trying to win a lot of money. I was really playing for the time it gave me to think.

The times that I did play were when I had nothing to do, such as between training sessions. During the Super League period we would arrive at training at 9 a.m. and wouldn't leave until 5 p.m. so we trained in two blocks — 9–11 a.m. and then 1–4 p.m. That left a few hours to kill so I would pop into the club with a mate or two, have a chat and put some money in the pokies. I used to see some of the other guys pile in hundreds and hundreds of dollars and I would think to myself: 'Nah, I can't do that', because I couldn't afford it and didn't see it as the thing for me.

Then in 2000, Jo's uncle, Lee Walton, died and she had to go back to Roma for the funeral. At the same time we were in the process of moving to a new unit we had bought in Dulwich Hill, but there was a mix-up with the compliance papers so when we turned up to move in we were told that we would have to find somewhere else temporarily while everything was sorted out. We could move our furniture in, just not ourselves. It left us in a bit of a bind so we booked ourselves into the Park Royal at Darling Harbour expecting to be in our new place within a few days. We ended up staying there for a month!

It was while we were at the Park Royal that Jo and the kids went up to Roma for the week. I had pre-season training so each day I would head off to training, come back to the hotel and have nothing to do, so I would head over to Star City Casino and play the pokies. I didn't realise how much I was spending until the end of the week when I looked at my bank account and saw that I had burnt through $2000!

Straight away I thought: 'This isn't good, I've got to do something about this'. I wasn't out of control but I had heard stories about people that were and I didn't want to find myself in the same situation. I certainly didn't ever want to get to a point where I could lose my wife and family over it — nothing was worth risking that. I literally made a decision on the spot that I would put an end to playing the pokies.

I called my financial adviser, Richard Shaw, and said to him, 'Mate, this is what I did and I feel terrible'. I was really depressed about it. I felt like I was a dog. I had let my family down. Money that I'd earned had just been wasted and that's not what Steven Price is about.

I met with Richard and he was a huge help. We had a talk about what had happened and I said, 'I don't think it's out of control but I know this is how much I've spent this week and it's the most I've ever spent. I didn't like it, I don't feel good about it and it's not me'. He said, 'Alright, what do you want to do about it?' I told him, 'I think if I put some things in place that make it hard for me to play the poker machines it can only be a good thing. I still want to be able to play if I need some time to myself but I want to have limits. I don't want to be able to go to the ATM to get more money out'.

Now, this is the same guy that had helped us out when we had all of our problems during Super League. Richard helped us get from the point where we almost lost everything and were struggling to make repayments on our $160,000 loan to having a savings plan and being able to make payments on two or three properties at once. Thanks to him we had started budgeting very well.

Richard was glad to help out again. He said, 'What if I become a signatory of your account, if you trust me, and Jo becomes another so that if you want to write a cheque you need either of our signatures as well as yours to go with it and you're going to have to tell us what the money is for'. I said, 'Yep, no worries, I can handle that'.

Richard also suggested that I go and have a talk to Bob Hagan because he had dealt with a similar situation with someone he knew. Bob said, 'Alright, what if we stop you from playing the pokies at the Leagues Club'. Again I said, 'No worries, I've got no problem with that', because I didn't really like playing anywhere else and I was only playing at the club because it was close.

So that's what happened. I was up front with Jo about it as well which was really satisfying for me because I never wanted to lie to her about anything like that. I've seen plenty of guys that have and I just can't understand how they can do it. They were the alarm bells that woke me up that this could get out of hand if I allowed it to.

I've never done anything similar since. I have a couple of bets on the horses if I'm at a club. If I've got a bit of time or I'm bored I might play the pokies a little bit but that's very rare. 'Bullfrog' used to say to me all the time: 'I don't know why you're playing those things, you're never going to beat a computer. This club is not as big as it is because people win on the pokies!' But you learn your lessons in life.

What hurt me more were the stories that were written at the time. In 2005,

Cronulla hooker Michael Sullivan went public about how he had lost $150,000 on gambling. Not long after, I received a phone call from James Hooper at *The Daily Telegraph* to confirm a rumour he had heard from another journalist — a former *Telegraph* writer who is now with *Rugby League Week* — that I had lost two houses and a car over my own gambling addiction. Apparently they were talking about Sullivan and this journalist says, 'If you think that's bad, wait until you hear what Steven Price did'.

James wouldn't actually tell me who had told him the rumour but it wasn't too hard to figure out — *Rugby League Week* ran a story two days later as one of their lead stories for the week that said everything about me except my actual name. This journalist basically gave himself up by printing every single thing that James had told me about the rumour.

James obviously couldn't believe it though so he called me straight away which is what this other journalist should have done too. James asked me about it and I said, 'No mate, I've never had a gambling addiction. I've played the pokies but this was the situation'. I also told him that I wasn't too comfortable with him writing the story because it really wasn't a big issue. I didn't want to be brought into a comparison with Michael Sullivan's situation.

James said to me, 'No, no it's a feel good story about how you recognised it at an early stage before it got out of control and you did some things that helped you stop'. I don't know if I'm easily convinced or if I'm just naïve but I said, 'Alright, but I want to know what the story is before you put it out'. He said that was fine and called me back to read the story out but it just didn't seem like it was the full story. I asked him if there was more and he said, 'There is a little bit more but the editor is going to be looking over that'.

I probably should have realised something was amiss when I first mentioned that I wasn't comfortable and James responded with: 'No, the editor really likes what you said and he wants to use it'. I asked James about the headline. He said, 'The editor hasn't come up with that yet — we've got a couple of ideas but it will be alright'.

The next day the newspaper hit the stands and it was terrible from my perspective. At no stage did the story read like it was a feel good story or that I had beaten the gambling bug before it got to me. It actually read as though I had lost more money than Michael Sullivan.

I received a heap of phone calls after that — from the media obviously as well as people like Gamblers Anonymous. It was everything I had feared. People were assuming that I really did have an addiction. I even received a call from John Ballesty — CEO of the Canterbury Leagues club — who was distraught to think that I had become addicted to gambling while at the club. He ended up going through all of my records just to satisfy his own mind that I hadn't. We were close friends and he offered to give me that information to present to everybody else to prove I was telling the truth.

Even worse though was how the story affected my family. I had spoken to Mum the night James had called me and I told her there was probably going to be a story in the paper, just to warn her. She was really concerned and with good reason as it turned out. Not long afterwards Mum was at Toowoomba Hockey Club waiting for Gaz and filling in time by putting $5 in a poker machine. That's about the limit for Mum — $5. As she was playing, a lady walked past and said, 'Well, now I know where your son gets his problem from'. That broke Mum's heart. She called me in tears and that really hurt me.

When the story first came out I thought to myself: 'I'm a big boy, I can handle it — if someone says something to me I'll tell them exactly how it is', but it never occurred to me that people would say something like that to my mother. The person that said it probably meant no harm — it might have been a passing joke — but Mum didn't take it that way and neither did I. These are the side effects that come about from the things that we do as players and the stories that are written about us.

If the story James Hooper wrote had been the truth it would have been a great story but hopefully through this book I've been able to clear up exactly what happened. There certainly are people out there with genuine gambling problems and there are plenty of players that enjoy a punt. Everyone is different and I'm just glad that I recognised the danger signs early. It didn't cost me my family. I did lose some money and I wish I hadn't but I've lost money through investments too and they're all lessons in life. Provided you heed them they can only benefit you in the long run.

Gambling is a huge problem in Australia that causes marriages and families to break up. Unfortunately I became caught up in the middle of a story that struck at the heart of the issue because one journalist heard a rumour and told another that it was true. The whole thing has actually made me a little bit paranoid whenever I'm in an area where there are poker machines. I can't help but wonder if people are watching me and thinking: 'Hey, he *has* got a problem with gambling'.

Some people have told me that they were inspired by my story but I've had to say: 'I don't want you to be inspired by my story because it's not true. It wasn't the way it was supposed to be written. It was manipulated and twisted the way the editor wanted it to read so you should probably be thanking *The Daily Telegraph*. They just used me as a character.'

But it was a lesson for me. I *did* play the poker machines, I *did* reach a point where I felt terrible about what I was doing and I *did* make sure there were procedures in place to make sure it didn't happen again. One of the great things about coming to New Zealand is that I no longer have that spare time I used to fill in by playing the pokies. I'm actually so busy these days that I barely have enough time to spend with my family let alone sit in front of a machine for a few hours.

I can only hope that, by telling the truth about what actually took place, people will no longer consider me a reformed gambling addict but someone that recognised the danger signs and took immediate steps to prevent any damage being done. I also hope that if there is someone reading this book that recognises similar signs they actually do something about it before it spirals out of control.

23 Never Tough Enough

I KNOW for a fact that there are certain coaches out there who don't consider me tough enough for the NRL. I know that I've been tested a number of times through my career. I know that when Ricky Stuart was coach of the Sydney Roosters they certainly went out to target certain players and I was one of those.

There are certain qualities that people within the game expect from a player and, for my size and the position I play in, people often want me to be more aggressive than I am. It's the way I was brought up. I'm a caring person and I show my feelings at times but I'm also very passionate about playing within the rules. It bugs me that most of the guys that are considered to be 'tough' are also the guys that are regular visitors to the judiciary.

From the age of nine I was labelled the nice guy that would always finish last and it inspired me to prove people wrong. I wanted to be Steve Price and live my life the way I was brought up by my mother. It's something I'm very proud of and I won't change to please anyone else.

I'm sure there have been plenty of representative teams throughout the years that I've been overlooked for because certain coaches didn't think I was tough enough. The irony is that you definitely can't survive in the NRL if you haven't got some sort of toughness in you. The game is the easy part — it's the training and playing with injury that makes it so hard. That's what a lot of people can't get their head around when we talk about the length of the season — 26 rounds plus finals plus State of Origin and test matches with tours thrown on top.

If I was soft I wouldn't be playing State of Origin and I certainly wouldn't have played for Australia. But I have never changed anything that I stand for. There were times when I worked a lot more on my technique but I never changed the way I play the game. I'm more intimidated by a guy who doesn't say much, has a great technique and plays within the rules than someone who is likely to end up at the judiciary at any given time.

The guys who talk it up and say they're tough, they're not intimidating at all from my perspective. I look at a guy like Dallas Johnson. He's not known as a bad boy or spoken about when people name the 'tough guys' but I can tell you there is nobody I enjoy playing with and dread playing against as much as him. When you get hit by Dallas you know you've been hit — you're sucking in the big ones.

I've always been a bit frustrated by guys attracting publicity and being regarded as greats of our game just because they've been suspended so many times and have knocked out so many players. To me, the only way to knock a player out is to hit him in the head and if tackling to hit in the head was a prerequisite of the game then a lot of us wouldn't have lasted as long as we have.

How do you determine who is tough these days anyway? The interchange system is different to how it used to be so players don't play with injury as much as they once did. We *do* play injured and are needled up but it's a different sort of toughness.

Players from yesteryear would probably look at the game now and cringe compared to what they went through. At the same time, would a player from the past be able to survive in the current game? Even from when I started playing first grade the game is completely different. I've been lucky enough to be able to adapt but there are certainly a lot of players who have fallen by the wayside along the way because they haven't been able to keep up or they haven't had the skills or fitness levels to survive.

I suppose I was lucky enough in my early days to go to a club like the Bulldogs where we had 'tough' guys in our team — they didn't need me to be the tough guy that I was never going to be. I don't think I intimidate anybody. I don't think there are too many people shaking in their boots when they are marking up against Steven Price. A few years back Mark Geyer named five players he considered to be the softest in the NRL and I was one of them! That's fine by me because at the end of the day it's only the opinion of one person.

It's also a different game these days. Back in Mark's day it was about how tough you were and how many blokes you could run over or knock out. All of those aspects have changed — and for the better in my opinion. I wouldn't still be playing if the rules were the way they once were because I wouldn't have lasted.

That doesn't mean I'm not tough enough. To play in the NRL you have to be tough. I don't know of too many weak people that can actually run onto a rugby league field and be tackled by three or four guys 20 or 25 times a game, then have to turn around and tackle them as well while fatigued and battling injury.

I have always come across blokes calling me this, that and the other, saying I'm not tough enough. I don't say anything back to them because that's what they want me to do. If they're talking to me it is either because they aren't confident enough to be able to dominate me or they're trying to put me off my game.

There were times when I wasn't able to dominate as much as I wanted to because the other team had blokes that had been handed the task of hounding me, but that was always a great challenge. I didn't know it for certain at the time but I could feel it because, against teams like the Roosters, I was copping a lot more attention than usual. I'm not trying to pat myself on the back. I was made aware of it afterwards and that just confirmed my suspicions. Blokes would test me to see whether I would throw in the towel. I never did, even if injury sometimes prevented me from playing to the best of my ability.

I hate missing games. Even when I'm in State of Origin camp I hate sitting there watching the Warriors run around when I can't play. It kills me. Even during games I hate being taken off the field. I guess it comes down to people's definition of toughness because toughness can be viewed in so many different ways.

If you're an old guy who looks at the current game you would probably say that I'm not tough, but then when you look at what we have to go through with the standard of training every day — it's certainly tough. It's the mental toughness too of having one day off each week and training every other day. If you don't, you get left behind. People don't realise how draining it is to wake up early and go to training every day for nearly 11 months of the year. As I said, playing is the easy part and it's the part that everybody enjoys.

The pre-seasons are by far the hardest part of the year because it is when you train the hardest — and you don't even get to play a game for four months! It kills you because playing is the reason you took the game up when you were eight years old. The problem is that you need all of that training to be able to play the game.

The technology that clubs have now and the standards of fitness are so far ahead of where they were when I first started playing. Each individual is monitored and scrutinised with the latest technology that provides all sorts of readings for the trainers, coaches and doctors. After a few seasons they can recognise patterns and monitor a player's performance as a result. There is no longer any place to hide. That actually helps you with your toughness because you've got the techniques and your body is at a stage where you're very confident that you're fit, strong and fast enough to be able to handle most things in the current game.

Even the NRL season itself — it's no surprise that the young guys often struggle to play at the same level week in, week out. I was fortunate to have a player like Terry Lamb in my corner when I was younger. Terry gave me some tips about preparing for a game which were basically that if I set myself a level where my best game is, I need my worst game to be only marginally below it. The best players are the ones with the smallest gap between their best and worst games.

It's something that I took on board after 2001 and it is since then that I have played my most consistent football. Wherever you're playing, whoever you're playing against and whatever the conditions, there is no reason for you not to play as well as you can. You're still on a footy field with a referee and a football and 13 blokes on either side. There are games where you don't play your best football but you still need to be the best you can be on the day.

I reassess myself during games every couple of minutes to see where I'm at. I look at what I want to achieve in a game and whether I'm achieving it. If I'm not, I start making sure that I do achieve those things. I don't wait until half time to realise that I haven't done anything.

These are the sorts of things that keep your mind ticking over. It helps you forget about whether you just belted someone or someone smashed you. To me, the ability to improve during a game and play to your best even under difficult circumstances is the greatest test of toughness you can get.

24 Charge Downs

IN 2007, NSW halfback Brett Kimmorley accused me of a 'cheap shot' after he injured his knee as I tried to charge down one of his kicks during the third State of Origin game at Suncorp Stadium. It was the second time in 12 months that a player had been injured by one of my charge-downs following a similar incident involving Cronulla's Tony Caine, and Brett told *The Daily Telegraph*: 'It's a bigger cheap shot than hitting someone in the head'. Their Sharks team-mates Greg Bird and Paul Gallen also accused me of poor sportsmanship.

I put myself in Brett's shoes and I can understand his disappointment at being injured but I wasn't happy to be labelled a cheap-shot merchant. I'm nothing of the sort and all of these players are ignoring the facts about what actually happened. We're all at risk of injury every time we take the field and unfortunately a freakish circumstance saw two players pick up injuries from my charge-downs in consecutive years. I've been pressuring kickers throughout my entire career without any problems.

When I look at some of the hits other players have put on kickers over the years I'm amazed that it's me they focus on. On the rare occasions that I even make contact with a kicker it is because they have actually tripped over me as their momentum has moved forward. For me to be able to come in contact with the kicker means he has either been slow to get his kick away, is kicking from dummy half as in Tony's case, or is kicking at the line as with Brett. Brett likes to kick from these spots because he has already gained extra metres compared to those who prefer to stand deep in order to give themselves more time.

Charge Downs

I remember both incidents well. In Tony's situation he was kicking out of dummy-half having originally looked to pass back to Brett. I was starting to chase Brett out of marker but, when Tony decided to kick instead, I just leaned down with my back to him to charge the ball down, which I succeeded in doing. I didn't even realise what had happened at the time because I was replaced straight afterwards, but I was later told that he had suffered a terrible injury. I sent Tony a card the next day wishing him all the best because you never like to see players injured, but I didn't feel that I did anything wrong. It was an accident, one of those unfortunate incidents that can happen on a rugby league field.

I said at the time that I had been charging kicks down for 14 years and nothing like that had ever happened before, so it was a shame when people suddenly began to scrutinise my technique. When Brett hurt his knee 12 months later that scrutiny became twice as intense. I have studied every kicker in the NRL and I know all of their traits, just as I'm sure that they know about mine. Brett certainly would have known that I was coming.

On this particular occasion I dived at the ball as I usually do and Brett went over the top of me as he moved forward. It wasn't a case of Queensland coach Mal Meninga telling me to go and take him out or anything like that — it was an accident, just like Tony's situation.

I was disappointed that I was blamed for both injuries when they were the ones that took the advantage of kicking in the line. I have since had to change my technique simply because I put pressure on two kickers who were looking for the advantage of extra yardage. If they were concerned about me getting to them to charge the ball down they would have stood further back like most kickers. I can assure you that it is much harder to get to guys like Andrew Johns and Johnathan Thurston because they're so far back and can usually get their kick away.

I took exception to the comments made by a number of coaches and CEOs at the end-of-season conference last year. They brought up the issue of protecting kickers but all of the footage shown on the day was examples of kickers being taken out late. Not one was a situation involving my technique, yet the only player mentioned by Nathan Brown, Graham Murray and a few other coaches was me. They ended up bringing in a new rule this season because of me getting off the ground — despite the fact that my charge-downs were never the problem.

I make no apologies for the fact that I like to pressure kickers. It's something I started doing when I was 12 years old as a means of gaining an extra advantage over my opposition. I felt it was an area that not too many people were willing to put the extra effort into because you don't get too much praise for it — and it *is* a lot of extra effort. If you don't charge the ball down or don't force them to kick out on the full you've got to run back 50 metres after already sprinting up 10.

But I've continued to do so throughout my career. Nothing has changed. I've always had exactly the same technique and although I've received some negative publicity in recent years there have been far more times when *I've* been injured from doing it.

Most kickers, guys like Andrew Johns, are quite difficult to get to because they know you're coming and the ball is gone by the time you arrive. You have to be smarter about it and you have to prepare. I always try to be in the right position on the last tackle to challenge the kickers. If that's from marker, you tell the second marker that you're going to be chasing and you know where the kicker is standing. Obviously the dummy-half knows that too so he will try and fire the pass as quickly as possible. As soon as the ball leaves his hands I'm off to the races and I'm focusing on the space directly in front of the kicker's boot because that's all I can worry about.

My goal is to either charge the ball down, force the kicker to kick out on the full or to have our fullback catch the ball before it bounces. The worst-case scenario is to make contact with the ball and have the opposition regather for a repeat set. When I was younger, particularly at the Bulldogs, that happened quite a lot. I was just nuts — I wanted to charge down every ball I could. Then, as I grew older, I started to look for better opportunities — times in a game when I thought it might really benefit the team. I started speaking to the kickers in my team to get an idea of how other kickers felt about being chased. The general consensus was that they hated it. Ideally they wanted all the time in the world to get the perfect kick away — either a 40/20 or a kick that would make the fullback have to run back to pick the ball up.

Over the years, I've had coaches who have been extremely receptive to my charge-downs and others who have been quite negative. Some players I've played with would rather I didn't actually go for the ball but I know that, in the kicker's mind, if I'm actually going for the ball he is going to be aware of that. If I'm just trying to knock him over it won't worry him because he can still get his kick away. If I get a charge-down anything can happen and that will be going through his mind — the pressure intensifies.

Charge Downs

Particularly in my early days, I would always try to get either a touch or a charge-down early in the game — whether the ball bounced our way or not — in order to let the kickers know that I was going to be annoying them all day. There have been a few times where my team has scored off a charge-down although, more often than not, the other team gets six more tackles. A lot of coaches get upset by that because they say possession is such an important part of the game but I know for a fact that when your kicker has his kick charged down it rattles him a bit. It rattles the whole team. He gets to his kick and thinks: 'Okay, we're about to be downfield tackling', and then all of sudden, even if they get the ball back, they've gone backwards. It can really get to them. It's a momentum swing.

Some players believe otherwise. Shane Webcke was one who hated giving the opposition another set from a charge-down and in State of Origin it is generally considered suicide to do so. But one person I almost always have supporting my charge-down attempts is my fullback. Fullbacks love me pressuring the kicker so that the ball doesn't go where the kicker wants it to. Whether our fullback catches it on the full or the ball just doesn't go as deep, it's a huge advantage for us.

One game I remember in particular was game two of the 2002 State of Origin series at the old QEII Stadium — my first game back after a two-year hiatus. Andrew Johns had an unbelievable first game in which he mesmerised us with his kicking game and I said to Wayne Bennett, who was coach at the time, 'I'll chase 'Joey' all night long but if I do that I might be a bit too tired to do as many hit-ups as I normally would'. Wayne addressed the team and said, 'I've given Pricey full scope to chase Andrew Johns all game but if he does that it will put a bit more pressure on you guys to do a little bit more work'.

What ended up happening was that Andrew's kicks weren't anywhere near as effective which basically meant that I was taking a hit-up without actually doing one. He kept kicking to our fullback on the full or kicking short, so, although I might make one fewer hit-up each set, I was basically saving us 20 metres anyway.

I remember another game when the Warriors played Newcastle in Auckland and Andrew Johns was out injured. Kurt Gidley took over from him that day as first-choice kicker and I charged down his first three or four kicks of the day. It got to the point where the entire crowd cheered when he finally got a kick away. That's where charge-downs can be so valuable.

25 All That Glitters is Gold

IN EARLY 2007, Andrew Johns was invited by the New Zealand Rugby League to travel to England at the end of the year to play with a New Zealand 'All Golds' team against Great Britain's 'Northern Union'. The match celebrated 100 years since Australian superstar Dally Messenger toured with the original 'All Golds' in rugby league's first-ever international tour in 1907, and 'Joey' was the man the NZRL wanted to replicate Messenger's guest role in the Centenary clash. I knew that I was never going to be offered such a great opportunity ahead of a player of Andrew's calibre but I must admit the first thing I thought was 'I would love to be involved in that'.

Unfortunately for Andrew, a serious neck injury forced him into early retirement and he missed the chance to play for the 'All Golds' against the 'Northern Union'. The NZRL nominated Darren Lockyer as Andrew's replacement and it was around this time that I received a phone call from an NZRL official asking if I would be interested in going on the tour as well. I was told that both 'Locky' and Wayne Bennett had also been invited which blew me away — I had played a lot of footy with 'Locky' and had been coached by Wayne, so it was the ideal scenario.

I wasn't quite sure why I had been invited ahead of so many great players in the NRL but the NZRL explained that it was because of my relationship between New Zealand and Australia — I was representing the close relationship the two countries had enjoyed in rugby league's formation.

'Locky' was to play the role of Dally Messenger, which was a great honour for him, but I was even prouder to be invited to represent the link between our countries. I don't consider myself to be anywhere near the calibre of either Darren or Andrew but I ended up playing both roles in the end after 'Locky' was also ruled out with injury and third choice Johnathan Thurston opted to have end of season shoulder surgery. It's strange how things work out.

We finished our season at the Warriors when we were knocked out of the semi-finals by North Queensland and I went straight into the train-on squad with the Australian Test team.

I had some promotional commitments for the 'All Golds' tour but I was also wary of over-stepping my bounds. I was chosen in the Australian test team to play the Kiwis in Wellington on October 14 and I was very conscious not to do anything that would upset coach Ricky Stuart or any of my team-mates.

We ended up winning the test by a record score-line of 58–0 and I was due to link up with the 'All Golds' the following day. I had already made sure that I had read the book *All Blacks to All Golds* so that I understood the history of the 1907 tour and the whole thing blew me away. Rugby league was basically born because rugby union didn't pay their players, despite the fact that the governing body was making a lot of money from international tours. The players were frustrated because if they were injured and couldn't do their jobs, rugby union officials refused to compensate them. The players heard about this new game called rugby league in the Northern Union, had some rules books sent over and began scouting players. While rugby union remained a game for amateurs, this new sport of rugby league was considered to be professional. Unfortunately, those who defected to the new code sacrificed a lot and were basically labelled outcasts from then on.

I was rooming with Brett Stewart in Wellington and I had to sneak out of my room the morning after the test match dressed in my 'All Golds' tracksuit. It had been the final game of the year for the rest of the Australian players so they had a big night after our win which gave me a chance to leave early.

The problem was that it was the New Zealand team bus that was picking me up from the hotel and you can imagine how excited the Kiwi boys were to see me after we had just thrashed them 58–0! When I jumped on I said, 'Hi boys, how're you going?' — then it occurred to me that they probably weren't going that great after all. I thought: 'Right, I'll just put my head down, walk up the back and sit there quietly'.

The Kiwi squad was heading overseas for a three-test series with Great Britain with five of their players also selected for the 'All Golds' game. While the rest of the squad continued on up to Leeds to prepare for their series, we were off to link with Wayne Bennett and the other 'All Golds' players who had travelled to England a few days earlier.

My first assignment once we arrived was to learn the haka. I had made a conscious effort not to learn the haka before we left New Zealand because I was involved in the Wellington test match with the Aussies and I figured it would be a conflict of interest to point my energies towards the 'All Golds' when I had a test to play for Australia. So I didn't learn it, but, in not doing so, it put a lot of pressure on me once I arrived in England.

We were due to meet Queen Elizabeth that afternoon and it was the first time any team had performed the haka at Buckingham Palace or in front of the Royal Family! I headed straight up to my hotel room with the Kiwi social manager Bailey Mack, who had 25 minutes to teach me the words and actions. We started with the words and I went through them bit by bit — 'Ka Mate, Ka Mate, Ka Ora, Ka Ora' and so on.

Bailey said, 'Right, you've got those down pat, now we'll go through the actions'. Once I had a bit of a grasp on them he said, 'Okay . . . now we've got to put them together.' Well I was all over the shop! I was singing the wrong words and doing all of these weird actions. It was hilarious but we did the best we could and eventually headed off to do our first training session with the group. After that we went back to our rooms and had a shower — then it was off to Buckingham Palace.

What an unbelievable experience. I had been there in 2005 with my family, standing outside and wondering what it would be like on the inside.

We travelled to the New Zealand embassy first because they were the ones who had organised for us to do the haka in front of the Queen. The reason she had said 'yes' was because rugby league was celebrating 100 years and apparently the Royal Family is very into centenary-type celebrations.

We sat with the ambassador while he ran us through what to expect and what we were and weren't allowed to do. One rule was to always wait until we were spoken to and not to ask any questions ourselves. We were to refer to the Queen as Her Majesty and we weren't allowed to take photos. The Royal Family has one official photographer and he is the only person allowed to take photos on the premises.

We were all pretty nervous as we headed to the gates for our security check. As we drove through I looked back at hundreds of people standing outside looking in and imagined that they must have wondered who we were and what we were doing at Buckingham Palace.

We travelled underneath an arch and stopped in an internal square with the palace built right around the sides. A guard jumped onboard and ran us through the rules again before we finally headed inside.

The palace itself was amazing and the room that we entered first was the most unbelievable room I had ever seen. It had enormously high ceilings and huge stairways on either side leading up to another level. We walked up and entered another room that looked out into the backyard — acres and acres of greenery. The entire wall, from floor to ceiling, was made of glass.

The staff all stood on our left while we waited and we were told to make ourselves comfortable — the Queen would be down shortly. We were offered a cup of tea which I gladly accepted. I'm no tea connoisseur but I do love my tea and the one thing that my grandmother had told me, being born in England, was the rumour that there was no better tea than the tea served at Buckingham Palace. I drank that tea for Nan as much as for myself and it was easily the greatest cup of tea I have tasted in my entire life!

There were two types of cups there — a small one and a large mug — so I made sure I used the mug. It was made of the finest China and I enjoyed my tea so much that I asked if I could have a second, which was just as good.

We were standing around waiting for a few minutes before the corgis suddenly came flying down the stairs. The Queen and the Duke, Prince Philip, were following but nowhere near as fast as the corgis! There were seven or eight of them and they absolutely flew down to us.

We had no idea what the protocol was and whether we were supposed to pat them or not.

I remember one of the boys patting a corgi and saying: 'Damn, now I'm going to smell like dog when I meet the Queen', but when he smelt his hand it was like perfume — he smelled better than he did before! I couldn't help thinking: 'Here are these people looking after these dogs and they must be thinking that they'll have to wash them again because all these dirty footballers have touched them!' They really were immaculate.

The corgis ran around us for a few minutes and then the Queen and the Duke entered the room. We were split into two groups — forwards and backs — with Ruben introducing the forwards and Nigel Vagana introducing the backs.

My group met the Duke first and he was a magnificent guy, very down to earth. He was very interested in our being there, what we do, what it was like and so forth. I was blown away by that and I must admit I felt a bit uncomfortable because this was his house and here he was, having to start a conversation with these 17 blokes who were in his place. They had two more appointments that day too and this is what they had to do every single time.

The Duke spoke with us for about 15 minutes and then it was time to meet the Queen. Poor Ruben — he was so flustered that he forgot our names! But we shook the Queen's hand, introduced ourselves and started talking to her. That was amazing too. I don't know if it was a perceived thought that I had but she was so down to earth and was curious to know what we were about. She asked a question about our profession and we were all standing there silently because we didn't know who should answer back. I ended up chirping up, as I do.

She said, 'So, 100 years of this game of yours. Have many things changed over the years?' I said, 'Yeah, there have been a lot of rule changes. The teams used to stand close together and now they're separated by 10 metres on each play; we have a set number of tackles now whereas it used to be unlimited; we have interchange now and we didn't used to'.

I told her how privileged we were to be representing such an historic occasion — 100 years of rugby league — and that we were extremely grateful to be welcomed into Buckingham Palace.

Then it was time to perform the haka. We returned to the first room we had entered and the Queen and Duke stood at the top of the stairs looking down at us. The whole palace — around 200 staff — stood watching on each side with the Queen and the Duke up above.

The Queen had already noticed that I wasn't a Kiwi when we spoke and I had explained to her why I was part of the tour, but even if she hadn't picked up on my accent she would have realised I was Australian when she saw me do the haka! I'm just glad they stuck me at the back of the room because I was terrified. Having said that, the whole experience blew me away. It was the first time I had been part of the

One of the most emotional nights of my career as we celebrate our 2004 grand final win over the Sydney Roosters. A knee injury the previous week ruled me out of the game but replacement captain Andrew Ryan was kind enough to let me make a victory speech (top right).

I found Jo in the crowd after our 2004 grand final win in what was another emotional night for both of us. My brother Dan is standing directly behind Jo looking back into the stands.

Putting on a brave face while climbing Sydney Harbour Bridge for *The Footy Show*'s 'Face Your Fears' segment in 1999 to raise money for cancer research.

Craig Borrow/News Ltd

I was lucky enough to meet the former Head of State of the Soviet Union Mikhail Gorbachev in Brisbane while in camp with the Queensland State of Origin side in 1999.

Left: In 2006, I featured in an episode of popular New Zealand television series *bro'Town* alongside Russell Crowe and Rove McManus. My character appeared for two minutes singing a song with my colleagues. With my voice I'm surprised they showed me for that long!

Below: News Ltd cartoonist Scott 'Boo' Bailey drew this picture of me in 2002 after I was named Bulldogs captain. It appeared in *The Daily Telegraph* in Sydney.

29th May, 2000

The New Children's Hospital
Royal Alexandra Hospital for Children

Steven Price
C/- Garry Hughes
Canterbury Bulldogs

Dear Steven

Thank you so much for visiting Matthew last week here at The New Children's Hospital. Matthew has been sick for a long time and he needed a boost to help him remain positive.

You were able to give him exactly what he needed. He smiled all day the day you came and was so much more cheerful after your visit. It was perfect. He so enjoyed his time with you. A very big thank you from Matthew and his Mum Kim.

Thank you for making time at such short notice and making Matthew feel very special indeed.

Very best wishes

Kind regards,
Debra Fowler
Public Relations

I received this letter from The New Children's Hospital after my first visit to my mate Matthew Mitric in 2000.

Steve Price Collection

The Queensland State of Origin side visits Australia Zoo in 2006. Steve Irwin was a huge Maroons supporter and invited us up for a special tour.

Jamie-Lee, Riley, Jo and Kasey celebrate Riley's 2nd birthday in June 2002.

Jo and I at her brother Brent's wedding on Australia Day, 2007. I was MC that night and told the guests, 'It's fantastic to be here tonight because Brent Tate is paying for everything'.

Woman's Day / Stephanie Creagh

A family photo taken for New Zealand's *Woman's Day* in September 2007. Kasey sits between Jo and me, Riley behind and Jamie-Lee.

haka and to see how much effort goes into it and how it makes you feel was a real eye-opener. It wasn't something I was brought up with but I understood the passion when I looked over and saw tears running down Ruben's cheeks. It gave me a whole new respect for what it actually means to the Kiwi players.

I was relieved to make it through my first haka — in front of the Queen — without any major mishaps but I wasn't so lucky the following day. We travelled up to Leeds to do it all again at Leeds railway station where the 1907 'All Golds' had also performed a rendition — and I stuffed up big time! Most people have seen the Kiwis do the haka before a rugby league or rugby union test match — you start slapping your legs and the ringleader starts shouting before the rest come in with 'Ka Mate, Ka Mate'.

David Kidwell was leading us on this particular day and he started in with 'Ahhhhh' which I thought was leading into 'Ahhhhh Ka Mate, Ka Mate' so that's what I started doing. Well, I was wrong and poor Tame Tupou standing next to me just burst out laughing. There were hundreds of people around and I lost it as well. I was so embarrassed. Here were Tame and me trying to get through the haka and we were almost wetting ourselves — I put him completely off!

FROM THE moment it was confirmed that I would be playing in the 'All Golds' game I was looking forward to being coached by Wayne Bennett again. Wayne is very big on history and tradition and he knows a lot about rugby league back in the early days. He was an ideal choice to coach the 'All Golds' and the Kiwi guys loved being coached by him. Players such as Ruben Wiki and Stacey Jones had never been coached by Wayne before but had huge respect for him. Then there were the younger guys — Chase Stanley, Shaun Kenny-Dowall and Epalahame Lauaki — who learned so much. It was an amazing opportunity for them.

On a personal note, I was given the opportunity to play in what was basically a Kiwi test team and under a coach who I had always regarded very highly. It was the ultimate privilege.

Our jerseys were very tight though. When we were asked to try them on for sizing they were the standard make but the ones we wore in the game itself were tapered — by the time they arrived they were all about four sizes too small!

The game was played at Warrington and it was an unforgettable evening. The atmosphere was fantastic. I'm sure the officials would have liked a bigger crowd but with the Rugby Union World Cup on at the same time it was difficult to generate publicity.

Still, the Northern Union side was very good and it was a great game that we ended up winning 25–18. We played under the 1907 rules and it was a very enjoyable occasion.

Because we weren't playing for competition points or in a test series there wasn't the same pressure as there would be in any other game. It was a celebration as much as anything. All week we had attended luncheons and heard stories from former players about what they had to endure — it gave everyone an appreciation of just how good we've got it these days.

And the game itself had the perfect mix of intensity and fun. There certainly wasn't State of Origin intensity but the English players were playing for spots in the Great Britain side while a few of our guys were pushing for the Kiwi squad. Put it this way — I knew I was in a game of football and I was sore the next day — but there was no spite in the game. It was played in the right spirit and there were some great tries scored by both teams.

We did the haka again before the game and luckily for me the English televised it so the Kiwi cameramen couldn't focus on me the whole time! Everyone was looking to see if I stuffed it up again but I nailed that one, as well as another one after the game for Stacey because it was his last ever game.

Stacey followed the tradition of hanging his boots on the grandstand and I actually gave my boots to a little boy in the stands, because I knew if I took them back home I would have to clean them and go through all of the trouble of trying to get them through immigration. I still have my jersey though and I will always cherish it.

The whole 'All Golds' experience is something I'll never forget. It was the icing on a magnificent cake that was my 2007 season and I feel privileged that they even asked me. It was a career highlight and an absolutely unique situation. Whether the game will be remembered in years to come, I don't know and to be honest I don't really care — the fact is that I was there. Was I lucky? Probably. I was in the right place at the right time. I just happened to be around in rugby league's centenary year and was lucky enough to stay fit when three other magnificent players were injured.

It meant a lot to me and with the way the boys went about their preparations it was just a great week. We were all very proud of what we were representing and I was able to play alongside the likes of Nigel Vagana, Ali Lauiti'iti, Ruben Wiki and Stacey Jones. It was a tremendous squad.

The things that I learned on that tour you couldn't learn on any other rugby league tour and I don't think you could learn them on a holiday either. They were special occasions, one-off moments. When else will I get a chance to go to Buckingham Palace and be treated so well? It was all because of the occasion and will never happen again. I'll cherish the memories forever.

26 The Highest Honour

THERE IS one thing that has kept me going in the NRL all of these years — representative rugby league. If I had made the decision to retire from rep footy I wouldn't be playing in the NRL today. I wouldn't have that fire inside me. It's one of the main reasons I decided to come to the Warriors — they wanted me to aspire to be my best, while the Bulldogs tried to take that away.

Although there is no greater honour than representing your country, I must admit that it is State of Origin that really gets me going. From the moment I first saw Bob Lindner play for Queensland in 1985 I wanted to be a part of it.

Like every kid growing up north of the border, State of Origin was like a religion — something that you absolutely had to watch every single year. And every year it would always be the same — how could Queensland possibly beat these superstars from NSW? I would watch every game and I was always so inspired. I desperately wanted to don that Maroon jersey one day.

But I very nearly let the opportunity slip away. When I made my State of Origin debut in 1998 I felt I was just making up the numbers. It was as if we needed 17 blokes but only had 16 so my name was called out to fill the extra space. That's exactly how I played for the first three years of my Origin career and it really disappointed me.

It wasn't until I was dropped after we lost the first two games of the 2000 series that I realised just how important State of Origin was to me and that I had embarrassed myself and the jersey. I hadn't been doing what I did at club level. That's what you want to do. Origin is the biggest test there is for a rugby league player and I wasn't testing myself. I let myself get too comfortable.

My form went out the window with the Bulldogs that season too and I was dropped to the bench. The only reason I played the first two Origin games was because we had drawn the series the year before and the selectors stayed loyal. Once we lost the first two games their loyalty expired. That hurt and at the time I was in one of those moods where it was everyone else's fault — I wasn't doing anything wrong so why was I the one that was dropped?

Jo was the one that made me realise I only had myself to blame. She sat me down and told me that just because I had achieved everything I wanted to achieve didn't mean I had performed at a level to be proud of. I decided then and there that I was going to work as hard as I could to not only regain my form but to play the best football of my life.

In 2001 Queensland held a pre-Origin camp where about 25 guys who were in contention to play State of Origin that season gathered together to prepare for the upcoming series. We had lost 3–0 the year before so I knew I faced an uphill battle to be recalled. I felt that the selectors were blaming me and a couple of other guys for what had happened in 2000 and there was no guarantee that I would ever play Origin again.

Wayne Bennett took over again as coach that year and actually said to me at that camp, 'Mate, you're probably not going to be much of a show this series. I really think you need to go back and get everything back in order — play some consistent footy so that if something does go wrong and the players we have earmarked to play Origin this year get injured or don't step up, you have put yourself in a position to take their place'. That very same night I ran into Wally Fullerton-Smith, who played 12 games for Queensland between 1983-90, and I'll never forget what he said to me. I asked him, 'What do you miss most about footy? Do you miss it at all?' and he said, 'There is only one thing that I miss — playing State of Origin. That time of the year, every year, is the hardest time of the year for me because I know how enjoyable it is to play and what a test it is as a player. Every Origin game goes down in history and you love being a part of it.

'I'll give you some advice because you're still quite young — don't regret not having achieved what you should have achieved. Don't let it slip. You've still got an opportunity to get back in there but it's up to you'.

From that day on I never, ever thought of anything else but wanting to work as hard as possible to be the best player I could. If I was ever given another chance in a Queensland jersey I was going to make sure I gave it my best shot.

I didn't earn a recall in 2001 which was disappointing because I was playing much better football and didn't receive any reward for the work that I had put in, but I guess that goes to show just how far I had fallen. I was there, I let it go and I had to start from scratch to earn a second chance.

It was an important lesson because that second chance certainly didn't come easy. It took a lot of hard work to get to where I had been and then I forgot to continue that hard work. It's still something I hold onto today — just because you're where you want to be doesn't mean you can take your foot off the accelerator.

Queensland ended up winning the series in 2001 and the following year Wayne said to me, 'You've done some great things but we're going to go with the same team that won it last year out of respect to them because I think they deserve that'. I understood that line of thinking but I also felt that I was a lot closer to a recall than I had been 12 months earlier.

When we were thrashed 32–4 in game one my chance finally arrived — I was on the bench for game two. This time I made sure my preparation was perfect and that I would enjoy the game more than any before. I wanted to act as if it was my last game rather than letting myself get comfortable or complacent, because playing Origin is a privilege and every game you play *could* be your last.

This was the game that Wayne assigned me with the task of harassing Andrew Johns because he had ripped us to shreds with his kicking in the series opener. We ended up winning game two 26–18 and game three was a draw so we retained the trophy.

Playing Origin again — and making a difference — provided a huge boost to my form at club level too and it's been that way ever since. A perfect example of that was my 2007 season when we won Origin and it lifted my form to a standard I had never reached before and will probably never reach again. I've really appreciated that while trying to back it up this year — to average 200 metres per game across the entire 2007 season was unbelievable. Teams were trying to stop me every week and I was still able to do it. They talk about people being in the zone, well, I was in the zone.

I'VE ALWAYS been disappointed by players who have fallen by the wayside because they didn't give it their best shot. There have been a lot of players who have been good enough to play Origin but have failed to live up to the talent they possessed.

The big thing for me when I went into my first few State of Origin camps was my preparation. I would be hanging out with the boys until midnight or one o'clock in the morning because I thought that was what Origin was all about, when, in fact, it's about making sure you spend the week preparing to play the game of your life.

When I returned to the Queensland side in 2002 I knew that the best thing to do was simulate exactly what I had been doing at club level that had been working for me. I also realised just how special the opportunity was because I'd had something that I loved taken away from me, and I wasn't going to let it happen again.

My worst performance since then has still been better than my best performance before that. Part of it is knowing I deserve to be there. I didn't used to think that I was as good as the players I was playing with or against and until I started to believe I was, I couldn't compete with them. I needed to realise that I was picked in those teams because I'm Steven Price, not because I'm Darren Lockyer. It's having the confidence that you can not only compete but actually make a difference.

I was named Queensland's player of the series in 2003, won man of the match in game one of 2005 and played what I believe to be my finest ever game in the series opener in 2007. I received my first players' player in that game and my second in game three. Those are massive achievements for me and a huge improvement on the Steven Price that first played State of Origin. I've learnt as I've gone along.

This year I equalled the most number of games by a Queensland forward alongside my idol, Bob Lindner. If you had told me back in 1998 or 2000 that I would play 25 State of Origins I would have laughed, but it all comes down to why I'm still playing and enjoying my footy at 34 — because I love State of Origin. I've always said that I'll never, ever retire from rep footy and I stand by that view. The selectors can make that decision for me.

IF I HAD to name my single greatest ally on a rugby league field, it would be hard to go past Petero Civoniceva. We've been through a lot together — from being blamed for State of Origin's potential demise to helping Queensland win the past three State of Origin series in a row — but, no matter what, I've always felt better just for knowing he was on the field alongside me.

After we came back from 1–0 down to win this year's series, Jo was talking to

Petero's mum, Tima, and she said, 'Petero missed Steven so much in game one, he was so excited when he came back for games two and three'. I understand exactly how he felt. I know we have 15 other team-mates who all make huge contributions but since Petero and I have been Queensland's starting front-rowers I've played the best football of my life. I think Petero has too.

We've won eight out of 10 games since we've been the starting props and I believe that is because you sometimes build successful relationships with people that are similar. Neither of us is the sort that goes out to grab a headline. We don't make huge statements, we just go out and do our best. We care about what we want to achieve and what we represent.

We actually sit in our hotel rooms each night during an Origin camp and have a cup of tea before bed. We enjoy each other's company and we know what each other is going to do. You know what to expect and you're very comfortable that you've got an ally there that will do his absolute best every time he goes out there. Hopefully Petero feels the same.

It's strange because before we became Queensland's starting front-rowers we were actually battling it out for the second spot alongside Shane Webcke, but neither of us enjoyed as close a relationship with Shane as we do with each other — even if Petero has stolen my favourite No 10 jumper!

It was never a problem when Shane was playing because he always wore No 8, but, once he retired, Petero and I would clash about who would wear that big one-zero. Before the Anzac Test in 2005 we both walked up to Steve Walters, who was the team manager for the Kangaroos, and he decided that the only way to solve the problem was with rock-paper-scissors! We were on the Gold Coast, standing out the front of the Marriott, with me thinking it was best of three but Petero won the first one and Steve said, 'Okay Pet, you've got No 10'. Ever since that day when we've made a rep side Petero has been No 10 and I've been No 8. I think we should do rock-paper-scissors every game but Petero's argument is that ever since then we've barely lost a game together. Fair enough.

Anyway, when Shane retired from rep football there were huge panic stations about what Queensland was going to do in the front row and it very nearly saw the representative careers of both Petero and me killed off.

Queensland headed into game one of 2006 on the back of three consecutive series losses. We lost that game too, albeit by one point (17–16) but afterwards everyone was saying that we had been completely dominated in the forwards. Petero and I bore the brunt of the criticism because we were the senior members who were supposed to be leading the way for our young forwards. The general consensus was that our time was up, we were too old and it was time to bring in the new breed.

Before State of Origin II we had a team dinner at which Paul Vautin was a guest speaker and he told us what the NSW forwards had been saying about me and Petero. It was without doubt the most embarrassing moment of my entire career. I know Paul didn't mean for that to be the case but this was a time when I was trying to earn the confidence and respect of the young guys in the team and for a Queensland legend to come in and destroy that in three minutes — I was scared to even look at the younger boys.

As I said to Pet, because we were both really upset, I would have preferred 'Fatty' to pull us aside and tell us one on one. I still would have been upset but when he said it in front of the whole playing group — I've never been more embarrassed or devastated in my whole life.

I didn't know how to react. I started to doubt myself. I was actually in a really bad way. We were down 1–0, we had lost the previous three series and people were saying that, if Queensland lost this one as well, State of Origin could be dead forever. Not only that, Petero and I both knew that a loss in game two would almost certainly end our representative careers.

If you're talking about a career-defining moment, that was it for both of us. You couldn't have your backs up against the wall any more than we did. We even had legends of Queensland questioning whether we should be in the team — and the blame was wholly and solely on our shoulders. Even though we lost by only one point in game one, the talk was that NSW was so dominant it was embarrassing. But that one moment has inspired me and Petero to be in the situation that we're in now. That moment was our turning point. I know that Petero hasn't forgotten about it and I *certainly* haven't.

Mum and Jo were the only ones who knew how depressed I was at the time and it wasn't pretty. I actually walked down to a hairdressing salon at the Myer centre in Queen Street in Brisbane before the game and said to the lady, 'I want you to shave the whole thing off'. The reason I did that was because it was the haircut I used to have when I was a kid when I really loved my footy. Mum always said to me: 'No matter what is happening or what people are saying, if you're not enjoying yourself then that is your biggest problem'.

I went to the hairdresser to give me that feeling of being nine years old again and loving playing rugby league. That's not to say that I *wasn't* loving footy — I really was — but shaving my head showed just how negative I was feeling ahead of game two.

As it turned out it was the greatest game I've ever played in for Queensland. We belted NSW 30–6 and it was one of the most dominant defensive performances that I've ever been involved with in regards to ferocious defence. It started right from the kick-off. I can assure you that not one NSW forward wanted to be on the field that night. When you've got guys like Carl Webb, Nate Myles, Dallas Johnson, Neville Costigan and Petero with fire absolutely flaming from their nostrils — at Suncorp Stadium — it's a fearsome sight. What could have been the worst night of my Origin career turned out to be the best. That game could have been my last. It's quite remarkable how close things can get.

But I think Petero and I have silenced the doubters and we've been able to build up an unbelievable partnership. Cameron Smith has had a fair bit to do with that too — I really enjoy playing with Cameron — and having the Australian No 7 in Johnathan Thurston, No 1 in Billy Slater, and guys like Karmichael Hunt, doesn't hurt either, but all good teams boast successful combinations and I'm lucky enough to have that with big Pet.

THERE WAS one other occasion when I felt similar to that terrible time in 2006 — and it happened this year. I was out for 10 weeks and missed the opening State of Origin game because of a hamstring injury I picked up against Melbourne in round one. I had only been back for two games with the Warriors when I was selected for game two. Just like two years earlier, I experienced a lot of anxiety and self-doubt before the game, which was created a little bit, albeit accidentally, by my Warriors coach Ivan Cleary.

We played Newcastle in round 12 and after the game Ivan asked me how I felt things had gone. I told him I was very disappointed. I took soft options. I felt fatigued and instead of toughing through it, which I pride myself on, I actually listened to the little devil on my shoulder telling me it was too hard. I haven't done that for a long,

long time. I had been sick for a few days before but it's no excuse — when you're on the field you have to do your job.

Ivan knew that it was very uncharacteristic of me and when I was picked in the Queensland team he basically implied that I should pull out because he wasn't sure I could go out and do the job I was required to do — particularly being 1–0 down and needing to win to keep the series alive. I think he actually had fears that it could be a very bad night for Steven Price.

The main concern for me before Origin II was my match fitness and there was talk that NSW was going to target me. It even got to the stage on the Monday that I thought I had the flu and missed training. The doctor checked me out and said, 'You haven't got the flu mate, it's actually symptoms of depression'.

I sent a text to Jo before the game questioning whether I would be able to perform at the level I was expected to. It was quite hard too because 'Locky' had pulled out and the Queensland media had been saying we would be right now because Darren Lockyer and Steve Price were back. Mum told me that there was a photo in the paper on the Sunday of me and 'Locky' charging and the headline read, 'The cavalry is coming'. When you talk about pressure and expectation, it's a bit scary to think that everyone is relying on you when you've played only two games and 'Locky' has pulled out. The Queensland media was saying, 'It's okay, Pricey is still there', and I was thinking: 'Oh, great'.

In terms of the pressure and the impact that had on me it ran a close second to the 2006 game.

I'VE ENJOYED some unbelievable times playing for Queensland since returning in 2002. One that stands out was my 'no try' in 2003. I received the ball on the halfway line with nothing but space ahead and the only thing that was going through my head was 'run as fast as you can' . . . then I tripped over! To end up a metre short probably epitomises my career — so close to greatness without ever getting there. The 2004 grand final was an example of that. People say it would have been one of the greatest tries scored in State of Origin history because front-rowers don't run 50 metres to score!

But I have plenty of fond memories. My try on debut in 1998 was special because of what I went through in that game. Certainly game two in 2006 was a huge highlight with the pressure that was on me. And every time I've played at the new Suncorp Stadium has been memorable. I love playing there for Queensland and I've probably played my best ever footy at that stadium, whether it be for Queensland, Australia or at NRL level. It's the most beautiful stadium ever built.

I've spent time with some wonderful people too. I used to love being on the team bus with Chris 'Choppy' Close and Gorden Tallis when they got stuck into one another. Gordy would say: 'Hey Choppy, you're so fat you need a boomerang to put your belt on!'

One day we were driving along the expressway in Brisbane when 'Choppy' jumped on the microphone and said, 'Boys, just over to our right we've got the Imax Theatre. We've just had a phone call from the manager to say that the big screen has cracked. They were wondering if we could drop in there so that they can use Gordy's forehead as the screen'.

There have been some great people involved with Queensland. I'll never forget Dick 'Tosser' Turner coming around the dressing rooms in his wheelchair after game two earlier this year. All of the boys were sitting around in a circle and I was having a massage. Jim Banaghan, one of the NRL's player managers, was wheeling him around and I asked if he could bring him over. I almost started to cry because of the health that 'Tosser' was in. I had seen it before and I knew that it was probably the last time I was going to see him. 'Tosser' used to call me 'The Special One' — which I'm sure he has done to every single player that has played for Queensland — but that's how he made you feel.

And even though his body was frail, his mental strength was still there. He even told me he was going to be in Sydney for game three — I'm sure that he was there in spirit when we wrapped up the series. 'Tosser' was a real character and for him to make the effort that he did to be at Suncorp that night was a huge testament to the guy. To find out a few days later that he had died was very sad but I was very privileged that I got to spend that short moment with him.

Radio broadcaster Alan Jones is an ambassador for the Queensland team and he said to me afterwards, 'You were the last player to talk to 'Tosser' after game two. I know that he thought a lot of you'. Little things like that make you realise that it's more than a game and you realise what it means to people. When we win the whole state is on a high and when we lose the whole state is in depression.

The Highest Honour

'Tosser's' life was about to come to an end yet the most important thing to him a couple of nights before he died was to be at a State of Origin game. It's quite humbling — no wonder he had such a huge influence on the Maroons. He certainly influenced me over the years, as did Wayne Bennett who had the confidence to pick me early on and give me a second chance four years later.

I learnt a lot from Michael Hagan too when he was in charge in 2004-05 and over the past three seasons Mal Meninga has come into the job at the ideal time in regards to my career. Those three years under Mal have been the most enjoyable time I've had in State of Origin. I'm really proud that we've achieved what we have because it's a special group of guys. To have won three in a row is fully deserved from the coach right down to the last player chosen. There are no egos, the players are super-talented and they're all quite young too which bodes well for the future.

Being one of the older generation, I've enjoyed our success — even though I tend to sit around talking to Mal, Petero and Kevin Walters these days. The young guys just bring a tremendous skill level and excitement to the squad and it is that which gives the likes of myself and Petero a new lease on life.

I'VE ALWAYS treasured representing my country. State of Origin may be the pinnacle in terms of testing yourself against the very best but there is no higher individual honour than playing for Australia. That's why I was so disappointed with my performance in the 2005 Tri-Nations series. When I talk about letting myself down in my early days of Origin, these were my darkest days while wearing the green and gold.

I had played well in the Anzac Test that year and then won man of the match in State of Origin I, but I re-injured my knee straight after and was ruled out for seven weeks. I returned with six weeks of the season remaining, the Warriors missed the finals and that meant another six weeks without playing before the first test against New Zealand.

I didn't do a lot of training in that time because I had a lot of pain in my knee. When we eventually went into camp Billy Johnstone absolutely flogged us and I could hardly walk for the whole week. It was like returning from pre-season.

We played the first test that week and were beaten 38–28. I was the heaviest I'd been at 110 kg and I certainly wasn't match fit. But Wayne stuck with me for every game until we got to the last game against England when he called me up to his room and said he was going to rest me. I was pretty disappointed. He told me the reason was because I had aggravated my knee against New Zealand but the real reason was that I wasn't playing good footy.

I didn't have an argument with him but I told him what I thought. It was one of those times where I was blaming everyone else and had all of the excuses in the world. I look back on it now as being like the Origin situation — I was embarrassed by how I was playing.

So I didn't play in that game but Wayne recalled me for the final against the Kiwis when we were smashed 24–0. That series very nearly cost me my test career and the fact that I had helped convince Stacey Jones to come out of international retirement for the Tri-Nations series that year didn't help. Wayne wasn't too pleased with me but I thought it was important that he played.

I had lived in New Zealand for 12 months by then and I knew what sort of impact Stacey had on the game there. He was worried that people would accuse him of reneging on his word by coming out of retirement but I explained to him that nobody could have a problem with that if he was doing it to help out the team and his country. He would be making a huge contribution and that's exactly what happened. It's just ironic that my conversation with Stacey almost ended my Kangaroos career — I didn't play again for two years!

Unfortunately New Zealand's Tri-Nations win *did* cost Wayne his test career and he stepped down soon after the final. When Ricky Stuart took over we spoke about the fact that it was important for him to have experience in the squad and what he wanted me to do as part of that.

I wasn't picked in the test team in 2006 and the rumours started straight away that I didn't like Ricky and he didn't like me, but that was never the case. I knew from a few people that he didn't think I was the toughest nut on the tree but I'd had that all my life. I would have been disappointed if that was the reason he overlooked me but I look back now and that 2005 tour didn't help my cause. I didn't play well. If it wasn't for Wayne I probably wouldn't have played as many tests as I did. I'm disappointed that I let him down. He trusted in me and I didn't back him up. I'm not saying I'm the reason we lost the final but I contributed to it by the way I went into the tour and my form throughout.

From Ricky's perspective, he could only go by what he had seen and I can totally understand why he formed the opinion that he did. It just took me a while to realise that. I knew it would take time to win my spot back too because Ricky has his opinions and once they're formed they can be very hard to change.

It's why being named in the side to play New Zealand in Wellington last October was so special. We won by a record scoreline, 58–0, and it was a great moment to be part of. The first thing Ricky said to me when I came into camp was 'Mate, I've got absolutely no issue with you. I want to bury the hatchet right now because none of that media was initiated by me. They asked me questions and took what they wanted from it'. I appreciated that and I told him the same thing from my perspective.

I really enjoyed it because whenever you have something like that taken away, you have to work 300 times harder to get it back. It's true that you can have a black line drawn through your name so you have to convince the coach or the selectors to take you back — and that's hard to do. If you failed last time, why should anyone think you won't fail this time? That's something I'm really proud of — to have regained that privilege and performed at the level the Kangaroos jersey deserves.

27 My Son Steve
— By Margaret Sullivan

I HAVE always told Steve that he has been blessed. While most of us stumble through our lives looking for something we'll never find, my eldest son knew from a very young age what he wanted to do in life.

I was watching Rafael Nadal's amazing victory over Roger Federer at Wimbledon earlier this year and when interviewed after the match he said: 'From when I was six or seven I knew that I wanted to achieve this — I wanted to win Wimbledon'. There are only a lucky few in this world that know, but my Steve was one of them. And there have been no half measures ever since.

I recall him being absolutely devastated one day while playing junior football when a so-called expert said: 'Steve won't amount to anything in this sport, he hasn't got what it takes'. Those words filtered back to Steve and they really upset him, but rather than give up they only made him more determined. He thought to himself 'Right, that's all I need to prove them wrong'.

Having said that, it took Steve a while to realise his own potential. He was a tall kid and very quick but there was always something missing. I would tell him 'When you get the ball you should just run'. He would reply, 'Oh, but there are some big boys out there'. I'd say, 'But Steve, you're a big boy too'. It wasn't until somebody showed him a tape of a game that he went, 'Wow', and that seemed to be the turning point where he realised, 'Hey, I can do this'.

But Steve has always strived to be his best. I remember when we first started talking with Peter Moore about the Bulldogs and Peter flew my other son Dan and me from Adelaide for the Commonwealth Bank Cup final in 1992. I told Peter that Steve did some refereeing on the side and he was absolutely horrified! He said, 'Why on earth would he do that?' I told him, 'Well, it's so that he can get a perspective of what's on the other side — you can show respect for that person because you have been in their shoes'. After I explained his thoughts behind it Peter said, 'Oh okay, I never thought of it that way'.

But that was always Steve's way — he wanted to learn everything he could. He wanted to understand other people. It's what has made him the man he is today.

We were sitting at Brisbane airport one day when Steve was younger and he came running over with great delight to say that Ray Price was there with his wife. Like all little boys back then in the 1980s, Steve was a Parramatta fan and he wanted an autograph. I said, 'Be forthright then. If you want something you go and ask for it. He can only say yes or no'. So he went over, got the autograph and came back with his chest all puffed out.

When he signed with the Bulldogs and made it through to first grade I said to him, 'Remember that little boy at Brisbane airport and how you felt when you got that signature and a pat on the shoulder? Don't forget that there are all sorts of little Steve Prices all over the place and how *you* felt is how *they're* feeling now. Always remember that'.

I truly believe that he has too. Whether he is tired or has things on his mind, he always makes time for his fans. When he was the face of the Bulldogs during the salary cap and Coffs Harbour he considered everybody. It was never about what was best for Steve Price, it was about families, the fans, the club and the game as well. It was amazing to watch him bring all of those people together. It was something that he was chosen for.

When Kevin Stewart — the former Leagues Club chairman — was sick in 2006, Steve called me and said, 'Mum, Kevin is very sick — do you think I should go and visit him?' I told him, 'Darling, at the end of your life you don't want any regrets. Do you want to look back and think that you should have gone to see him but didn't?' Steve said, 'You're right. I don't want to have any regrets'. And Kevin was absolutely delighted. When they spoke about the Bulldogs situation Kevin said, 'Steve, it was you. You're the one that got the Bulldogs through. Without you standing there I don't think they would have survived'.

I hear these stories about Steve all the time. He does those special things. One thing I always say is that you can go through your life and have all of the praise and people patting you on the back, but at the end of the day the important thing is whether you can look in the mirror and be content with the person you see looking back. Steven can certainly do that. He has always been there for people.

I was always inclined to shield Steve and his sister Wen from the breakdown of my first marriage but there was one particular night when he was about six that I've never forgotten. There was an awful incident on this night and I was terribly upset but I wasn't aware that he saw me. I thought he was safely tucked away in bed. To my shock and horror he was standing there in the doorway and as soon as he saw me he ran over, hugged me and said, 'It's okay Mumma, I'll look after you'. That little man and those few words have stayed with me forever.

And it wasn't easy for him. Our family was blessed when Garry came into our lives a few years later — he gave us stability when we needed it most — but it took a long time for Steve to accept that. Here was this boy saying, 'Don't be frightened Mumma, I'm here to look after you', and then this adult man came into our lives. Steve thought, 'No, it's me!'

That was quite difficult and Garry found it hard to deal with too. Like all children, Steve wanted his mum and dad to get back together again even though that was never going to happen. Garry would say to him: 'Mate, I'm here for you when your dad isn't here. I'm not going to try and be your dad and I can't be but I'm your mate. You can count on me'.

Garry has always been there for me during the tough times, particularly as Steve became more determined to follow his rugby league dreams. When we were offered an opportunity to move to Adelaide for Garry's work, Steve refused to come with us. It was a huge decision but he was so determined to succeed. We weren't in a financial position to stay — there was an opportunity there and it had to be taken. We didn't know where the next dollar was coming from but Steve dug his heels in and said, 'I'm not going!' I thought: 'Oh my God'. It was absolutely heartbreaking — 'Do I follow the husband or stay with the son?' They were very difficult times. But maybe if it was different Peter Moore wouldn't have looked or been so intrigued by this young kid from Toowoomba.

Being so far away from Steve was awful and I was a wreck. I longed for him so much that I really couldn't function. One weekend when Steve was playing in a state final on the Gold Coast, Garry and I managed to scramble together enough money for me to fly to Coolangatta and surprise him. Steve was dumbfounded, but little did I know — and in hindsight I should have — that young people make plans and on this particular day he had planned a huge weekend with his mates after their footy match. I spoiled it all! I ended up trying to find a lift home to Toowoomba so it was a disaster. And leaving him behind again was terrible. I remember getting back on the plane after the visit and bursting into tears. I sobbed from Brisbane all the way to our stop-over in Melbourne, then from Melbourne all the way back to Adelaide. I only started coming good when I touched down in Adelaide and when I saw Garry waiting for me in the terminal I started all over again! It was heartbreaking.

It was similar when Steve moved to Sydney. Of everything that he has been through during his career, those early years in Sydney were by far the toughest. He was terribly homesick.

Darren Smith was his 'big brother' back then and I made more than a few phone calls to him that Steve doesn't know about saying, 'Please, can you just give him a little bit more support? There is something wrong. I don't know what exactly but I can hear it in his voice. Can you just check on him for me?' That was really tough. Peter Moore helped him a lot but it wasn't until his soul mate, Jo, went down to Sydney that he finally seemed complete again.

I've always been concerned about their welfare — Steve, Jo and the children being by themselves and having to deal with everything without their family network. There have been some hard times but it shows the strength of character between the two of them — both Steve and Jo — and what a great partnership they've got. The fact that Jo is so down-to-earth has helped.

As a high-profile rugby league player it can be easy to feel a little bit self important but Jo has never allowed that to happen to Steve. I always said to Steve, 'Don't forget the humble beginnings you came from', because times *were* really tough when he was a kid — to the point where I would be thinking: 'How am I going to be able to afford to buy them meat this week?'

Then again I don't think that hurt — it gives you strength of character. And Steve has come through all of that to do what he always said he would. It's a wonderful achievement.

But Steve is more than a Bulldog, a Warrior, a Maroon or a Kangaroo. When he eventually calls it a day on his career I'll be sad for him because rugby league has played such a huge part in his life, but ask Garry, Wen or Dan and they will tell you that we love him for Steve — not for all of the bells and whistles that have come with it. Of course we are all very proud of him and what he has achieved but at the end of the day he will always be Steve Price — our son and our brother.

28 State of the Game

THE NRL has made tremendous strides since the trauma of Super League and there have been a number of positive steps taken.

Believe it or not, despite the salary cap nightmares that I've endured on two occasions, I do see merit in the concept of a cap to even out the competition although it could certainly do with some tweaking. The salary cap will always be a sticking point with certain parties — be it club bosses, players or supporters — but I think it's important that we have a system in place to regulate the competition.

You will always have some people trying to push the boundaries because at the end of the day success is determined by what happens on the field. You don't get sponsors, you don't get people coming to the games and you don't sell merchandise — the three primary revenue streams for any club — if your team doesn't perform on the field. Every club is looking for an advantage to put the best possible team on the field to win that elusive premiership.

Unfortunately, as has been shown over the past six to seven years, whichever side has won the premiership has been decimated within the next three years. One of the main reasons for that is players tend to have a far greater chance of representing their state or country if their side performs well and once that happens they can demand a lot more money. It leads to players changing clubs to chase top dollar and ultimately that's what the NRL wants. I spoke to David Gallop a number of years ago about loyalty and trying to keep players at clubs and he said they want players to move around to level the competition out.

Personally, I believe there should be a better system for rewarding loyalty and long-serving players. I'm a bit of a fan of the NFL system whereby you can re-sign your current players to whatever amount you can afford but if you are over the cap you can't sign new players from outside. A system like that would have some merit.

Another concern is that the landscape of the NRL has changed dramatically over the last few years to the point where a player's future is no longer in their control. It used to be up to the player whether he stayed where he was. Now it is largely in favour of the club. If there is a player on the market who is seen as a genuine target and can make a positive difference to a club, they'll do whatever they can to land that player and make the tough decisions later.

Previously, if a club had $200,000 left in the cap and a player demanded $400,000, they wouldn't even bother chasing him. Now they will spend $600,000 and if they're successful they will then get rid of two or three of their current players in order to make room. That's unfortunate because the players that are punished tend to be those lower-profile, loyal guys that would love to stay at the club forever. They're rarely the highest-profile players.

That really hit home to me in 2006 when Matt Orford and Steve Bell signed with Manly and the club let go of Sam Harris, Chad Randall and Scott Donald. They seemed to me to be guys that would give anything to play out their careers at the club yet overnight they had their aspirations decimated. That's how the business of rugby league operates these days.

The Warriors did a similar thing when they decided they needed me and Ruben Wiki. I doubt they ever expected to get both of us and when they did they had to make some tough decisions elsewhere. As it turned out they were still over the cap and Ruben and I were the ones blamed for it, despite the fact that the Warriors had been over the year before as well.

My time at the Bulldogs and now the Warriors has certainly awakened me to the different thought processes of a rugby league club and I realise now that the most important team is the one that I come home to every day. You're only in the game for a short period and at the end of the day you have to look out for the most important thing — your family. It's why I joined the Warriors in the first place.

But I'm disappointed that player salaries have become public these days. When I started out it would be written into your contract that the only people who knew the details of your deal were you, your manager and the club. If there was a breach of that confidentiality you knew exactly where it came from.

It's a shame that went out the window because straight away people's perceptions of players changed for the worse. Professionalism brought with it much more focus on players. The public knew we were on big money and wanted to know what we were doing with it when we weren't playing.

Having said that, I'm happy with where the game is going in regards to player education and welfare. There is far better security against situations such as when the Warriors or Northern Eagles went broke and players didn't get paid. The NRL now guarantees the salary cap of each club and that's a huge step in the right direction.

The Under-20s competition is another great idea and provides young players with a taste of the NRL without quite as much pressure. There have been plenty of players come through the Under-20s this year to play in the NRL and that will only become more frequent as the years go by because we'll have 17, 18, 19 and 20 year-olds that will have spent years in the system before they play first grade. It used to be such a huge contrast between the grades and it was very difficult to adapt education programs in order to prepare all players for what they are going to come across. This system is certainly a move in the right direction.

THE NRL recently introduced an accreditation system for player managers in order to protect all of the parties involved but I believe their role in the game still needs to be looked at.

There are a number of players in the Telstra Premiership who would be far better off with 'negotiators' rather than full-time player managers.

Ideally you would pay them an agreed fee to perform a certain task — such as negotiating a new contract — and that would be the end of it. You might say to them: 'If you can get me a $200,000-per-year, three-year deal I'll give you $10,000. If you get me more I'll give you a percentage for every dollar on top'. That's an incentive for the negotiator and he only needs to worry about you for that short period.

At the moment we've got managers who take between five and 10 percent of a player's contractual money for the entire duration of the contract and the only time you hear from them is when your contract is coming to an end. If you want any extra information or help you've got to pay for that as well.

In line with that, the NRL should also implement some sort of forced savings plan so that during your period of competition you have had to put a certain amount of your contract money into a locked account. If you negotiate a $200,000 contract, why can't they pay you $170,000 and put $30,000 away into an account that grows?

At present we have a similar sort of plan in place for representative fixtures but we could extend that further because there are too many players who come out of their careers with nothing to show for it financially.

There aren't too many who play 300 games in their career or who have a profile that enables them to go out and get a job straight away. Some aren't even in the competition long enough to take advantage of the NRL's education allowance. When their careers come to an end they have no idea what to do. They've gone from earning good money to earning no money whatsoever.

The representative superannuation is a great concept. A guy like Israel Folau is going to come out of the game with a great reward if he stays with rugby league. How good would it be if you had, for example, a $250,000 loan on your house and when you retire you have enough money in your superannuation fund to pay the whole thing off in one hit?

At least there is now an education programme in place that enables clubs to help players study without affecting their salary cap but, again, more could be done. There are still too many players that take their football for granted and think it's going to last forever. It's not until it's too late that they regret missing out on an education. I'm very passionate about education because I still regret not getting in there and studying earlier.

I'm studying now and should be fully qualified by the end of next year but if I had started earlier I would already have my qualifications. Still, it has certainly helped my football because it's given me an outlet. It helps with time management and it's an interest that I know will benefit me in the long term.

I FELT great disappointment when the Bulldogs stopped playing at Belmore Oval in 1998. It was a sad day for me because it was a place I just loved playing footy at. I understand that there were reasons — crowds were down and the NRL was introducing new rules regarding the quality of grounds — but I believe the NRL could have put more thought into it.

State of the Game

The suburban ground is sorely missed in the modern game. I find it hard to watch Wests Tigers playing the Bulldogs at ANZ Stadium. That's nothing against ANZ Stadium but I would rather see it played at Belmore or Leichhardt Oval or Campbelltown Stadium. Why can't we play more games at Kogarah or WIN Stadium?

I remember talking to fans when I was at the Bulldogs who had grown up watching their side play at Belmore. They had sat on the hill with their dads as six- or seven-year-olds watching their favourite players running around for the Bulldogs. It's not the same today.

There is an aura to the suburban grounds. I love playing at Kogarah, Toyota Park and EnergyAustralia Stadium. There is a time and a place for the big stadiums but your regular season games aren't it. Unless you know that it's a huge game and you'll get 70,000 there to watch, what's the point? There is nothing wrong with having 20,000 people at Belmore Oval.

Clubs are losing their identity. ANZ Stadium isn't even a home ground anymore, it's just a venue to play football. I know that when the Bulldogs started playing at the Sydney Showground and then ANZ Stadium it just didn't feel like our home ground. When we played at Belmore it was our home ground and other teams hated playing there. *Hated* it. Sometimes we would have them beaten before they even turned up.

That's why I've loved playing in New Zealand — because teams don't like coming to Mt Smart Stadium. Brookvale Oval is another that intimidates people.

There is no reason why we shouldn't be playing at these grounds and that was highlighted earlier this year when a group came out pushing for a return to Belmore. I'm very passionate about that. It's one area that the NRL needs to look at in regards to getting back to the grass roots. I realise there are some problems with some of these grounds, but they've improved Kogarah and EnergyAustralia Stadium over the years.

Belmore is dilapidated these days but that can be fixed. It's so sad that we've lost that from our game. We've lost touch with the community. Too many clubs no longer have an association with their area. Parramatta, the Bulldogs, St George Illawarra, South Sydney, Wests Tigers — they're all playing games out of the same place. How can that be regarded as your region? It breaks your heart. How can someone who lives in Wollongong consider Homebush to be their area? I just hope we can turn back the clock because the game needs those suburban grounds.

I had been pushing for a number of years with referees boss Robert Finch to make all referees full-time. Why haven't they been recognised as the 17th team in the competition? They've got a head coach, they've got a trainer and they're just as important — if not more important — than any other franchise in the competition. How is it fair to expect them to be out there each week without making any mistakes when they're not full-time and the players are professional full-time athletes?

I had a talk to Steven Clark about it a few years back and he told me that, depending on what sort of season you had, you could earn anywhere from $30,000 up to $150,000 if you refereed Origin and the grand final. The problem with that was not knowing how much you stood to earn. You can't tell me that if you go into a bank to apply for a loan and tell them, 'I'm guaranteed $30,000 but I could earn up to $150,000', they're going to say yes. That problem still exists to a certain extent today although I believe the minimum wage has risen substantially which gives those referees a lot more security.

But I believe young referees need more to aspire to. I've also spoken to Robert, David Gallop and the NRL's chief operating officer Graham Annesley about having a Dally M-type medal awarded to the best referee, with points awarded each week based on performance. Robert told me that he had implemented a similar system whereby the referee who officiates the grand final is awarded a medal. I said to him, 'That's fantastic but that doesn't mean he is necessarily the best referee all year'.

We see with the Dally M medal that the player who wins doesn't always play in the grand final. There are any number of things that can go wrong. What if the referee does his hamstring in the grand final qualifier or suffers a form slump during the finals? Why is it that only the referee who officiates the grand final is recognised?

Graham has his reservations about it too but I hope it's something they implement one day so that young referees have something to aspire to. We need pathways for young referees to take and it's crucial that we target young people.

Now that we've got the Under-20s competition there is no reason we can't target players who don't quite make it to the NRL to become referees instead. They're fit, they're young, they love the game and it's a way for them to still be involved at the highest level.

If we do that we could have guys refereeing in the NRL who are 24 or 25 — a similar age to those actually playing — and they'll be able to keep up. At present we have referees who are 32 years old making their debuts and, although they're doing a great job, we're not going to have them for too long.

I recall Robert asking me how his referees would fill their weeks if they were all full-time. I said, 'Get them to do what we do. The more training they do the better because the fitter they are the better decisions they'll make. You could have a review and a preview about how they've performed and what they need to work on during the week'.

The other thing that would be a huge advantage would be to hold clinics in the country. Why can't they go out and hold coaching development clinics in the country for aspiring referees? After all, these are the guys that don't get paid. They do it for the love of it and probably cop more grief than anyone in the game.

If we showed them that kind of support by making them more confident and giving them those skills to make the right decisions in the right situations it would only make the game better overall.

DEVELOPING RUGBY league is crucial to the game's survival and one place I am passionate about is Papua New Guinea. I've played in two Prime Minister's XIII teams in PNG in recent years and it's something I will never, ever forget. It was a fantastic experience and made me realise just what rugby league means to people.

PNG is the only country in the world where rugby league is the number one sport. The locals aren't very well off — a lot of people live in terrible conditions — but they absolutely idolise rugby league and particularly the NRL. When you go there they swarm around you wanting to touch you.

To be given the honour of going over there to play as well as promote the war against AIDS and to help prevent violence towards women is an absolute privilege. I spoke with some of the Australian aid workers over there last time I went and they told me that in two years they didn't have anywhere near as much impact on the community as our football team had in two days. They idolise us so when we say something, the people listen. They respect what we say.

They're great games too. The first year I went over, in 2005, Luke Ricketson was captain, Mal Meninga was coach and Brad Fittler was his assistant. We had young guys like John Sutton in the team who learnt a lot about responsibility and being a role-model. The second year I was captain of a side that boasted Johnathan Thurston, Brett Stewart and Jarryd Hayne.

They were both very tough games with us winning 34–0 and 28–8. Last year I didn't play, because the Warriors were in the finals, but PNG drew 24-all. That would have given the locals a massive boost and it's why these games need to continue. I spoke to Mal during Origin this year about it and he said that he has the backing of the government again which is great news.

For us, it's a different way to represent your country. You're there as more than just a rugby league player and it's a great grounding for young players. You're there as an ambassador, an educator and a role model. To see how other people live gives you a real understanding of the world. I've done two tours and I will put my hand up every time.

PNG often gets a bad rap. We flew to Cairns in 2005 where they gave us a briefing about what to expect and what we should be concerned about. I was terrified of going and actually rang Jo to say: 'I don't think this is a good idea'. Apparently it is second only to Afghanistan for violence. I couldn't understand why we were going but when we got there it was the complete opposite. Obviously the fact that we were their idols helped — these people don't have a lot of money but they're all wearing footy jerseys!

It's an unbelievable experience. The stadiums are surrounded by barbed wire. You actually get dressed at the hotel and then jump on the bus which is an old school bus from about 1970. Going through traffic is like parting the sea — there are people everywhere. It's a bit like Caxton Street on Origin night but with more police and tear gas!

The dressing rooms at the ground are just walls and a toilet and the toilet is full of wastage so we didn't spend much time in there. When you run out the place is absolutely packed despite the fact that a ticket to the game is worth three weeks' wages. You can imagine how much it means to these people.

After the game they all race onto the ground and you just run for your life back to the dressing room, lock the door and say: 'Okay, what are we going to do now?' They're like crocodiles waiting at the bottom of the tree for you to fall out! They don't need to go anywhere either so you spend a lot of time wondering how you're going to get out again. The police eventually settle everyone down — I don't know how and I don't want to know how — and you finally exit safely and return to the hotel. But it is incredible. They're fanatical. They don't want to hurt us but they do want our clothes and our boots. They're actually very, very kind people and rugby league means so much. It's crucial for the game that we keep developing these areas.

29 The Future

I'VE OFTEN looked into my little crystal ball and envisioned myself as the future CEO of a rugby league club or boss of the NRL. That was certainly the goal before the dramas that engulfed the Bulldogs in 2002. The salary cap saga and Coffs Harbour two years later gave me a whole new insight into the business of rugby league — both at club level and the NRL — and it's very different to what I had originally perceived.

BUT I haven't ruled those challenges out and could well find myself following that very path once my rugby league career comes to an end. I love the pressure of leading people and it's something I look forward to post-football.

The key for me, though, is to keep my options open. I had been trying for a number of years when I was at the Bulldogs to initiate some form of education in preparation for the future but it wasn't until the NRL introduced salary cap exemptions for educational purposes that my wish was finally granted.

My final contract with the Bulldogs had a $20,000 education allowance written in so I undertook a Certificate in Small Business through NSW TAFE. The tutor would come out to Belmore Oval and I would study between training sessions. It worked really well and in 12 months I had finished a course that was supposed to take two or three years.

When I joined the Warriors I wanted to continue on with my education and spoke to the club about setting up a similar programme to the Bulldogs', because there wasn't a lot being done back in 2005. I wasn't quite sure where to go from my TAFE studies but after examining my options I settled on a Masters in Business

Management. I spoke to a few people about it first including Mick Watson and Don Mann.

Mick told me not to do it, that it would be too hard and that I wouldn't be able to finish it. A few other people said, 'Nah, I wouldn't do it'. But I've never been one to back down from a challenge. I applied through Southern Cross University in Lismore and lodged my application on the pretence that I had never had any tertiary education before but held a Certificate in Small Business and had earned a high distinction in doing so.

The University also took into account what I had to deal with at the Bulldogs with the salary cap and Coffs Harbour. They felt that I had the skills to be able to handle this course, so I started in 2005 and have now completed nine of my 12 subjects.

Your qualifications grow as you finish each subject — after four subjects I had a Certificate in Business Management, after eight I had my diploma and after 12 I'll have my Masters. Even if I finish now I will at least have a piece of paper that says I do have some skills.

The most obvious development in me has been learning to write academically. I scored 14 out of 30 in my first assignment and I was shattered. I put absolutely everything into it and I could only muster 14! I thought: 'There is absolutely no way I can do this — I tried my absolute hardest and I still failed'. Jo said to me, 'Don't worry about it, you don't need it, you'll be able to get a job because of the person that you are', but I knew that wasn't the case.

I've had a lot of ex-team-mates who have told me that reputation and profile won't get you a job. They might give you a head-start but you need the qualifications to reinforce that. It's what inspired me to go down that path in the first place.

Thankfully my tutor Wayne Dreyer was very positive. He convinced me to continue and suggested that working on my writing skills would make the world of difference — and it did. As tough as the course was to begin with, as I've gone through I've passed all of my subjects. It's nice to look back and think: 'I've been able to survive and I'm that much closer to getting that little piece of paper that I set out to get so long ago'. If I do aspire to be the CEO of the NRL or a club one day it will be a tremendous qualification to have.

Whether I target the business world instead of the sporting one, only time will tell. I do a lot of speaking engagements now and I enjoy the fact that business is

The Future

actually very similar to sport. I feel quite confident that in the next stage of my life I'll be able to make that transition, whereas three years ago I was very nervous about it and really didn't know what I was going to do.

Already Bruce Sharrock and George Mimis are putting a plan together with me looking at what I might want to do, what lifestyle I want and where I want to live. There are a number of options but at the end of the day it's going to come down to what is best for my family and my career development. We want to utilise my profile coming out of the game and I enjoy working in the media so I would like to be involved in both television and radio.

I enjoy helping out on the coaching side of things too but I don't see myself as a head coach. I don't enjoy the stress of not being able to control your own future so I wouldn't want to put myself in that situation.

Could I actually become CEO of a club, the NRL or a corporate company? None of those will happen overnight and I know that I'll need experience but, however long that takes, I'm more than willing to do it. I want to strive to be the top dog in whatever field it happens to be. I'd love to be involved in a couple of corporate businesses in an ambassadorial type of role.

At this stage it looks as if I'll be staying in New Zealand when my playing career comes to an end. Jamie begins high school soon and Kasey and Riley will be following on after that. I don't want to uproot them from school and drag them all over the place. Unless an opportunity presents itself that is simply too good to refuse we'll stay in New Zealand for a couple of years at least.

I thought I was going to be at the Bulldogs forever but once I made the decision to leave, I came to New Zealand with open eyes. It taught me to always be conscious of what's best for my family rather than making any grand long-term decisions about what we're going to do. The Bulldogs situation taught me that things don't always work out the way you anticipate.

In fact, before I signed my 2009 contract with the Warriors earlier this season I actually spoke with Bulldogs CEO Todd Greenberg about returning to the club that launched my first grade career. I told Todd that I would consider it because at the end of the day it could have been the best decision for me and my family. George met with the club but we were thinking of greater numbers than what the Bulldogs had in mind and it didn't go much further than that. Still, it was important that we considered our options before I re-signed with the Warriors.

At the moment it looks as though my best opportunities in the immediate future will be in New Zealand and hopefully I will have finished my studies by the end of next year, which may well be my last season. Even that's no certainty — I'll never say never. If you had asked me straight after this year's State of Origin decider I would have said: 'Yeah, I want to keep playing', but if you were to ask me the following morning I'd have said: 'Nope, next year is definitely my last', because I was very, very sore!

As it is, to go and play another season after 2009 might not fit in with the opportunities that are offered anyway. The longer you keep playing the fewer opportunities are going to be waiting for you once you finally decide to retire. That has to be a consideration as well as my enjoyment of the game.

But I don't want to get ahead of myself. We're not at the finish line yet. I still have goals and aspirations, such as winning the first premiership for the Warriors. That hasn't changed.

I would also love to join the select group of players to have played 300 first grade games and I'll hit that mark next year if I stay injury-free. I'd love to achieve that just for my own satisfaction — for all the people who haven't believed that I was good enough. It will really be gratifying to be able to look back and say: 'Wow, I played 300 games'. There will be others who reach 300 too but so far only 10 have made it in 100 years of rugby league in Australia.

And if I could play Origin next year it would start pushing my numbers up near the top of the list for most-capped Queenslanders too. Cameron Smith is already on 15 and I'm sure he will go on to become the most-capped-ever but for me to have reached 25 Origin games — I'm extremely proud of that. I was presented with a medal last year called 'The Dick Turner medal' for players who have played over 20 games for Queensland, and there were only 11 of us who had done it. To be one of those is pretty special.

I always had the thought in the back of my mind that if I ever played for Australia or Queensland, I wanted to hit double figures for both. There was a time when it didn't look as if that would happen at test level but in 2005 I was able to get there. I'm very proud that I've been able to achieve that. It's those little things that I'll look back on once my career is over and know that, no matter the hurdles along the way, I was the best that I could be.